Negotiating Gender, Policy and Politics in the Caribbean

Negotiating Gender, Policy and Politics in the Caribbean

Feminist Strategies, Masculinist Resistance and Transformational Possibilities

Edited by
Gabrielle Jamela Hosein and Jane Parpart

ROWMAN &
LITTLEFIELD
INTERNATIONAL

London • New York

Published by Rowman & Littlefield International, Ltd.
Unit A, Whitacre Mews, 26-34 Stannary Street, London SE11 4AB
www.rowmaninternational.com

Rowman & Littlefield International, Ltd. is an affiliate of Rowman & Littlefield
4501 Forbes Boulevard, Suite 200, Lanham, Maryland 20706, USA
With additional offices in Boulder, New York, Toronto (Canada), and Plymouth (UK)
www.rowman.com

British Library Cataloguing In Publication Data
A catalogue record for this book is available from the British Library

ISBN: HB 978-1-7834-8750-9
      PB 978-1-7834-8751-6

Library of Congress Cataloging-in-Publication Data

Names: Hosein, Gabrielle, editor. | Parpart, Jane L., editor.
Title: Negotiating gender, policy and politics in the Caribbean : feminist strategies,
    masculinist resistance and transformational possibilities / [edited by] Gabrielle Hosein
    and Jane Parpart.
Description: London ; New York : Rowman & Littlefield International, [2016] | Includes
    bibliographical references and index.
Identifiers: LCCN 2016040138 (print) | LCCN 2016051219 (ebook) |
    ISBN 9781783487509 (cloth : alk. paper) | ISBN 9781783487516 (pbk. : alk. paper) |
    ISBN 9781783487523 (electronic)
Subjects: LCSH: Feminism—Caribbean Area. | Women's rights—Caribbean Area. |
    Sex discrimination—Caribbean Area. | Women—Political activity—Caribbean Area
Classification: LCC HQ1501 .N44 2016 (print) | LCC HQ1501 (ebook) |
    DDC 305.4209729—dc23 LC record available at https://lccn.loc.gov/2016040138

∞™ The paper used in this publication meets the minimum requirements of American
National Standard for Information Sciences—Permanence of Paper for Printed Library
Materials, ANSI/NISO Z39.48-1992.

Printed in the United States of America

*To Caribbean feminists whose fearless
vision for justice is our guide.*

Contents

List of Tables

TABLES

List of Acronyms

ACWM	Anglophone Caribbean Women's Movement
APNU/AFC	A Partnership for National Unity + Alliance for Change
BGA	Bureau of Gender Affairs
BWA	Bureau of Women's Affairs
CAFRA	Caribbean Association for Feminist Research and Action
CARICOM	Caribbean Community
CariMAN	Caribbean Male Action Network
CBO	Community-Based Organization
CEDAW	Convention on the Elimination of All Forms of Discrimination against Women
CDB	Caribbean Development Bank
CIWiL	Caribbean Institute for Women in Leadership
COP	Congress of the People
CPDC	Caribbean Policy Development Centre
CRC	Constitution Reform Commission
CSO	Civil Society Organization
CONCACAF	Confederation of North, Central American and Caribbean Association Football
DACAMEN	Dominica Association of Catholic Men
DLP	Dominica Labour Party
DNGP	Dominica National Gender Policy
DNCW	Dominica National Council of Women
ECLAC	(UN) Economic Commission on Latin America and the Caribbean
FGD	Focus Group Discussion

List of Acronyms

GAD	Gender and Development
GIS	Government Information Service
GFP	Gender Focal Point
GOCD	Government of the Commonwealth of Dominica
HATT	Housewives Association of Trinidad and Tobago
IDRC	International Development Research Centre
IGDS	Institute for Gender and Development Studies
ILP	Independent Liberal Party
IPU	International Parliamentary Union
IWC	International Whaling Commission
HWO	Hindu Women's Organization
JCSC	Jamaica Civil Society Coalition
JWPC	Jamaica Women's Political Caucus
LGPT	lesbian, gay, bisexual and transgender
List PR	List Proportional Representation
MOA	Ministry of Agriculture
MOE	Ministry of Education
MOH	Ministry of Health
MSJ	Movement for Social Justice
Network of NGOs	Network of NGOs of Trinidad and Tobago for the Advancement of Women
NGO	Non-governmental Organization
NGP	National Gender Policy
NGPE	National Gender Policy for Gender Equality
NJAC	National Joint Action Committee
NOW	National Organisation of Women
NPGE	National Policy for Gender Equality
NPW	National Policy on Women
NVM	New Vision Movement
OAS	Organisation of American States
OC	Oversight Committee
OECS	Organisation of Eastern Caribbean States
OPM	Office of the Prime Minister
PNC	People's National Congress
PNM	People's National Movement
PNP	People's National Party
PP	People's Partnership
PPP	People Progressive Party
PPP/C	People Progressive Party/Civic
PS	Permanent Secretary
PSSC	Parliamentary Special Select Committee
SIA	Security Intelligence Agency

SM	Social Movement
SMMA	Soufriere Marine Management Association
TL	Transformational Leadership
TOP	Tobago Organization of the People
TTPR	Tunapuna/Piarco Regional Corporation
UNC	United National Congress
UNDP	United Nations Development Fund
UNIFEM	United Nations Development Fund for Women
UN Women	United Nations Entity for Gender Equality and the Empowerment of Women
UWI	The University of the West Indies
WAND	Women and Development Unit at the University of the West Indies
WICP	Women in the Caribbean Project
WID	Women in Development
WIN	Women's Issues Network
Workingwomen	Women Working for Social Progress
World YWCA	World Young Women's Christian Association
WPA	Working People's Alliance
WPP	Women's Political Participation
WPEO	Women's Political and Economic Organisation

Preface

This collection of essays was borne out of an academic commitment to the Caribbean feminist movement and its work over more than a century. The women who originally sat around the table at UN Women in Barbados in 2010, initiating the space and funding for this project, included Rawwida Baksh, Roberta Clarke, Jane Parpart, Camille Samuel and Gabrielle Jamela Hosein. As a young scholar, Gabrielle was invited by Jane to lead the project, with her support, and to build on the work of Rawwida Baksh and the Commonwealth Secretariat, in particular the conference Rawwida organized, which was titled 'Decentralization, Local Power and Women's Rights: Global Trends in Participation, Representation and Access to Public Services', held in 2008, in Mexico City.

Jane's work as a feminist development scholar had long focused on gender and development, gender mainstreaming, empowerment and, more recently, on gender and security with particular attention to gender relations and hierarchies, and the role of masculinities in conflict zones. She came to the Institute for Gender and Development Studies (IGDS) in 2006, where she led an expanding graduate programme, taught and benefited from working with colleagues and students. Her long-standing connections with Southern feminists concerned with questions on gender and development had included work in Africa, Asia and the Caribbean. When she moved to Trinidad and Tobago she welcomed the opportunity to work with IGDS students and faculty to explore gender, masculinities, development and insecurity. She found the IGDS a congenial and exciting place to rethink gender and development both intellectually and through policy building. She welcomed the opportunity to join Patricia Mohammed and Deborah McFee on the British Virgin Islands team advising the government on the creation of a national gender plan. This project provided welcome opportunities to operationalize theories on gender, femininities, masculinities and the search for gender justice.

By 2010, Gabrielle had been close to the Caribbean women's movement's efforts to advance women's political participation for fifteen years, particularly through the work of the Network of NGOs of Trinidad and Tobago for the Advancement of Women, and through her 'Steppin Up': A Feminist Movement-Building Game workshops for the Caribbean Institute for Women in Leadership (CIWiL). She came to the project as a younger feminist mentored and trained by the many activist efforts that had emerged from more senior feminists' collaborations. She also came as a young scholar at the IGDS, University of the West Indies (UWI), St. Augustine Unit. Indeed, one part of the IGDS' mission is to document and analyse the work and impact of Caribbean feminist activism and women's movements, and the historical contexts that shape their strategies and successes.

As a regional institute, the IGDS also sought to encourage work that sees social movements through a transnational lens, understanding the Caribbean as criss-crossed by ideas, politics and people, particularly with regard to rights, freedom, citizenship and justice. Caribbean feminist history is no less regional, with struggles in one country part of wider trends and mobilization that traverse the global before returning to the local. This collection's aim reflects this transnational Caribbean feminist grounding, the many women whose support made this collection possible, and the legacy of scholarship of those women themselves.

Following the initial meeting, Rawwida Baksh, then at the International Development Research Council (IDRC), guided the process of securing a grant to conduct regional research. After her, Francisco Cos Monteil, at IDRC, maintained oversight of the project until its completion in 2014. We thank him for his guidance throughout. We also thank the IDRC, whose funding made this research project possible.

The research project, Politics, Power and Gender Justice in the Anglophone Caribbean, was conceptualized one Saturday morning by Gabrielle Hosein, who sought to bring together the different threads of women's scholarly mentorship, Caribbean feminist history, and ethnographic interest in politics and governance, which followed from her PhD on authority in Trinidadian public life. That morning, the four feminist strategies and the four countries in which they were going to be explored (Trinidad and Tobago, Guyana, Dominica and St. Lucia, Jamaica came later based on the work of Maziki Thame and Dhanraj Thakur), the methodological break-up into a first historical and second ethnographic phase, and the core research question were decided. Tisha Nickenig, who went on to coordinate the project over the next four years was to first to hear about it on the way to Yarra River that morning. Tisha's endless support over the project's life was invaluable and irreplaceable as was her immediate understanding of, and excitement about, what we hoped to accomplish. It's not possible to thank Tisha enough for overseeing the project through from then to completion of the research reports in 2014.

The aim was to gather original data that examined four feminist strategies to advance gender justice – women's political leadership, national gender policies, electoral quota systems and transformational leadership – from a regional and historical perspective. The second phase of the project would then engage in ethnographic national case studies of each strategy, focusing on those countries where they were seemingly successful. Over the next weeks of proposal writing, Jane Parpart and Camille Samuel, who had recently completed her PhD, the institute's first, on gender and corporate turnaround leadership, helped to refine the research questions, deepening focus on the project's subtitle: 'Women's Understandings of Politics, Experiences of Political Contestation and the Possibilities for Gender Transformation'. Their work to secure the final grant was crucial, making the project design a truly collective and collaborative effort.

After conceptualizing the project's core research questions, methodology and research sites, a research team was hired and supported between 2011 and 2014 to produce nine research reports, with Gabrielle Hosein as principal investigator and Jane Parpart as lead researcher. The project's researchers were Deborah McFee, Natalie Persadie, Shirley Campbell, Aleah Ranjitsingh, Denise Blackstock, Iman Khan, Ramona Biholar, Maziki Thame and Dhanaraj Thakur. The researchers primarily comprised early career scholars, recent PhD and MSc graduates, and IGDS graduate students. We thank them for their investment in the project's concerns and for their intellectual contribution to the scholarship that the project generated.

In keeping with the mandate of the IGDS, and indeed Caribbean feminism, the research methodology also sought to build capacity among emerging scholars to analyse statehood and citizenship from a gendered perspective, in ways that compare historical, quantitative, discursive and ethnographic data, and ways that put the perspectives and experiences of feminist activists (both female and male) at the centre of rethinking solidarities, strategies and struggles over meaning and practice. To this end, a Project Advisory Committee comprised of experienced feminist scholars and activists, and Caribbean political scientists, met in 2011 and in 2012, first to review all four of the regional and historical review chapters, and second to review the national case studies. Its members were Eudine Barriteau, Patricia Mohammed, Selwyn Ryan, Cynthia Barrow-Giles, Rawwida Baksh and Linnette Vassell. Each of the chapters received detailed reading by one of the advisory committee members, plus continuous feedback by the principal investigator and lead researcher. We thank our advisory committee members for their guidance and mentorship. These chapters should each be seen as part of an overall, integrated project that sought to invest in and build younger scholars' knowledge, networks and capacity in the region.

There were many other aspects of this project that do not appear in this collection, but are worth noting precisely because the life of Caribbean feminist scholarship doesn't exist only on paper, but also finds form in workshop organizing, supervision of students, popular cultural engagement, public addresses and more. Thus, the Politics, Power and Gender Justice in the Anglophone Caribbean research project should be seen within its wider context as producing more than an edited collection, and instead as contributing to regional public discourse in multiple ways.

On June 29, 2011, Gabrielle Hosein made a presentation about the project to the 'Women Leaders as Agents of Change' Regional Colloquium for female political leaders, parliamentarians and civil society representatives, held in Port of Spain, Trinidad. The colloquium was hosted by CIWiL, the Office of the Prime Minister, the Organisation of American States (OAS), UN Women and the Commonwealth Secretariat, and resulted in the Port of Spain Consensus on Transformational Leadership for Gender Equality. On March 14, 2012, as part of the IGDS' International Women's Day activities, the project organized a public lecture at the UWI, St. Augustine, by Dr. Martina Rieker of the American University in Cairo. Her lecture is available for viewing on the IGDS YouTube page. On March 16, 2012, Deborah McFee, in her role as IGDS Research and Outreach Officer, helped to organize a conversation and roundtable discussion with women parliamentarians, in collaboration with the Women's Institute for Alternative Development (WINAD). Women politicians and feminist activists participated in this gathering. On October 23, 2012, the IGDS, St. Augustine Unit, hosted a visit by Her Excellency Ms. Penny Williams, Global Ambassador for Women and Girls.

'Click Power': An Online Photo Exhibition of Women in Caribbean Politics was developed to build an online archive of images of women's participation and power in Caribbean politics. This project commissioned original photographs from elections taking place in 2010 in Guyana, St. Lucia, Jamaica and Trinidad and Tobago. These are now housed in IGDS' archives along with the transcripts of more than eighty original interviews with feminist activists, bureaucrats and scholars, and others such as men and women in civil society organizations (CSOs) and in-state machineries. Regarding additional research, in 2015, Sabrina Mowlah Baksh completed her MSc project, titled 'The Decision to Run: Experiences of Women Who Have Succeeded in Winning Elected Public Office'. Nicole Hosein produced a research report on the status of women in government in the cabinet and the 10th Parliament of Trinidad and Tobago from May 2010. Deborah McFee is finalizing a PhD dissertation on gender and policymaking that has been advanced by the production of her chapter for this collection. Finally, a team of researchers, including Tisha Nickenig, Aleah Ranjitsingh and Anusha Ragbir, collected data on campaigning during the 2015 Chaguanas West by-election in Trinidad and Tobago. This led to four articles on gender and the election published in Gabrielle Jamela Hosein's *Guardian* newspaper column, taking writing on these issues into the more open-access public domain.

In addition to this output, as principal investigator, Gabrielle presented findings from the project at various stages, for example, in a paper titled, 'The Woman in the State: Trinidadian Feminism and the State under a Woman Prime Minister', on November 14, 2012 to the American Anthropological Association. Another paper, 'On Sexual Rights and the Limits of Gender Mainstreaming Strategies to Advance Gender Justice in the Anglophone Caribbean', was presented at the American Anthropological Association Conference on December 3, 2014. This presentation developed on the research on national gender policies produced by Deborah McFee, Ramona Biholar, Maziki Thame and Dhanaraj Thakur. And, a paper documenting the methodology of the project titled, 'Feminist Approaches to the Anthropology of Caribbean Citizenship', was presented on June 11, 2015 at the Workshop on Political Anthropology: Power, Subjectivity, and Citizenship in the Contemporary Caribbean, held in Trinidad.

In addition, four public fora continued the work of the project. The first was the IGDS public panel, 'Women and Political Power: A Right to Lead', held on the UWI St. Augustine Campus on March 19, 2014. Speakers were Sunity Maharaj, Paula Morgan, Winford James and Gabrielle Jamela Hosein. The second was the panel on women and politics held as part of the 'Fearless Politics: The Life and Times of Hazel Brown' conference on March 27–28, 2015. Speakers included Terry Ince, Khadijah Ameen, Nicole Dyer-Griffith and Penelope Beckles. The third forum was on 'Gender and Politics in the 2015 General Election'. Held on September 30, 2015, the speakers were Khadijah Ameen, Nafeesa Mohammed, Jowelle de Souza, Colin Robinson, Luke Sinnette and Sabrina Mowlah-Baksh. Finally on June 16, 2016, Gabrielle Jamela Hosein gave the feature address on 'Women, Politics and Transformational Leadership' at the UWI Open Campus in St. Lucia as part of the IGDS Regional Lecture Series, drawing specifically on the research produced by Shirley Campbell and Denise Blackstock. These presentations are available on the IGDS YouTube page.

In the years between the project's initialization and the publication of this collection, many persons have helped sustain the interest and energy needed to see this research and its dissemination through to completion. First, the IGDS, its staff and the heads of the institute deserve our sincere thanks, for supporting this research from within, taking on this project as its own. From within the IGDS, Patricia Mohammed's wise and ethical guidance made managing a range of challenges a true learning experience. We would also like to acknowledge the contribution of Tessa Ottley and Amilcar Sanatan for their assistance.

To end on a personal note, we must thank our families, friends and colleagues for their love and patience with us, without which we couldn't have balanced all that seemed necessary to accomplish. Jane Parpart would particularly like to thank her spouse Professor Timothy Shaw, her family and her colleagues at IGDS and other institutions around the world. In particular, the Anglophone Caribbean continues to influence her thinking and writing and to inspire new ways of approaching gender in an increasingly complicated global world. Above all, she would like to thank her students, who continue to inform and inspire her work.

Gabrielle Jamela Hosein would like to thank her mother, whose weekly help with baby Ziya, born over the course of this project, made completion possible with much less guilt about the number of hours spent at her desk, rather than with her family. She would also like to thank her husband, Lyndon 'Stonez' Livingstone, who has provided quiet love and many sandwiches over a seemingly endless production cycle, and her badass, feminist friends, who know who they are, and who were generous with food, faith and fiery cuss on her behalf when needed. Finally, Yarra River, where everything is put into perspective, deserves special mention.

This collection is another step in a long movement to end hierarchies and biases that limit our experience of being equal, human and Caribbean. May the collection stimulate global conversations, critiques and collaborations, and future feminist activist, bureaucratic and scholarly work. These will add necessary steps forward in a struggle whose emancipatory possibilities are now ours to envision and fearlessly pursue.

Chapter 1

Feminist Strategies, Masculinist Resistances and Gendered Transformations in Caribbean Perspective

Gabrielle Jamela Hosein and Jane Parpart

INTRODUCTION

While women's political representation and state commitment to gender mainstreaming have been increasing around the world steadily, albeit marginally, since the Fourth World Conference on Women in 1995, they have only produced mixed results. This highlights the need for further research into the relationship between strengthening democracy and struggles for women's rights and gender equality. For example, to what extent has women's participation in democratic governance changed inequitable and undemocratic practices within governmental bodies and civil society? Have quota systems helped to increase women's leadership and effective representation of women's interests in democratic processes? Has the turn to policy solutions been productive for gender mainstreaming? Has feminist advocacy empowered women leaders and transformed power relations? And have these practices challenged the influence of colonial perceptions and practices of democracy and governance in postcolonies, translating into gender justice for women and marginalized men in public life?

A substantial body of Caribbean feminist scholarship has examined women's political leadership, gender and citizenship, constitution making and various issues characterizing mainstreaming gender in policy and planning. However, very little of this work has pulled these different areas together, seeing them as complementary parts of feminist activism for gender justice, and the opportunities and resistances it negotiates. Taken individually, each area elucidates one aspect of how policy and politics are gendered. Taken together, a series of pictures emerge which attend to governance structures, campaign discourses, state machineries, policy text analysis, men's gender consciousness and individual women's narratives which, layered onto each other, show the depth of the multiple levels of feminist strategizing, success, refusal and containment.

This collection is such an integrated project, drawing on decades of Caribbean feminist analysis, while uniquely interconnecting disparate areas of focus into one picture of more than a century of feminist struggle to promote democratic governance, women's rights and gender equality in the Anglophone Caribbean. Four feminist strategies to advance gender justice are explored here. First, women's political leadership is examined for the extent to which women have been able to enter representative politics, and challenge masculinism while there. Second, electoral quotas are assessed for their impact on effective women's participation and leadership in representative government. Third, the capacity of national gender policy documents to promote gender equality is evaluated, both from a policymaking and from a policy implementation perspective. Finally, the impact of feminist organizing around a vision of transformational leadership, in and out of the state, is investigated. As is now well established, getting numerical parity in representative politics is only one step towards securing a space within representative politics for women and men to make decisions which transform inequities in public life.

Each of these strategies expands spaces for women and men to alter gender relations and to shift the gender ideologies that limit women's effective political participation and leadership. Together, they reflect a core set of historical struggles waged across the Anglophone Caribbean. This collection documents this history as it has been experienced in five Caribbean countries, focusing specifically and ethnographically on countries where these struggles appeared to have been won. The five-year administration of Kamla Persad-Bissessar, Trinidad and Tobago's first woman prime minister, is therefore the subject of the national case study on women's political leadership. A focus on Guyana follows, as this is the only Anglophone Caribbean country to adopt an electoral quota system. From here, the collection turns to Dominica and Jamaica to explore gender policymaking and implementation. Dominica was one of the first countries to approve of such a policy and Jamaica is one of the most recent. Finally, the collection stays within the Eastern Caribbean for the national case study on transformational leadership, as two women, trained by the Caribbean Institute for Women in Leadership (CIWiL), who have been involved in public life, were willing to share their life histories. Together, these five in-depth case studies of four feminist strategies provide insights into transnational, regional and national alliances between states, international organizations, non-governmental organizations (NGOs) and feminist movements, and demonstrate the lived experiences of feminist activists, and women and men both enacting and confronting masculinist resistances in the region.

For example, while the structural and political resistances to women's transformational leadership are explored in regard to the constitutional change in Guyana, the individual, in-depth narratives from St. Lucia provide nuances of women's experience, and their feelings and dilemmas that help to explain the limitations facing advocates of Guyana's quota system. While the draft national gender policy process was partially explored in relation to Kamla Persad-Bissessar's manoeuvring of femininity discourses in Trinidad and Tobago, the case studies of Jamaica and Dominica provide greater insight into the way masculinism influences policy politics from the perspective of feminist bureaucrats and those in civil society. Thus, the project's comparative approach demonstrates how a broad Anglophone Caribbean effort, led by feminists in civil society and the state, took different forms at different times and through different networks across the region. It is a multifaceted story focusing on parts of a whole, showing their interrelatedness while giving constituent elements, from discourses to bureaucratic processes, and from policy texts and laws to individual narratives, more or less focus in each chapter.

The significance of the collection's historical approach is its acknowledgement of many decades of women's organizing, which emerged in response to the hierarchical conditions of colonial, Caribbean plantation economies, in which women and men were both adversaries and allies. It was this experience which would lead intellectuals like Trinidadian-born Claudia Jones to theorize the multiple interlocking jeopardies of gender, race and class as early as the 1930s, and it is to this activist-intellectual legacy of globally connected praxis that the collection traces its genealogy. More to the present, the Caribbean has been the area outside of North America, par excellence, for an early and 'frontal' masculinist backlash in the form of an overwhelmingly popular concern about male marginalization. Thus, it contributes to the scholarship on contemporary masculinism and the limits of gender mainstreaming by analysing gender relations, negotiations and transformations from the perspective of a transnational feminist movement, which, over three decades, has explicitly engaged male allies and questions of masculinities while destabilizing the homogenous category 'woman' on the basis of race, class and sexuality. Indeed, given its ethnic and religious heterogeneity and uneven development as well as long experience of women's educational and occupational advancement and autonomy, the Caribbean provides an ideal site for detailing the contradictions of women and men's reproduction of and challenge to hetero-patriarchal norms as well as both the uptake and containment of a language of women's rights and equality by state and society. Essentially, tracking and qualifying 'successes' are another beginning for stories about the tensions, limits, challenges and transformations experienced by feminist advocacy in public life.

The chapters therefore take different angles to regional feminist strategies to engender democracy and governance, but are propelled by three central questions:

1. How are the twenty-first century shifts in gender ideologies, stimulated by women's movements, shaping access to, exercise and redistributions of rights and power among groups of Caribbean women and men?
2. Have feminist strategies to engender democracy and good governance, with particular attention to women's political leadership, electoral quota systems, national gender policies and transformational leadership, effectively advanced gender justice in the Anglophone Caribbean?
3. What are the lessons for feminist analysis and advocacy with regard to feminist institutionalization and feminist movement-building?

These questions emerged as an entry for our engagement with the international feminist literature on women's political power in the state, the role of quotas in women's political advancement, the role of national gender policies and gender mainstreaming, and the potential of transformational leadership to foster gender equality.

CARIBBEAN FEMINIST STRATEGIES IN GLOBAL PERSPECTIVE

The three questions explored in this book are situated in and speak to international debates on women's political participation, the role of female quotas in women's political participation and activism and the impact of national gender plans and women's activism around political issues, including gender justice. The research in this book thus not only speaks to issues of women, gender justice, political power and transformational leadership in the Anglophone Caribbean, but also contributes to ongoing debates around the world. These debates not only reflect the growing concern with global trends, forces and perspectives, but also are deeply affected by scholarship on postcolonial and decolonial realities, global governance and the impact of cultural differences in a complex globalizing world.

Women's low levels of participation in political institutions have been an ongoing feminist concern. Quotas have been seen as a key mechanism for ensuring greater female participation in parliaments and political parties everywhere. First introduced in the 1970s in Western Europe to influence political selection processes (Dahlerup 1998), by 2006 around 40 countries had introduced quotas for women in elections to national political institutions. Many major political parties have voluntarily created party quotas to encourage women's participation in political elections and institutions (Tadros 2011, 1; Squires 2007). Quotas have played a role in improving gender ratios in many national parliaments, and have highlighted the importance of greater gender balance in political parties and institutions. At the same time, the quota systems have often been disappointing. In India, improvement in women's participation in local elections and parliaments has failed to address the reluctance to apply this strategy to women's entry into national political institutions (Jayal 2006). Moreover, the literature on quotas for women suggests that no technical formula, including the use of quotas, can ensure significant participation in national political institutions. Quotas have often been used to improve the gender balance of political candidates with little concern for how many women are actually elected to serve in national legislatures and parliaments. Indeed, global research suggests that quotas have often been used as a proxy for a genuine commitment to gender justice. They also do not guarantee elections of women who are committed to gender equality and gender justice rather than simply providing places for supporters of local political parties and their leaders, who may or may not be concerned with gender issues (Squires 2007; Franceschet, Krook and Piscopo 2012). Thus quotas remain a contested vehicle for change around the world, suggesting the need for a more in-depth analysis of the way they work or do not work in specific contexts. The chapter on quotas in Guyana contributes to this body of literature, and provides evidence of the limits of quotas as vehicles for social change and gender justice.

Feminists around the world have also been concerned with increasing the number of women in positions of political power at the national level. The number of women who have been heads of state remains relatively small, so their impact continues to be an ongoing concern that calls for further research. Many of the most well-known female political leaders, such as Margaret Thatcher of the United Kingdom and Indira Gandhi of India, have displayed little concern for or commitment to gender issues. They have achieved power by being 'the best man in the cabinet', fitting in with the masculinist culture of power politics. These leaders have done little to challenge that culture, and may have even strengthened it (Squires 2007; Genovese and Steckenrider, 2013). Sometimes women have been placed in political leadership positions when a party is in decline. Witness the election of a female head of the Canadian state just as her party was about to lose its grip on power. Considerable interest has been focused on the rise of female presidents in Latin America, particularly in Brazil, Argentina, Costa Rica and Chile. A number of these leaders have experienced considerable pushback, have not been re-elected or have been ejected from power, such as the recent case of Rousseff in Brazil (Jalalzai 2016; Franceschet, Krook and Piscopo 2012; Tadros 2014; Schmidt-Bayer 2012; Thomas 2011).

The Anglophone Caribbean provides an interesting case study as it has experienced a number of very powerful women political leaders who have managed to rule and survive within the masculinist political cultures of their political parties. Eugenia Charles, who led Dominica from 1980 to 1995, is one of a number of such leaders in the region (Barriteau and Cobley 2006). Trinidad and Tobago's previous president, Kamla Persad-Bissessar, provides a recent example along with the past woman prime minister of Jamaica. The number of female leaders in the Anglophone Caribbean makes it a particularly interesting site for exploring the possibilities, and challenges, facing female political leadership in the region. The chapters on political leadership contribute to the vibrant discussions on female political leadership in Latin America and the Caribbean, as well as global debates on this very complicated and important issue.

Gender equality and gender justice have also been sought through policy instruments, particularly a concern with mainstreaming gender into all insti-tutions and practices around the world. This effort was influenced by the Beijing Platform for Action that emerged from the 1995 United Nations World Conference on Women in Beijing and called for a global approach to gender inequality. Gender mainstreaming was quickly taken up by supranational institutions, international development agencies and national governments (Walby 2005; Squires 2007). While sometimes criticized as too ambitious and optimistic about the possibilities for fundamental change (Parpart 2014), gender mainstreaming remains a fundamental mechanism for encouraging social change and gender equality (Squires 2007). Supranational institutions and international development agencies continue to be key players in this process. The UN has been particularly influential, encouraging development initiatives globally but also seeking national solutions to gender equality challenges. One of the UN's key strategies has centred on encouraging the adoption of national gender policies around the world. These policies are seen as key instruments for encouraging national commitment to gender equal-ity and for establishing legal structures that will define and shape national governance processes aimed at improving it. National gender policies have emerged in many parts of the world, but critical scholarly attention to their impact is still developing. Efforts to address these issues through case studies in Africa continue to be an important challenge (Chauraya 2012). Clearly a global discussion is needed. The three chapters on national gender policies in the Anglophone Caribbean provide important overviews and case studies to analyse this important legal effort to legislate gender equality. These chap-ters bring masculinities, gender relations and hierarchies as well as cultural, political and economic issues into the discussion, reminding the reader that gender is a primary conduit for shaping access to material and social benefits in particular societies. National efforts to legislate more gender-equitable processes are important issues that call out for further comparative work. The three chapters are a contribution to this ongoing debate.

The chapters on political advocacy for enhancing gender equality and gender justice in the Anglophone Caribbean raise important questions that are often ignored or subsumed in development praxis. The chapters explore the impact of efforts to develop transformational leadership that has the potential to enhance gender awareness and foster more gender-equitable behaviour in a variety of institutions. This is a relatively understudied area that has important implications for social change. The chapter on St. Lucia reminds us that transformational leadership has to take local contexts into consideration, including understanding the limits, as well as the possibilities, for fostering gender justice in particular contexts. This is pathbreaking work and hopefully will inspire and contribute to further exploration of transformational efforts around the world. It should bring together the large literature on women's empowerment, peace-building and development with new approaches to transformational leadership, masculinities, gender relations and gendered hierarchies. Aili Tripp has provided a useful overview of these trends (Tripp 2012). The work on transitional justice and peacemaking also provides insights into new ways of understanding conflict, including gender conflicts (Buckley-Zisel and Stanley 2011; Cheldelin and Eliatamby 2011; Tadros 2014). These discussions cross disciplines and contexts and promise to develop into new approaches to agency, subjectivities, gender relations and transformational leadership. The Anglophone Caribbean is a fertile site for continuing and expanding this debate. This book is intended to contribute to this conversation.

MASCULINIST RESISTANCES AND GENDERED TRANSFORMATIONS: CARIBBEAN FEMINIST CONCEPTUALIZATIONS

Our collective study of Caribbean feminist strategies contributes to this global literature by drawing on the strength of Caribbean feminist theorizing of masculinist resistance; the tensions that characterize varying conceptualizations of 'gender'; and the goal of gender justice in a context where feminist politics are both culturally included and contained.

Caribbean feminist engagement with masculinist backlash has been well developed in scholarship over the last thirty years. While feminists were already talking about male anxieties in response to the establishment of women's desks, commissions and bureaus in the 1970s, Caribbean feminist scholarship in the field was stimulated by the publication of two books – the *Marginalisation of the Black Male* (1986) and *Men at Risk* (1991). In these books, Errol Miller argues that schooling and other prestigious occupations in Jamaica were taken over by women as part of a larger colonial effort to disempower black men and prevent them from challenging white colonial men for power. 'In a real sense', writes Miller, 'the black woman was used against the black man' (Miller 1991, 125). In his theorizing of patriarchy, women's increasing power, including their independence and power at home, are intimately connected to men's marginalization. What is significant for the Anglophone Caribbean is that this thesis swept across the region as a generalized experience of *all* Caribbean men in the face of women's education and occupational gains, and a concern with male marginalization became a flag for a successful backlash against Caribbean feminist institutionalization. This, despite the fact that many Caribbean men do not experience economic, political, institutional, familial, religious, legal or other forms of 'marginalization' while the majority of women have not been among those able to 'reverse' roles. The question of male marginalization has also never been popularly or bureaucratically taken up in the context of gay, transgender and queer men's experiences of unequal sexual citizenship, or indeed in terms of dismantling class hierarchies which create relations of dominance and marginality among men.

Miller's thesis also was critiqued by a range of scholars from the region, and their critiques have global relevance as other postcolonies move into similar gender demographics. Barbara Bailey (1997) and Janet Brown (1995) pointed to greater complexity in the schooling data, suggesting that boys remained high performing in specific subjects and that gender stereotyping in school curricula continued. Christine Barrow showed that men are not marginal to Caribbean female-headed households by pointing to the role that uncles, brothers, grandfathers and sons play. Barry Chevannes (1999) argued that women continue to be elected or allowed to function in leadership positions far less than men, whether in relation to university student government, community-level governance, religion and so on. Even where there are shifts in numbers, Keisha Lindsay points out that to 'argue that women can overpower men simply on the basis of increased income or occupational status is to incorrectly presume that income or occupational dominance form the sole basis of men's control over women' (Lindsay 2002, 76). Mark Figueroa (2004) countered that 'male privileging' reinforced a sexual division of labour at home, which then provides girls with the kind of socialization that has enabled them to function with greater docility and focus at school. Andaiye (2003) pointed to globalization's effects on insecure livelihoods such that 'men's losses are not women's gains' (Barriteau 2003, 216). Mondesire and Dunn (1995, 86) concluded that the majority of mechanisms to achieve the strategic objectives of the Beijing Platform for Action in 1995 had never 'been implemented nor even attempted by the majority of regional governments' and that 'political will to do so seems to have evaporated' (Barriteau 2003, 202).

This collection is situated in Eudine Barriteau's approach to this debate regarding male marginalization because it provides a framework for assessing what reconstruction of the institutions of civil and political society requires, particularly because entrenched gender roles normalize political injustice across public life. Barriteau's conceptualization of gender relations usefully refers to 'the continuous social, political, economic, cultural, and psychological expressions of the material and ideological dimensions of a gender system' (Barriteau 1998, 189; 1994; 1998, 188; 2000, 2). While 'the material dimension exposes how men or women gain access to or are allocated the material and non-material resources within a state and society' (Barriteau 1998, 191), 'the ideological dimension indicates how Caribbean societies construct and maintain beliefs and expressions of masculinity and femininity' (2000, 6). Inequality is rooted in asymmetries of power that have differential ideological and material outcomes (Barriteau 1996). Barriteau thus suggests using this approach to assess the extent to which gendered power relations are shifting, and their implications for women and men. She specifically suggests asking:

> What are the policies, legislation, prejudices, practices that penalize or reward men? What are the deeply entrenched, policies of the state and its institutions that marginalize men? What are the contents and effects of the gender identities men subscribe to? What part do they play in expressions of masculinity that are viewed as problematic? What are the recommendations in the literature for dealing with marginality if it exists? And how do these address concerns for gender justice and equality? (2000, 7)

These questions are useful for moving discussion from whether there are individual male adversaries or allies to a focus instead on the ideological and material conditions within which gendered transformations are being sought.

What has been the Caribbean feminist experience of such transformations? First, it is worth noting the extent to which the struggle has been over the meanings of the word 'gender' itself. Barriteau observes a proliferation of competing meanings for gender, including 'women', 'new, slick feminist strategies for dominating and emasculating men' and 'programmes and policies to introduce and maintain a focus on men' (Barriteau 2004, 30). For her, gender meant the loss of a focus on 'women' in public discourse and a way of neutering feminist politics. As Barriteau continues, 'When we focus equally on men, as national machineries are now being mandated to do, will we see women accepted as equals or will we see attempts to contain the long-overdue gains that women have made?' (2004, 42–43). As early as 2000, Peggy Antrobus (2000, 25) wrote,

> My conclusion is that there are currently efforts to de-politicize the field and the movement by removing the feminist political agenda. I see evidence of this in the co-option of feminist language (e.g. empowerment), feminist concepts (e.g. gender) and feminist visions (e.g. transformational leadership) and by the various bureaucratic devices such as gender mainstreaming, gender analysis, and the substitution of the word 'gender' for 'women' in so many programmes.

This view opposes one that claims gender has been a substitute term for women, and highlights the specificity of the Caribbean experience of masculinist uptake of gender in and out of the state.

Tracy Robinson (2004) similarly refers to 'gender somethings' 'whose meaning though nebulous, was understood to be antithetical to a feminist politics' (Haynes 2011, 189). Patricia Mohammed (2003) observes the development of everyday gender consciousness among women and men that has come without feminist consciousness and even with a fear of feminist activism. Tonya Haynes suggests that gender equality discourses have been absurd with the women's movement 'recast as the "gender movement" and accused of excluding the concerns of men' (Ibid 87). Michelle Rowley (2011, 86) describes 'rhetorical practices of gender mainstreaming and the lack of substantive moves toward gender equity' as a form of inclusion as containment. What is the significance of this for understanding the nexus of feminist strategies and masculinist resistances? Haynes writes,

> The production of different gendered subjectivities for men serves as a location from which they make demands of the state.... In short, three positions from which men make claims to the state have emerged: from a position of gendered subjectivities, as genderless citizens and by rejecting formal socializing institutions which are considered key for the production of responsible middle-class masculinity. Furthermore, Barriteau highlights the fact that the Caribbean state now leads the discourse on addressing men as gendered beings when in the past, discussions on gender were never initiated by the state. In the past, the state's response to issues of gender occurred only as a result of activism by women's NGOs and transnational changes in the gender regime. (Haynes 2011, 90–91)

Noting 'the emergence of new gendered subjectivities and the resilience of old forms of domination' (Haynes 2011, 86), Tonya Haynes conceptualizes contemporary gender consciousness as

> the mainstream, broad-based, awareness of gender as an idea, concept, term, *something* – whose understanding includes that which may be considered feminist and that which is vaguely understood as related to women, men, sex and sexuality and questions of equality. The more prevalent understanding of gender, however, is not a neatly feminist one. Gender consciousness then is not necessarily a consciousness of the existence of gendered power relations or an awareness of sexist oppression with the acknowledgement that this needs to be redressed.... The swift uptake of 'gender' by state manager has been credited to its understanding of being apolitical and its distance from women and feminism. The proliferation of gender talk in everyday life may also be due to the conceptual fuzziness of the term with its 'vagueness and open-endedness' being the key to its invocation by a range of constituencies and to very different, often mutually antagonistic, political ends. (Haynes 2011, 97–98)

This collection is situated in this historical and conceptual context with its focus on tracing the possibilities for a gender just system as one in which there are no asymmetries of access to, or allocations of status, power and material resources in a society, or in the control over and the capacity to benefit from these resources. There are no hierarchies of gender identities or the meanings Caribbean society give to masculinity and femininity. In an unjust gender system there is unequal access to and distribution of material resources and power (Barriteau 1998, 191). This conceptualization of gender justice requires assessing the power relations within which women and men may be seeking to transform representative, bureaucratic, legal, policy-centred, discursive and other forms of power. The following summaries show that this is exactly what the collection's chapters do.

CHAPTER CONTRIBUTIONS

Drawing on these concepts as threads tying together the chapters, the collection's chapters' main findings should be read in relation to each other.

WOMEN'S POLITICAL LEADERSHIP: POSSIBILITIES AND LIMITS FOR WOMEN IN THE STATE

Women remain a statistical minority in the parliaments and in local government bodies across the Anglophone Caribbean. Gabrielle Jamela Hosein shows that this significant gender bias in the Anglophone Caribbean reveals ideological and structural barriers that continue to powerfully influence political leadership. It is therefore not surprising that women who occupy the highest level of political leadership, the office of prime minister or president, have not significantly advanced women's access to and effective participation in parliamentary and local government systems, whether in Dominica, Guyana, Jamaica or Trinidad and Tobago, the four countries which have been led by women prime ministers. Elected female representatives, as well as those on boards, commissions and other high-level fora, remain largely unable to undermine and redefine masculinist power relations or inequitable and undemocratic practices within governmental bodies and civil society, despite the incremental but important growth in the visibility and number of women in democratic governance. Women's political leadership has stimulated shifts in governmental approaches to women's rights, and ideologies and practices regarding gender equality, but these are fraught at every turn with ideological, bureaucratic and other kinds of policy implementation confusion, drag and backlash, including resistance generated by popular belief in the myth of male marginalization. Although a few women have managed to slip through the tiny fissures in the glass ceiling, they do so at a very high cost, and face disproportionate public attacks that cast them as weak and incompetent. Such regional feminist struggles highlight how sexuality, gender, class, ethnicity and middle-class politics of respectability remain challenges for women political leaders, even those with male allies.

The historical issues introduced in chapter 1 are explored here in a case study of cabinet- and state-board appointments, the making of the draft national gender policy, gender-responsive national budgeting, legislation that challenges sexism and homophobia, and women's experiences of campaigning under the leadership of Trinidad and Tobago's prime minister Kamla Persad-Bissessar. Aleah Ranjitsingh brings together textual analysis with ethnographic observation and interviews with activists and political leaders to detail how dominant ideologies which allocate gendered spaces are resilient enough to allow women to shift the discourse of women's political leadership, creating historical cracks that are significant in their own right, while being disciplined by the political unpopularity to do much more than speak a language of women's rights on paper or on political platforms. Kamla Persad-Bissessar's engagement with feminist issues has been uneven. She has expanded the social safety net, and made children's health and education her cause celebre. Yet, the qualitative transformations or even interruptions of Caribbean gender systems, hoped for by feminists, remain elusive. The invoking of femininity and womanhood and the presence of a female body, in what has predominantly been seen as a male space, is powerfully inspirational and problematic as possibilities and limitations to women's political leadership exist in difficult contradiction. Looking specifically at campaigning, for example, this chapter examines how discourses regarding femininity shape the embodiment and exercise as well as limitations placed on women's political leadership. Individual women politicians are then blamed for what are seen as personal failures of leadership by publics that deny the significance of gender inequalities, which are tightly interwoven with state and political party structures, and the status quo.

GENDER QUOTAS:
PARLIAMENTARY PROVISIONS WITHOUT POWER?

Deepening the historical picture of individual women leaders' experiences and state policy processes with one focused on structural reform, Natalie Persadie reviews the Anglophone Caribbean struggle to secure gender quotas, and explains the significant role of international forces, such as the Beijing Platform for Action and regional feminist networking. In Guyana, the only Anglophone Caribbean nation that adopted a quota of one-third of female candidates on each political party's electoral list, the push came from a few women activists, supported by a much larger transnational network, who strategically intervened in broader discussions about democracy and constitutional reform in the late 1990s and early 2000s, reacted to many years of non-democratic rule (1964–1992) with resulting concern for individual rights and democratic processes. The revised Constitution addressed three main issues regarding women's representation: extraction of women's names from the list, the minimum proportion of female candidates to be placed on a party's list and the maximum proportion of geographical constituencies in which a party may contest without a female candidate. The Elections Law, passed in 2000, adopted a candidate quota to ensure at least a third of female candidates on each electoral list. This chapter documents this success, for gender quotas are a critical step towards the feminization of parliament, and can provide a basis for legislative activism around gender equality and gender justice.

An in-depth view of how Guyana's gender quotas are experienced and negotiated shows that while one-third of the total number of candidates in each political party's national list are required to be women, the same percentage do not have to be extracted from the list and placed in parliament. It has thus taken continual women's movement pressure on Guyana's parties to ensure that almost one-third of parliamentarians are women. Iman Khan shows that the quota system has been successful in increasing the visibility and embodied representation of women in parliament, as well as in potentially disrupting the discursive terrain of a masculinist institution. Yet, women in parliament are left trying to negotiate the masculinist terrain of their parties while women's rights activists criticize them for ignoring injustices against grassroots families and undermining efforts to empower women. The focus on getting women into parliament has not significantly advanced the gendered norms and relations that ensure patriarchal discipline and control despite the quota system. Drawing on interviews, parliamentary debates and analyses of legislative and budgetary commitments, this chapter echoes the collection's conclusions, highlighting that even when women access office and even when structural shifts are secured, state politics remain embedded in ethnic, class and geographical power struggles in which women need more than a 'critical mass' to fearlessly pursue transformed gender relations amid masculinist exercise of authority. The degree to which this is both a colonial heritage as well as a reflection of gendered practices raises important questions about the limits of current analyses of gender transformation in the Global South and elsewhere.

NATIONAL GENDER POLICIES: NEGOTIATING MASCULINITIES IN GENDER MAINSTREAMING

Whereas the first four chapters examined individual women's struggles to exercise political leadership and their implications for democracy, women's

rights and gender equality, this chapter explores the politics of national gender policymaking as a process of controlling narratives about gender. Framed
by a complex interplay of belief systems, resistances, actors and silences,
Deborah McFee's study of feminist activism in the region suggests that most
national gender policies grew out of a concern about the position of women.
The problem of women was subsequently reframed to be about the need to
achieve gender equality, for example, in 'balancing' attention to women with
attention to men. Yet, the politics of difference, assertion of multiple identities
as well as negotiation of various norms of gender and sexuality, signal deeply
contested policy spaces, explaining why gender policies were approved in
some Anglophone Caribbean countries while remaining disallowed in others.
Again, taking a regional and historical view, the gender policymaking experiences of the Cayman Islands, Trinidad and Tobago, Dominica, Jamaica, the
Bahamas and Belize are surveyed.

Deepening and narrowing the analytic lens to a case study of Dominica,
Ramona Biholar examines the centrality of the discourse and the practice
of masculinities to the implementation of the Dominica National Gender
Policy (DNGP), which was approved in 2005. The DNGP's definition and
operationalization of gender highlighted the benefits of moving the discussion
beyond women to include men, the multiple and competing interpretations
of women's and men's gendered realities, and the gender power relations
in the policy document and in public discourse. While women's advancements are visible, the continuing hegemony of patriarchal ideologies and
asymmetric power relations illuminates their power as organizing forces in
everyday life and state bureaucratic practice. This highlights the need to theorize men and masculinities' incorporation in national gender policy's efforts
to advance gender justice in Dominica. This chapter complements the case
study of Trinidad and Tobago by examining the implications of masculinist
discourses, not just for women in politics, but for state processes such as policymaking, for media and civic participation in governance, and for gendered
popular discourse on specific areas such as education. It also raises questions
about competing notions of gender, particularly their framing in Western/
colonial and/or decolonial/postcolonial discourses.

While the regional review focused on regional experiences of policymaking and the Dominica case study focused on the politics of policy implementation, Maziki Thame and Dhanaraj Thakur examine the text of the Jamaican
National Gender Policy for Gender Equality (NGPE), approved in 2011.
Also drawing on interviews and parliamentary Hansard records, it analyses
the policy as a statist and feminist strategy for establishing an official vision
for public and private life. Critical interrogation of the policy text shows
how the deeply patriarchal nature of the Jamaican state affected policy production *and* implementation. The policy failed to sufficiently challenge the

patriarchal status quo because, as an instrument of the state, it was charged with changing the same organizations and institutions responsible for its implementation. It therefore remains unclear where the momentum to create change beyond the text may be found, particularly in relation to sexuality, reproduction and women's rights. This chapter, then, redirects attention away from the processes of policymaking and implementation, back to the resilient, if unstable, masculinist ideologies in state and society, and the nuanced ways they limit the transformational possibilities of feminist, mainstreaming strategies.

TRANSFORMATIONAL LEADERSHIP: FEMINIST PEDAGOGIES, NEO-LIBERAL EMPOWERMENT

Coming after the collection's examination of embodied discourses of femininity in women's political leadership and electoral campaigning, myths regarding 'male marginalization' in processes of state policymaking, and masculinist resistances to structural shifts in favour of women's leadership, this chapter charts the late twentieth-century struggle to transform notions of power available to women (and many men). The Anglophone Caribbean search for an alternative transformational style of leadership emerged in the 1970s and 1980s amid biases that viewed leadership as a male domain dominated by favoured kinds of masculinities, women's reluctance to engage in political campaigns requiring behaviours considered anti-feminine, women's conceptions of leadership as corrupt and authoritarian, and higher levels of women's impoverishment. Addressing the need to transform the 'content' and 'conduct' of leadership, passionate regional feminist advocacy invested in creating a gender-sensitive, critical mass of women knowledgeable, competent and committed to running for political and other publically elected positions, taking appropriate action to influence gender-sensitive policymaking and implementation, and redefining leadership in ways that could further gender justice. This historical view highlights the depth of masculinist resistances to feminist political power given that women have found greater success in the micro practices of their personal and professional lives, but as Shirley Campbell suggests, they are less able to successfully and confidently build a feminist movement for women's rights within the broader discourses of the rights of men, children and the community.

In order to complement the budgetary, legislative, participant-observation and quantitative data on politics, policy and the state, the chapter on the St. Lucia case narrates the life histories of two women trained to be transformational leaders in order to illustrate how gender relations manifest in different and contradictory ways, for example in their conflicting viewpoints on whether there is a place in society for gender roles or whether these should be discarded because they limit both sexes' full potential. While cognizant of the importance of analysing discourses, texts, structures and processes, this chapter focuses on women's own negotiations with the personal as political. Both women are described by colleagues, as well as themselves, as adopting a democratic leadership style that is consultative, involves networking, seeks consensus, is community-based, promotes teamwork and group ownership of ideas, and attempts to facilitate and engage others in the pursuit of individual and social transformation. This approach is different from customary practices under previous masculinist regimes, which were autocratic, hierarchical, divisive and disempowering. Yet, both women share narratives about persistent gender stereotypes, resistance to bottom-up community development, personal struggles balancing work and family, and compromises to their health. Beyond pursuing empowerment at individual and interpersonal levels, their narratives also detail the barriers they face without sufficient strategies for collective movement-building against structural and institutionalized gender hierarchies. They also illustrate the need to understand the local gender dynamics and to shape approaches to transformational strategies within these contexts. Continued training needs to focus on strategies for women transformational leaders to deal with gender-based discrimination directed at them even as they work to break down these barriers for others, as well as the complexities of daily gendered power struggles and hierarchies. Once again, Denise Blackstock raises questions about the transformative agenda of the present-day political elite, particularly regarding gender equality.

CONCLUSION

The edited collection aims to explore the experiences and understandings of women and men to determine the factors which enable or impede transformation of public leadership and gendered power relations. It investigates the impact and effectiveness of feminist strategies to promote democratic governance, women's rights and gender equality in the Caribbean, with particular attention to legislative, budgetary, policy and programme creation and implementation. It shows how resistant gender ideologies limit women's political participation, leadership and commitments to gender mainstreaming despite greater capacity among individual women and men as well as civil society and state bureaucracies to transform gender and sexual relations. The following nine chapters in the collection therefore highlight the resilience of masculinist resistance to feminist struggles for gender-just citizenship while at the same time revealing potential spaces and opportunities for change.

Focusing on case studies of five Caribbean countries, this unique collection draws together a panoramic view spanning election campaigning, policymaking and implementation, men's rights movements as well as pro-feminist men's alliances, structural and constitutional reforms such as quota systems, transnational feminist activism and the personal politics of transformational leadership. This picture is drawn from a rich combination of historical reviews, ethnographic observations, textual and media analyses, quantitative data collection and life history interviews, which together create an historical, regionally comparative and national case-study approach to questions of gender policy and politics in the Anglophone Caribbean. The book thus reinforces concerns about the limits of decades of gender mainstreaming. Indeed, the Anglophone Caribbean history of uneven female representation at parliamentary and local government levels, limited success with implementing national gender policies, failures of advocacy regarding transformational leadership, and on-the-ground challenges to greater democracy reveal the importance of reshaping effective strategies through thorough analyses of existing and past impediments.

Women's participation in public life expands the bases for women and men working together, and women's agency, even if they are not working in gender-equitable contexts. This collection highlights how patriarchal forces undermine such agency, illuminating how statist policies and practices reinforce gender hierarchies. Formal protections, such as legislation and policies, are an incremental and necessary step for providing institutional, official recognition and protection. Expanded gender consciousness has meant that women and men in the region act as change agents to create new definitions of gender relations. Yet, masculinism, in the forms of male dominance and myths of male marginalization, its support from many women and men as well as the sexual division of labour in public and private spheres, continues to undermine the potential of feminist strategies. The way forward is a more robust analysis of how patriarchal forces undermine such agency, creating a discourse of women's failures, rather than illuminating how statist policies and practices reinforce gender hierarchies. Just as there is a danger in treating gender as referring only to women, there is also a danger in shifting gender from women to men without an analysis of masculine power and a critique of the gender relations and hierarchies established among men, among women, and between women and men, which are well established in the social relations of gender.

A number of questions are therefore suggested by these chapters. What can we learn about the limits of gender mainstreaming and the kinds of new approaches needed? In what ways can the issues of men as gendered beings be incorporated in struggles for gender equality without undermining the struggle for women's rights? This is a question that is acutely experienced in the Anglophone Caribbean. How can feminist efforts to transform the numbers and quality of leadership change gender and class imbalances not only between women and men, but also among women and among men? What are the strategies that can successfully pressure structures and institutions to change so that women leaders in politics and civil society are not individually or entirely blamed for their failures to be transformational? What are the possibilities for, and limits on, individual women's agency? How can feminist movements of women and men advocating gender justice continue to be strengthened? Finally, how does a focus on these questions point analysis to further thinking about strategies for their effective implementation? And how can these cases inform efforts in other parts of the world to achieve gender justice?

The struggle remains to integrate women into key decision-making institutions, but to also identify the forms of power that would facilitate and enable women's ability to negotiate and exercise power while there. Getting women into political institutions, whether as prime minister or through a quota system, has not solved the problem of female disempowerment in political spaces. Consequently, continued efforts to promote a gender analysis of domination and exclusion in political arenas are a crucial step towards gender equality. Such an analysis will enable an exploration of the role of material and ideological inequities in maintaining masculine hierarchies and will provide new ways of thinking about altering this imbalance and transforming politics into more hospitable places for women and for gender equality. Global and regional feminist activism therefore remains paramount. Bringing men into the discourse of development, as seen in Dominica, has been a successful approach to policy implementation, but this needs to be enacted creatively and without disavowing a transnational gender analysis of state practice that reveals neo-liberal forms of global capital and development, and the ways these exacerbate inequalities and tensions related to differences in class, religion, race and sexual preference, as lived and experienced in distinctive ways in nation states in the Anglophone Caribbean region.

Disjunctures and contradictions among policy, political leadership and transformation of gender relations remain difficult to negotiate, illustrating that national gender policies, women's political leadership, electoral quota systems and training of transformational leaders continue to challenge masculinist and hetero-patriarchal ideologies, even if in incremental ways. The collection highlights that these strategies may be insufficient, but are crucial, necessary and undeniably worth protecting. The factors that contribute to the success of the strategies in specific countries such as Trinidad and Tobago, Dominica, Jamaica, Guyana and St. Lucia do not provide in-depth explanations for why other countries have not succeeded in adopting quotas, achieving transformational leadership, or passing gender-equality plans, but they do provide detailed and nuanced cartographies of how gender, the state, policymaking and implementation, political leadership, and feminist visions for equality, democracy and women's rights have been and will have to be negotiated by any countries pursuing similar strategies in and beyond the region. The lesson remains one of learning from past strategies and successes while bringing creativity and commitment to new approaches for a more gender-equitable future.

REFERENCES

Andaiye. 2003. 'Smoke and Mirrors: The Illusion of CARICOM Women's Growing Economic Empowerment, Post-Beijing', in *Gender Equality in the Caribbean: Reality or Illusion*, edited by Gemma Tang Nain and Barbara Bailey, 73–107. Kingston, Jamaica: Ian Randle Publishers.

Antrobus, Peggy. 2000. 'The Rise and Fall of Feminist Politics in the Caribbean Women's Movement 1975–1995'. The Lucille Mathurin Mair Lecture 2000. The University of the West Indies, Mona Campus.

Bailey, Barbara. (1997). 'Sexist Patterns of Formal and Non-formal Education Programmes: The Case of Jamaica', in *Gender: A Caribbean Multidisciplinary Perspective* edited by Elsa Leo-Rhynie, Barbara Bailey and Christine Barrow, 144–58. Kingston, Jamaica: Ian Randle Publishers.

Barriteau, Eudine and Alan Cobley (eds). 2006. *Enjoying Power: Eugenia Charles and Political Leadership in the Commonwealth Caribbean*. Kingston, Jamaica: University of the West Indies Press.

Barriteau, Eudine. 1994. 'Gender and Development Planning in the Postcolonial Caribbean: Female Entrepreneurs and the Barbadian State'. PhD. diss., Department of Political Science, Howard University.

_____. 1996. 'Gender Systems and the Project of Modernity in the Post-Colonial Caribbean'. Paper presented at the 1st SEPHIS Workshop on the Forging of Nationhood and the Contest over Citizenship, Ethnicity and History, New Delhi, India, 1996.

_____. 1998. 'Theorizing Gender Systems and the Project of Modernity in the Twentieth-Century Caribbean'. *Feminist Review* 59 (Summer): 186–209.

_____. 2000. 'Examining the Issues of Men, Male Marginalization and Masculinity in the Caribbean: Policy Implications'. Working Paper No. 4 (September), Centre for Gender and Development Studies, The University of the West Indies, Cave Hill Campus, Barbados.

_____. 2003. 'Conclusion: Beyond a Backlash – The Frontal Assault on Caribbean Women in the Decade of the 1990s', in *Gender Equality in the Caribbean: Reality or Illusion?*, edited by Gemma Tang Nain and Barbara Bailey, 201–32. Kingston, Jamaica: Ian Randle Publishers.

_____. 2004. 'Theorizing the Shift from Women to Gender in Caribbean Feminist Discourse: The Power Relations of Creating Knowledge', in *Confronting Power,*

Theorizing Gender: Interdisciplinary Perspectives in the Caribbean edited by Eudine Barriteau, 27–45. Kingston, Jamaica: Ian Randle Publishers.

Brown, Janet. 1995. *'Why man stay so, why woman stay so': Findings of the gender socialization project.* St, Michael, Barbados: Women and Development Unit, The University of the West Indies.

Buckley-Zistel, Suzanne and Ruth Stanley (eds). 2011. *Gender in Transitional Justice,* New York: Palgrave Macmillan.

Chauraya, Eforitha. 2012. 'The African View on Gender and its Impact on Implemented Gender Policies and Peace in Africa'. *Journal of Sustainable Development* 14(3): 252–61.

Cheldelin, Sandra and Maneshka Eliatamby (eds). 2011. *Women Waging War and Peace: International Perspectives of Women's Roles in Conflict and Post-conflict Reconstruction.* New York: Continuum International Publishers.

Chevannes, Barry. 1999. 'What We Sow and What We Reap: The Cultivation of Male Identity in Jamaica'. Lecture delivered at The Grace Kennedy Foundation Lecture Series, Kingston, Jamaica.

———. 2001. *Learning to be a Man: Culture, Socialization and Gender Identity in Five Caribbean Communities.* Kingston, Jamaica: University of the West Indies Press.

Dahlerup, Drude. 1998. 'Using Quotas to Increase Women's Political Representation', in *Women in Parliament: Beyond Numbers,* edited by Julie Ballington and Azza Karam, 140–53. Stockholm: IDEA.

Figueroa, Mark. 2004. 'Male Privileging and Male Academic Underperformance in Jamaica', in *Interrogating Caribbean Masculinities*, edited by Rhoda Reddock, 137–66. Kingston, Jamaica: UWI Press.

Franceschet, Susan, Mona Lena Krook, and Jennifer M. Piscopo (eds). 2012. *The Impact of Gender Quotas.* New York: Oxford University Press.

Genovese, Michael A. and Jamie S. Steckenrider (eds). 2013. *Women as Political Leaders*. London: Sage.

Haynes, Tonya. 2011. 'Mapping the Knowledge Economy of Gender in the Caribbean, 1975–2010: Feminist Thought, Gender Consciousness and the Politics of Knowledge'. PhD. diss., The University of the West Indies, Cave Hill Campus.

Jalalzai, Farida. 2016. *Women Presidents of Latin America: beyond family ties.* New York: Routledge.

Jayal, Niraja Gopal. 2006, 'Engendering Local Democracy: The Impact of Quotas for Women in India's Panchayats'. *Democratization* 13(1): 15–35.

Lindsay, Keisha. 2002. 'Is the Caribbean Male an Endangered Species?' in *Gendered Realities: Essays in Caribbean Feminist Thought*, edited by Patricia Mohammed, 56–82. Kingston, Jamaica: University of the West Indies Press.

Miller, Errol. 1991. *Men at Risk.* Kingston, Jamaica: Jamaica Publishing House.

Mohammed, Patricia. 2003. 'Like Sugar in Coffee: Third Wave Feminism and the Caribbean'. Social and Economic Studies 52(3): 5–30. http://www.jstor.org/stable/27865339. Accessed June 30, 2016.

Mondesire, Alicia and Leith Dunn. 1995. 'Towards Equity in Development. A Report on the Status of Women in Sixteen Commonwealth Caribbean Countries'. CARICOM Secretariat/Commonwealth, Georgetown, Guyana.

Parpart, Jane. 2014. 'Exploring the Transformative Potential of Gender Mainstreaming in International Development Institutions'. *Journal of International Development* 26(3): 382–95.

Robinson, Tracy. 2004. 'Gender, Feminism and Constitutional Reform in the Caribbean', in *Gender in the 21st Century: Caribbean Perspectives, Visions and Possibilities*, edited by Barbara Bailey and Elsa Leo-Rhynie, 592–625. Kingston, Jamaica: Ian Randle Publishers.

Rowley, Michelle. 2011. *Feminist Advocacy and Gender Equity in the Anglophone Caribbean: Envisioning a Politics of Coalition*. New York: Routledge.

Schmidt-Bayer, Leslie (ed). 2012. *Political Power and Women's Representation in Latin America*. Oxford: Oxford University Press.

Squires, Judith. 2007. *The New Politics of Gender Equality*. London: Palgrave Macmillan.

Tadros, Maria. 2011. 'Women Engaging Politically: Beyond Magic Bullets and Motorways'. Brighton Pathways of Women's Empowerment. Pathways Policy Paper

_____. (ed). 2014. *Women in Politics: Gender, Power and Development*. London: Zed Books.

Thomas, Gwynn. 2011. 'Michelle Bachelet's Liderazgo Feminino (Feminine Leadership)'. *International Feminist Journal of Politics* 13(1): 63–82.

Tripp, Aili Mari. 2012. 'Women's Political Empowerment on Statebuilding and Peacebuilding: A Baseline Study'. Accessed June 30, 2016. https://ailitripp.files. wordpress.com/2014/11/women_s-political-empowerment-in-statebuilding-and-peacebuilding.pdf.

Walby, Sylvia. 2005. 'Introduction: Comparative Mainstreaming in a Global Era'. *International Feminist Journal of Politics*, 7(4): 453–70.

Chapter 2

A Will to Power

The Anglophone Caribbean Struggle to Advance Women's Political Leadership

Gabrielle Jamela Hosein

Because women who hold power are generally resented, and women and power have an ambiguous, uneasy relationship, women's leadership occupies a contradictory political space. Women who are leaders exist and operate in the borderlands of power. They are within the paradigms of leadership because of the positions they hold; simultaneously they are on the borders because ideologies of gender encode their sex to be the objects of power and not the initiators of decisions. (Barriteau 2003a, 26)

We do not wish to be regarded as rebellious, but we would point out to you that to cling sullenly or timidly to ancient, outmoded ways of government is not in the best interests of our country. (Dame Doris Louise Johnson cited in Barrow-Giles 2011, 73)

INTRODUCTION

In the Anglophone Caribbean, only four women have become heads of state through electoral politics. The first was Eugenia Charles, who held the position of prime minister of Dominica, from July 21, 1980, until June 14, 1995. The second, Janet Jagan, served as prime minister of Guyana from March 17, 1997, to December 19, 1997, and later as president from December 19, 1997, to August 11, 1999. Of the final two, Kamla Persad-Bissessar of Trinidad and Tobago won the general election on May 24, 2010, and lost five years later on September 7, 2015. Portia Simpson-Miller of Jamaica became prime minister from March 30, 2006, until general elections were held on September 3, 2007. She held office again after winning the election on January 5, 2012 until she lost power on February 25, 2016. Currently, there are no women heads of state in the thirteen countries of the Anglophone region.

How should these women's moments of power be historicized and what is the story of regional feminist struggle that preceded them? How does an understanding of this collective history help to contextualize contemporary women's political leadership and show why its analysis matters?

To answer these questions, this chapter provides a regional perspective to women's political leadership in the Anglophone Caribbean over the twentieth and twenty-first centuries. It situates itself between the two opening quotes. On the one hand, it recognizes that the struggle to advance women's political leadership has and continues to contend with great ambivalence regarding women's exercise of power, while on the other hand it traces women's efforts to challenge what they considered outmoded hierarchies and exclusions. This is the context within which the material relations of gender, 'or the distribution of political, economic and social power, and material resources', and the ideological relations of gender, 'or the ways in which a society constructs what it accepts (and contests) as the appropriate expression of masculinity and femininity', come to have significance for achievement of gender justice (Barriteau 1998a, 440). Here, gender justice is understood as commitment and work to 'end hierarchies embedded in the current gender ideologies that construct and maintain particular configurations of gender identities and the often punitive roles that flow from these for women and men' (Ibid. 440).

After briefly surveying the main debates about push and pull factors regarding women's political participation and leadership, I review early twentieth-century efforts by women to enter representative politics, highlighting the long history of this struggle in the Anglophone Caribbean region. Much of the major regional feminist work to advance women's political leadership began from the 1970s onwards. The second half of the chapter details some of these efforts before assessing their implications for increasing the numbers of women in politics, thus strengthening political representatives' commitment to women's empowerment and gender justice. I conclude with major considerations facing Caribbean feminist advocates given this history of individual and collective aspiration and struggle. Given the resilience of androcentric ideologies, processes and distribution of power over this period, indeed the rise of a masculinist backlash, the conclusion sets a sober context for understanding the hopes and disappointments experienced under these four women heads of state over their terms in office.

PUSH AND PULL FACTORS

Explanatory factors for women's political participation usually focus on the sexual division of labour; cultural attitudes towards the place and power of women in society; a country's governance structures, electoral systems and development status; the level of women's ambition and readiness; and women's acceptance of the existing order as natural and beneficial or, instead, as limiting the legitimacy of women's grievances. These factors, reproduced through historical structures and relationships, establish the bases for gender arrangements (Pfall Effinger 1998, 150) and patriarchal bargaining. They shape women's interest, knowledge, time, networks, civic skills, education and finances, as well as how women see themselves and are seen by men (Reynolds 1999, Fox and Lawless 2005, 2010, Lovenduski 2005, Paxton, Kunovich and Hughes 2007).

Historically two other factors have been considered significant. The first is women's levels of secondary and tertiary education and the second is women's labour force participation. In the Anglophone Caribbean, both of these present a paradox as women have always had high levels of labour force participation and have recorded higher levels of tertiary enrolment than men over the last twenty years. Of course, both areas – education and employment – present a more nuanced picture of women's participation based on sex-segregated vertical and horizontal clustering in the waged economy in addition to higher levels of reproductive labour within the household as well as clustering in stereotypically gendered disciplines of study.

Debate continues about the significance of dynamics such as socio-economic development, population and country size, level of urbanization, extent of religiosity and persistence of gender discrimination as well as candidate recruitment, candidate confidence, family obligations and support, participation in social and political movements and organizations, and career pathways. Caribbean scholarship suggests that personal independence, reliable support systems, mentorship, marital status, economic autonomy and tertiary-level education may all be enabling factors in addition to male approval and strategic alliances with men (Mowlah-Baksh 2015).

The trajectories of individual women deepen our understanding of entering into leadership positions and exercising power while there. The following section therefore provides a selective regional survey of individual women's pathways in order to explore the Anglophone Caribbean experience of these push and pull factors in terms of women's descriptive representation, or their numbers in electoral political bodies; their substantive representation, meaning their agendas while in office; and their symbolic representation, or the implications of their presence for belief and attitudes to women in power. These women's stories point to the importance of political apprenticeship (Cornwall and Goetz 2005) through early exposure to politics via informal networks, family, civic associations, unions and women's organizations (Barrow-Giles 2011, Tadros 2014). They also point to the challenges of pursuing women's equality and empowerment, and gender justice, through formal politics, a point picked up in the discussion on Caribbean feminism's will to power.

WOMEN IN EARLY TWENTIETH-CENTURY
ANGLOPHONE CARIBBEAN POLITICS

Scholarship on Caribbean women's political leadership records women's long participation in resistance to the political-economic systems of slavery and indentureship, and the *longue durée* of colonialism (Beckles 1989, Reddock 2011a). The androcentrism of Caribbean statehood was constituted within this political-economic model, which varied across the region. The place of women was one of super-exploitation as subjects whose bodies, fertility and labour were racialized, gendered and sexualized in ways that positioned them as outside the terms of equal citizenship, either with men of their own race and class or with colonial rulers (Reddock 1994; Beckles 1998; Kempadoo 1999; Boyce Davies 2008; Smith 2011; Sheller 2012). As Tracy Robinson (2004, 596) notes, even in anti-colonial movements, concern was primarily with manhood, 'meaning establishing that Caribbean men were ready to self-govern'. Yet, women were also political, spiritual and military leaders whose struggle for political rights was 'a necessary weapon in their struggle for civil and economic rights' (Reddock 1998; Stevens 2007, 47).

Their intersecting approach to challenging domination followed women into their engagement with formal politics in the twentieth century. Political strategies have differed significantly by class, with working-class women having long documented involvement in public rebellion while middle-class women were more closely associated with church, charity and social welfare activities. These middle-strata activities 'did not work to change the status quo, nor even to question the role and place of women within it ... they did not pose a threat to male-based formal institutions engaged in the exercise of official authority' (Peake 2011, 644). Yet, 'they opened public space for women to maneuver for power, introduce issues into public debate, enter commerce, the public sector and governmental committees, and begin to demand both expansion of the franchise and women's representation, and even the establishment of women's political parties' (Ibid. 644). For example, in examining women's political organizations in Guyana, Linda Peake observes 'the emergence of a large and varied network of primarily social welfare organisations, designed to promote an increased participation by women as citizens' over the early nineteenth century, which later evolved into the women's auxiliaries of political parties (Ibid. 642). This era in Caribbean feminism can be understood in the context of labour, pan-African, post-indentureship, socialist, and independence struggles across the colonial world (Antrobus 2004a).

Across the region and through to the 1940s, women voters had age, income, property tax and literacy requirements more oppressive than those applied to men, and were often barred from national-level representative politics (Vassell 1993; Reddock 1994). It took mass meetings, letters to the editors of newspapers, petitions to colonial governors, formations of women's organizations and street marches to secure 'the unconditional right to vote irrespective of literacy or any other restrictions' for women (Jagan 2009). This is the experience of women like Audrey Jeffers in Trinidad, Nellie Latrielle in Jamaica and Janet Jagan in Guyana.

In 1946, Janet Jagan, the US-born wife of Cheddi Jagan, co-founded the Women's Political and Economic Organisation (WPEO), whose aim was 'to ensure the political organisation and education of the women of British Guiana in order to promote their economic welfare and their political and social emancipation and betterment' (Peake 2011, 647). With both middle- and working-class membership, WPEO advocated for improvements in social welfare, but also 'set about encouraging women to register as voters' for the 1947 election. Three WPEO members unsuccessfully contested the 1947 legislative elections. Although WPEO had a short life, writes Linda Peake (Ibid. 647), it 'was successful in its broad aims of educating women about their political and economic rights as members of the community, and in training leaders for future elections at municipal and national levels'. Following the granting of universal suffrage in 1953, Jagan was one of the first women to enter parliament as an MP, returning to parliament in successive elections in 1973, 1980, 1985 and 1992. Her Marxist–Leninist politics influenced the centralizing hand she wielded over her party as well as the development of the working-class women identified, cross-race, feminist organizations which critiqued her leadership.

Referring to Trinidad and Tobago, Rhoda Reddock observes that 'no popular movement had ever been successful or even become a popular movement without a large following of active and committed women' (Reddock 2011, 672). The 'party's support base among working class and lower middle-strata Afro-Trinidadian women gave them a sense of selfhood, importance and inclusion', yet this group never seriously challenged 'male party leadership or the oppressive sexual division of labour in the party and society' (Reddock 2011b, 673) emphasizing the participation of women in the nation and community as 'better homemakers and citizens' (Reddock 2011b, 674).

For example, although universal adult suffrage in Trinidad and Tobago was granted since 1946, and women such as Audrey Jeffers had run for election to the Port of Spain City Council in 1936, the 1956 'electoral slate of 24 PNM candidates contained no women, although women were active in the campaign'. Indeed, Audrey Jeffers herself voted against a motion for immediate granting of adult suffrage to all women and men over 21 years of age (Reddock 2011b, 679). While women's grassroots leadership was acknowledged by political and economic elites, such women did not participate in campaigns to advance women's interests or to challenge male chauvinism.

Reddock describes this as a clear example of a trend that has remained steadfast, one that 'could be termed a "feminist conservatism" which seeks to change the system while "working actively for its maintenance"' (Reddock 2011b, 679).

Grace Augustin, St. Lucia's first woman legislator, was also a defender of the colonial order, and her propertied status shaped her approach to labour issues. Augustin, who was trained both as a nurse and as a lawyer, rode a motorcycle, wore trousers, was the only woman to join the St. Lucia Cricket Club; she managed the family estate and became an expert in tropical agriculture, and never married. She founded the Caribbean Women's Association, and was the first president of the St. Lucia Women's Association which 'sought to draw the St. Lucian women out of the home, away from traditional social welfare activities and into the world of civics and government' (Joseph 2011, 41). Yet, in a debate in the Legislative Council in 1955, Augustin opposed constitutional reform towards self-government. Tennyson Joseph comments, 'Thus whilst she may have developed a strong feminist consciousness, she failed to make the necessary leap to understanding colonialism as a masculinized European expression of power' (Joseph 2011, 51).

In Dominica, others such as Mabel Moir James, who won her second contested election in 1966, closely combined political leadership with trade unionism, working-class solidarity and women's rights. A member of the Dominica Labour Party (DLP), James, formed a Women's Guild because there were no women in the party executive or parliament at that time. James was neither the first woman to serve in Dominica's government nor the only one to contest elections. She supported sick benefits, pensions and decent housing for the working class, and addressed issues such as domestic violence, child maintenance and women's right to employment, wages and proper representation. Her ministerial portfolio of Home Affairs served as a de facto Ministry of Gender Affairs, illustrating her example of substantive representation.

Eugenia Charles, who rose to prime ministership in Dominica, combined a concern for freedom of speech with the violent oppression of Rastafarians, and a welfare-type approach to women and constituency needs with a neo-liberal, trickle-down model of development (Barriteau 2006, 23–24). An elite, whose symbolic representation was associated with opening space in politics and the public service for women, Eugenia Charles remained unmarried and childless, and endured public attacks for not meeting ideals of patriarchal conjugality and motherhood. Reflecting the gender ideologies she was navigating, John Compton, former prime minister of St. Lucia, said of her, 'It was not a woman that was there.... She transcended womanhood. She was an intellect, in woman's clothes' (Compton 2002 cited in Barriteau 2006, 15). Yet, she was also imaged as 'Mama' or 'Mamo', the mother of the nation, showing the tension between gendered representations and contradictions regarding a politics of gender justice.

In Barbados, Edna Ermyntrude Foster, best known as Ermie Bourne, was the first woman elected to the House of Assembly in 1951, in the first general election after the introduction of universal adult suffrage. She followed in her father's footsteps as a member of the Barbados Parliament. It was another twenty years before another woman, Gertrude Eastmond entered the lower house of Barbados's Parliament in 1971, and it wasn't until 1976 that Dame Billie Miller, also from a political family, would be appointed to the Barbados Cabinet. Bourne's legacy is associated with 'improving the conditions of the rural poor; paving the way for female politicians; and for women to be involved at the highest levels of political office' (Barrow-Giles and Branford 2011, 34). Miller is renowned for her leadership in liberalizing abortion law in Barbados in 1983.

Women's solidarity with the labour movement also cost them their political lives. Ivy Joshua, born in Grenada in 1924, went on to form the People's Political Party as an arm of the Federated Industrial and Agricultural Workers Union after she moved to St. Vincent with her husband Ebenezer and they both became involved in politics. They were strongly influenced by the Uriah Butler Movement, and its pan-African, working-class politics. In St. Vincent, Ivy Joshua was victorious in the 1957 elections, entering the Legislative Council as its first woman member at thirty-two years of age. Her career was marked by her involvement in public demonstrations and strikes against low wages and poor working conditions, particularly for sugar workers, and she faced continual elite attack over her decorum and language skills, establishing classed assumptions about qualifications to lead (Barrow-Giles and Robinson Hazell 2011, 63).

Yet, as the decades have worn on, involvement in trade unions have become seen as part of a political legacy, for example, in relation to women such as Penelope Beckles in Trinidad and Tobago, whose grandfather was also a Butlerite and whose father was general secretary of the Oilfield Workers' Trade Union during the 1970 labour riots. Beckles' mother was involved with village council meetings and community work, and Beckles herself became president of the Rape Crisis Society. Her understanding of women's experiences in politics led her to face criticism from her party colleagues for congratulating Kamla Persad-Bissessar when she became Leader of the Opposition. Beckles won four consecutive general elections, from 1995 to 2007, but fell out of favour with party hierarchy during her bid for Political Leader in 2015.

Such class and racial tensions also defined the political life of Doris Johnson, born in 1921, in Nassau, Bahamas. Johnson was a leader in the women's suffrage movement of the Bahamas, agitating for women's right to vote. Between 1959 and 1962, the movement engaged in continuous appeals to the parliament in the Bahamas and even the British Colonial Office, arguing that women's exclusion was outmoded, against the interests of the country, and reflected taxation without representation, a denial of women's rights, and failure to give the fundamentally different and more humane approach of women to social issues a place in public life.

Supporting them on gendered terms, House of Assembly member Ronald Fawkes argued, 'None of us, Mr. Speaker, would deny that our wives perform the legislative and executive functions in our homes. Mr. Speaker, if government is about good housekeeping, then it is time that we bring into the House of Assembly some good housekeepers. Let the women in, Mr. Speaker' (Barrow-Giles 2011, 73). Johnson established the National Woman's Movement and later became regional director of the Caribbean Women's Association. Although she never won an election, she served in the cabinet and Senate, and paved the way for Janet Bostwick to become the first woman elected to the House of Assembly in 1982. Bostwick sponsored legislation on marriage, maternity leave, sexual offences and domestic violence. She served as the minister for women's affairs (1995–2001) and as the Attorney General. She was also president of the Free National Movement Women's Association, and the International Caribbean Women for Democracy.

The inclusion of indigenous women here is also important. Sylvia Flores was raised by her maternal grandmother, who was a Garinagu community leader, and her mother, who was a community organizer and president of the United Women's Group – the women's arm of the People's United Party – one of Belize's two main parties. First serving in local government and as Speaker of the House of Representatives, Flores won the general elections in 2003, serving in the Cabinet of Ministers until 2008, a first for Garinagu Carib – descended women. Her reflections point to the significance of women's marginalization in politics and, particularly, their lack of mentorship and support systems at the top, leading to their greater vulnerability (Neal and Goldson 2011, 90). Indeed, women's greater vulnerability, even when in power, partly explains their conservatism in the face of the hetero-patriarchal definition of legitimate citizenship and rule.

The vulnerability stems from the ease with which women are locked out of office. In Jamaica between 1962 and 1983, the proportion of female candidates never exceeded 13% (Henry-Wilson 1989, 242). In 2016, nowhere in the region do women comprise more than 30% of elected representatives. When parties run women as candidates, the majority are sacrificed in seats the parties have privately surrendered and are frequently placed against the strongest candidates of rival political parties (Barriteau 1998b). Regional governments have preferred to seat women as ceremonial heads of states, for example, as governors general in Grenada, Barbados, Bahamas, St. Lucia and Belize. Women have also been assigned positions such as president or vice president of the Senate, or as Speaker of the House of Representatives, appointments which carry no decision-making power (Vassell 2003). Further, as Michelle Rowley points out, although 'Caribbean political parties have also historically exploited the canvassing done by their female supporters ... they have yet to become the benefactors of increased levels of access to formalized corridors of power' (Rowley 2004, 658–59).

It seems reasonable to conclude that 'women's participation in party politics may be a necessary, but not a sufficient condition for their emancipation' (Reddock 2011b, 675). While individual women have been able to enter the highest levels of decision making, many others work unnoticed, reflecting 'sexist discrimination' or 'female socialization and sex-stereotyping which advocated selfless hard work in the background without honour or overt power' (Reddock 2011b, 684). These biographical snapshots illuminate the extent to which increasing women's political leadership can be a valid strategy for advancing gender justice. Yet, by the 1970s, Caribbean feminist movements were also deeply aware of the resilience of androcentric ideologies in political structures, which ultimately reined in women's possibilities for civil, political and economic transformation.

CARIBBEAN FEMINISM'S WILL TO POWER: ACTIVITIES AND OUTCOMES

As the above section shows, women have been entering formal politics, or at least positioning themselves and petitioning to do so, over many decades. Many of them not only kept the interests of women in mind, but also the practical needs of the working poor. The early twentieth-century history of women's political leadership mainly involved elite women challenging the terms of their exclusion, with masses of working-class women being drawn into formal politics as nationalist movements began to cohere across the Anglophone region. Some women became serious political actors, but played within patriarchal rules, which reproduced the privileged status of dominant masculine attributes and naturalized elite male supremacy at the expense of feminized and marginalized women and men. Further, a vision for gender justice was articulated in struggles for universal suffrage, workers' rights, women's equality, social welfare services and full independence in the first half of the century, but there wasn't sufficient critique of 'the foundational assumptions of liberal political ideology to reveal its gendered construction of citizenship' (Barriteau 1998a, 441). As Hilary Beckles (1998, 53) has observed, 'Ongoing projects of nation-state building that promote allegedly gender free notions of nationalist cohesion should be contested and unmasked as skillful projections of modernizing masculine political power'.

In later decades, such deconstruction began to emerge in feminist manifestos, analyses, workshops, manuals, fora and campaigns to end asymmetries of power relations and relations of domination in order to alter the status quo (Barriteau 1996, Barriteau 1998a, 440). In both challenging and cooperating with Caribbean states and officials, as well as pressuring for the institutionalization of new state machineries and officials to advance gender mainstreaming, Caribbean feminist advocacy sought to provoke redistribution of political, economic and social power and material resources, and promote redefinitions of appropriate expressions of masculinity and femininity (Barriteau 1998c, 188; 2000, 2). By the early 1970s, the goal wasn't simply to increase the numbers of women or make public leadership more transformational, but 'to end hierarchies embedded in the current gender ideologies ... and the often punitive roles that flow from these for women and men' (Barriteau 2013, 206). By the 1990s, the women's movement had significant experience of and commitment to shifting the focus to gender relations and hierarchies, and had been engaged in encouraging women to transform economic and political institutions by their presence within them.

Such regional feminist activism reflected a conscious and collective feminist 'will to power'. Eudine Barriteau (2013, 196) writes, 'The first step in theorizing a will to power is to isolate the actions and outcomes implied by the term "will". What are the necessary actions feminists should undertake to work towards gender justice? How can that bring feminist influences closer to shaping the use of power in the public domains of the state, the economy and civic society?' These were fundamental questions guiding Anglophone Caribbean women activists as they attempted to open space for women and women's issues in political representation and decision making. This section attends to some of those actions and outcomes.

The period was marked by strong regional consultation and collaboration on the development of national machinery to integrate women's agendas in development planning. For example, a Women's Desk located in the Office of the Prime Minister (the OPM was established in Jamaica in 1974 as a precursor to a more integrated bureau (Henry-Wilson 1989, 246–47)). Between 1973 and 1976, on the basis of strong advocacy by women's groups both at international and national levels, Barbados, Guyana and Trinidad and Tobago established commissions to assess the status of women, make recommendations monitor their implementation. In St. Kitts and Nevis, women's affairs were established as areas of responsibility within ministerial portfolios (Reddock 2004, 26). In 1978, Grenada established the National Women's Organisation, with special oversight for women, youth, farmers and workers (Antrobus 1988). Mobilization in civil society and religious organizations as well as the introduction of more progressive legislation that addressed women's needs in relation to maternity leave, family court, domestic violence and rape highlighted the gains of feminist activism in the region. Antrobus (2004b) singles out the Women's Auxiliary of the People's National Party (PNP) in Jamaica as a leading movement to coalesce the energies of women across class lines and firmly place gender equality on the national agenda.

However, Michelle Rowley (2004, 662) argues that it was necessary to move beyond a model of 'partisan political campaigning by the women's arm of their perspective political parties', and to move from a welfare services and social safety net approach targeted to women as wives and mother's to one defined by women's empowerment. The Housewives Association of Trinidad and Tobago (HATT), which emerged in 1972, and focused, among other areas, on consumer issues, violence against women, and domestic workers' rights exemplifies such a shift (Shirley 2009). Five women from HATT contested the 1976 general elections representing four different political parties with the one running as an independent candidate. None of the women won their seat, but their strategy highlighted a focus on women's political participation to advance gender justice.

Over the following four decades, as women's empowerment became a theme taken up by United Nations' conferences and agreements, women's political participation and leadership also emerged as a global concern. By the 1990s, feminist movements began to gain the support of states and international institutions for electoral quota systems both at local government and national levels. However, feminists in the region were long aware that these wouldn't be enough. As Linda Peake points out for Guyana, issues such as 'unemployment, national debt and high levels of out-migrations ... acted as material and ideological constraints on the emancipation of women' and 'limited the impact of women's political organisations' (2011, 650–51).

Much of this momentum drew on the Post-Beijing Regional Plan of Action, which included strategic objectives to mainstream gender equity and transform structures of political representation (Bailey 2004, 630). Barbara Bailey posits that the constraints to success in challenging systemic gender arrangements included changes to political leadership and bureaux after elections, the myth of male marginalization and the impact of neo-liberal economic policies (Bailey 2004, 653). Nonetheless, from the 1990s onwards, often with support from the UN and international organizations, women's organizations produced political education materials and guidelines for successful campaigning, and sought to engage and develop the political leadership practices of women active at community levels and in media, representational politics, trade unions, the public service and private sector.

Shirley Campbell (2014) details the extent of these efforts: In 1991, the Barbados Bureau of Women's Affairs coordinated an intervention titled Training in Civic Education for National Leadership. In 1992, the Business and Professional Women's Club in Jamaica launched the Jamaica Women's Political Caucus (JWPC) to increase the number of women in politics, and established the Institute of Public Leadership to train political candidates and campaign teams. In 1995, a cross-race and cross-class coalition of women produced the Ten Points for Power manifesto, which they used for election advocacy. They called for a Code of Ethics for persons in public office, and an increase in women's representation to a minimum of 30% of political party candidates (Ellis 2003, 64–65, Reddock 2004, 38–39). The manifesto was refined through subsequent elections right up to 2016 and complemented other efforts such as the 'Put a Woman in the House ... of Parliament' and the '50:50' campaigns. Between 1995 and 1999, the Network of NGOs of Trinidad and Tobago for the Advancement of Women (Network of NGOs) completed the Engendering Local Government project to create a critical mass of women to serve in public leadership, to create greater opportunities for women to enter public leadership and decision making, and to conduct gender-sensitive analysis and planning among technical and administrative municipal staff.

Between 1997 and 1998, the National Organisation of Women (NOW) in Barbados implemented public education and outreach through the 'Share Power Programme' with women politicians and parliamentarians speaking publicly about their experiences and negotiations. In 1997, the JWPC and the Coalition for Community Participation in Local Government held a workshop titled 'Jamaica Local Government Leadership: Women and Community Empowerment'. In 1997, the Engendering Local Government symposium, held in St. Lucia, was attended by state, civil society and women's organizations' representatives from Antigua and Barbuda, the Bahamas, Barbados, Belize, Dominica, Grenada, Guyana, Jamaica, St. Kitts and Nevis, St. Lucia, Suriname, Trinidad and Tobago and St. Vincent and the Grenadines. In October 2002, women's and civil rights groups launched the Women's Manifesto against Sexual Violence in Jamaica in the run-up to the national elections. Issues of a 40% quota for women representatives and an institutionalized commission to advance women's rights and gender equality were also raised.

Between 2002 and 2005, the project Catalysts for Change: Caribbean Women in Governance implemented Women's Political Participation (WPP): Training in Governance and Democracy, which was held with participants from Antigua and Barbuda, Guyana and St. Kitts and Nevis. Between 2009 and 2011, the National Women's Commission, Women's Issues Network (WIN) Belize and the United Nations Development Fund for Women (UNIFEM) also engaged in transformational leadership and political campaign training. Shirley (2014) also details the work of the CIWiL to train women in campaigning, self-presentation, fundraising and networking. These are only a few examples, but they highlight the regional nature of continuous Caribbean feminist advocacy and strategizing from the 1970s onwards.

OUTCOMES: MASCULINIST RESISTANCES TO CARIBBEAN FEMINIST POWER

These decades of feminist advocacy to increase women's political representation had incremental successes in terms of numbers and contingent gains in terms of representation of women's interests (Andaiye 2009, 2). There has been greater success in increasing numbers at local government levels than in parliaments. For example, in Trinidad and Tobago, the number of women nominated to run for office increased from 41 candidates in 1996 to 91 candidates in 1999. Women won 28 seats in 1999, more than a 50% increase from 1996. The total representation of women increased from 17 to 26% and the number of women appointed as councillors, aldermen, vice-chairs of councils and deputy mayors also increased. Across the Anglophone Caribbean, women who have undergone training have been more likely than others to secure campaign funds, win in elections and enter Cabinet, to express more public confidence, to liaise in more empowering ways with communities and to engage in public dialogue about women's rights.

Yet, regional consensus is that women and men in political parties remain unwilling to publicly challenge hetero-patriarchal norms when in power and may only do so when it doesn't pose a risk to their parties, for example, when in opposition. Fearing penalization, they are unlikely to collaborate across party lines or prioritize economic positions taken from poor women's perspectives, highlighting political elite classism. This is not simply an issue of individual lack of will, but also of a lack of a constituency of support for women and women's rights, ambivalence about women's rights and women's capacity to lead, popular fear of women being 'too feminist' or of women's 'takeover' of the public domain, and few examples of truly transformational political leaders in the region. It remains true that women in political leadership have been closely aligned with political party agendas and male leaders, which has affected their ability to both climb the political ladder, or maintain position, and simultaneously challenge systemic racism, classism, sexism and homophobia within and outside their parties.

This, despite tireless collaboration among feminist activists and scholars, women's and gender bureaux, and international funding organizations to sensitize thousands of women and men from a range of organizations, classes and communities; and to provide campaign funds, training and support to hundreds of parliamentarians and local government representatives or aspirants to leadership whether in political parties, unions, media or other civil society groups. Speaking specifically about constitutional reform, Tracy Robinson observes that 'women have challenged prevailing conceptions of citizenship that rhetorically support "gender equality" and continue to place men at the heart of constitutional imagination' (Robinson 2004, 609). Yet, 'among feminists and women's organisations there is no consensus on the best way of securing fair representation and participation', particularly because gender justice goals are undermined by the political party and ethnic and class loyalties of both women and men (Andaiye 2002 cited in Robinson 2004, 617). Women politicians remain deeply ambivalent about feminist politics, instead combining liberal conceptions of individual advancement and respectability politics with welfarist programmes for women. Joycelin Massiah's (2003, xvi) sentiments are worth quoting here:

> How did a region, which was in the vanguard of commitment and action in the seventies, eighties and early nineties find itself at the turn of the century, unable to articulate a comprehensive program of action towards the achievement of gender justice? Does it mean that women and their gender concerns are only of value at a particular historical junctures? ... Does it mean that gender justice is considered irrelevant to social, economic and political development?

This is where scholarship on the persistent androcentrism, or male-centredness, of Caribbean states and citizenship must attend to contemporary masculinist resistance. As Blais and Dupuis-Déri describe (2012, 22), 'Masculinism asserts that since men are in crisis and suffering because of women in general and feminists in particular, the solution to their problems involves curbing the influence of feminism and revalorizing masculinity'. This is what feminists describe in terms of hetero-patriarchal resistance enabled by the terms of inclusion whether in law (Alexander 1991; 1994) or in state bureaucracies (Rowley 2004, 655; Rowley 2011); the denial of systemic inequalities in 'gender-neutral' lawmaking (Robinson 1999, Robinson 2004, 599); the uptake of the backlash myth of male marginalization in state discourse (Barriteau 2003b); and the illusion of economic empowerment in liberal notions of women's political and economic participation (Barriteau 1998a, 441, Andaiye 2003). These are strategies of containment, affecting both public will to gender equality and the language and forms it is allowed.

Indeed, Barriteau points to such 'ongoing attempts by institutions and individuals to maintain conditions of inequality for women' (Barriteau 2013, 189). Rowley's critique is even more decisive, describing obstructive hostility, which produces incapacity, incompetence and illegitimacy regarding effective realization of gender equity by Caribbean states (Rowley 2004,

664). Eugenia Charles, former prime minister of Dominica, noted this as early as 1985. She remarked, 'When I became Prime Minister one of the first things I did was to appoint a woman speaker to the House of Parliament.... On congratulating her some of the men Parliamentarians said that they were getting a little concerned about things in Dominica, and they felt that they should ask me to create a Men's Desk to look after the affairs of men because women were already so well looked after in Dominica' (Charles 1985, 6). In this context, Barriteau warns that women's transformational leadership is 'meaningless' (2001, 25) if it fails to address the sociopolitical reality of the region and challenge statist reproduction of masculine power as dominant (Mohammed 2010, 1).

Even where there are state-led and party-based strategies, Enloe (2004, 5) argues that these institutions are 'dominated by men and embody a perpetually ingrained ethos of masculinity', which contributes to women's lower access to corridors of political power, because they are seen as less suitable, are less networked, are penalized for being inappropriately feminine or masculine or are sacrificed in losing seats (Henry-Wilson 1989, 241; Barriteau 1998c, 191–205; Samuel 2010). Thus, in addition to women's exclusion from public life, 'when women are involved in politics, the convention is still to evaluate their public performance and relevance against the values and virtues of women in the private sphere' (Barriteau 2006, 6).

As former Jamaican politician Maxine Henry-Wilson (2004, 587) described,

> The conduct of politics is very male in its orientation. For example, most of it is done on a Sunday. Women's domestic lives invariably suffer while they are attending to political matters on a Sunday. The campaign trail is rigorous, almost to the point of being dangerous. After a while you begin to wonder 'Well, is this what I really want to do?' The norms of the campaign trail sometimes embody experiences and behaviors that are not seen as 'feminine'. I remember there was the case of a woman, who did what all men did, which was to go to the bar and drink, and it was used against her in the campaign. There are cases where you hear of women being described as very 'loose', and therefore you should not support them.

Expectations to be available twenty-four hours a day are also too demanding, and made more difficult by the low capacity of state institutions and resource inadequacies for parliamentarians.

CONCLUSION

The history of Caribbean women's political leadership points to how spaces for advancement or domestication of a feminist will to power are negotiated today. The story that unfolds is one that should focus attention on the contradictions of women's inclusion and containment on increasingly masculinist terms. Paradoxically, feminist advocacy to increase the numbers of women in power has been taken up by political parties and the state, with those women who are included expected to *not* challenge masculinism in politics, but rather to accommodate it for purposes of balance, equality, neutrality and inclusion *because* they are women. Second, that the numbers have translated to so little power highlights the precarity of political space over time, showing the relationship between resilient androcentrism, consistent hetero-patriarchal resistance and the structure of masculinized democracy, while feminists continue to advocate for women to be counted in. The result is visibility given to the inclusion of a minority of women while legislative, policy and budgetary accommodations to masculinist power undermine both welfare and feminist approaches, extending women's economic and political insecurity.

Almost a century after women began to individually and collectively agitate for the right to contest elections, the struggle to advance women's political leadership still has to secure women's power to advance gender justice. This power includes the ability to successfully challenge inequalities reproduced by legislation, policies and manifestos; to work across political parties and have influence on women's issues; to increase collaboration among feminist activists, women's arms of parties, and women and gender affairs bureaux; to redefine hetero-patriarchal relations between men and women, and within groups of men and groups of women; and to recognize reproductive rights, domestic labour, sexual autonomy. It also includes freedom from violence and class insecurity in all areas of decision-making, and an end to issues of unequal citizenship that negatively affect women and men.

A feminist will to power has been tirelessly and passionately pursued over these decades. In the Anglophone region, it has been propelled by intersections with 1920s socialism, 1930s Garveyism, 1940s–1960s suffrage and independence movements, 1970s black power, civil rights, environmental and peace organizing, and, from the 1970s onwards, transnational feminist advocacy that worked through UN conventions and grassroots research and activism. The last three decades of neo-liberal, structural adjustment policies in the region increased religious fundamentalism, community violence and masculinist resurgence making the terrain no less difficult than before. Amid this, Caribbean feminists' vision for justice is no less legitimate, and not yet fully achieved.

REFERENCES

Alexander, M. Jacqui. 1991. 'Redrafting Morality: The Postcolonial State and the Sexual Offences Bill of Trinidad and Tobago', in *Third World Women and the Politics of Feminism*, edited by Chandra Talpade Mohanty, Ann Russo and Lourdes Torres, 133–52. Bloomington and Indianapolis: Indiana University.

_____. 1994. 'Not Just (Any)Body Can Be a Citizen: The Politics of Law, Sexuality and Postcoloniality in Trinidad and Tobago and the Bahamas'. *Feminist Review* 48 (Autumn 1994): 133–49.

Andaiye. 2003. 'Smoke and Mirrors: The Illusion of CARICOM Women's Growing Economic Empowerment, Post-Beijing', in *Gender Equality in the Caribbean: Reality or Illusion*, edited by Gemma Tang Nain and Barbara Bailey, 73–107. Kingston, Jamaica: Ian Randle Publishers.

_____. 2009. 'Critical Review of Selected Interventions in Support of Women's Participation in Electoral Processes in the Caribbean in the period 2007–2008'. The University of the West Indies, Cave Hill Campus.

Antrobus, Peggy. 1988. 'Women in Development Programmes: The Caribbean Experience 1975–1985', in *Gender in Caribbean Development*, edited by Patricia Mohammed and Catherine Shepherd, 35–52. Cave Hill, Mona and St. Augustine: Women and Development Studies Project, UWI.

_____. 2004a. *The Global Women's Movement: Origins, Issues and Strategies*. Dhaka, Bangkok, Nova Scotia, Kingston, Bangalore, Kuala Lumpur, Cape Town, and London and New York: University Press, White Lotus Co., Fernwood Publishing, Ian Randle Publishers, Books for Change, SIRD, David Philip, Zed Books.

_____. 2004b. 'Feminist Activism: The CARICOM Experience', in *Gender in the 21st Century: Caribbean Perspectives, Visions and Possibilities*, edited by Barbara Bailey and Elsa Leo-Rhynie, 35–58. Kingston, Jamaica: Ian Randle Publishers.

Bailey, Barbara. 2004. 'The Caribbean Experience in the International Women's Movement: Issues, Process, Constraints and Possibilities', in *Gender in the 21st Century: Caribbean Perspectives, Visions and Possibilities*, edited by Barbara Bailey and Elsa Leo-Rhynie, 626–54. Kingston, Jamaica: Ian Randle Publishers.

Barriteau, Eudine. 1996. 'Gender Systems and the Project of Modernity in the Post-Colonial Caribbean'. Paper presented at the 1st SEPHIS Workshop on the Forging of Nationhood and the Contest over Citizenship, Ethnicity and History, New Delhi, India, 1996.

_____. 1998a. 'Liberal Ideology and Contradictions in Caribbean Gender Systems', in *Caribbean Portraits: Essays on Gender Ideologies and Identities*, edited by Christine Barrow, 436–56. Kingston, Jamaica: Ian Randle Publishers.

_____. 1998b. 'Engendering Local Government in the Commonwealth Caribbean'. Working Paper No. 1, April, Centre for Gender and Development Studies, The University of the West Indies, Cave Hill, Barbados.

_____. 1998c. 'Theorizing Gender Systems and the Project of Modernity in the Twentieth-Century Caribbean'. *Feminist Review* 59 (Summer): 186–209.

_____. 2000. 'Examining the Issues of Men, Male Marginalization and Masculinity in the Caribbean: Policy Implications'. Working Paper No. 4 (September), Centre for Gender and Development Studies, University of the West Indies, Cave Hill Campus, Barbados.

_____. 2001. *Stronger, Surer, Bolder Ruth Nita Barrow: Social Change and International Development*. Barbados: University of the West Indies Press.

_____. 2003a. *Confronting Power, Theorizing Gender: Interdisciplinary Perspectives in the Caribbean*. Kingston: University of the West Indies Press.

_____. 2003b. 'Conclusion: Beyond a Backlash – The Frontal Assault on Caribbean Women in the Decade of the 1990s', in *Gender Equality in the Caribbean: Reality or Illusion?* edited by Gemma Tang Nain and Barbara Bailey, 201–32. Kingston, Jamaica: Ian Randle Publishers.

_____. 2006. 'Enjoying Power, Challenging Gender', in *Enjoying Power: Eugenia Charles and Political Leadership in the Commonwealth Caribbean*, edited by Eudine Barriteau and Alan Cobley, 3–30. Kingston, Jamaica: University of the West Indies Press.

_____. 2013. 'Confronting Power and Politics: A Feminist Theorizing of Gender in Commonwealth Caribbean Societies', in *Caribbean Political Thought: Theories of the Post-Colonial State*, edited by Aaron Kamugisha, 189–213. Kingston, Jamaica: Ian Randle Publishers.

Barrow-Giles, Cynthia. 2011. *Women in Caribbean Politics*, ed. Kingston, Jamaica: Ian Randle Publishers

_____. 2011. 'Dame Doris Louise Johnson: A Bahamian Heroine', in *Women in Caribbean Politics*, edited by Cynthia Barrow-Giles, 67–78. Kingston, Jamaica: Ian Randle Publishers.

Barrow-Giles, Cynthia and Albert Branford. 2011. 'Edna Ermyntrude "Ernie" Bourne: Breaking the Ice: Barbadian Pioneer', in *Women in Caribbean Politics*, edited by Cynthia Barrow-Giles, 29-36. Kingston, Jamaica: Ian Randle Publishers.

Barrow-Giles, Cynthia and Nelcia Robinson Hazell. 2011. 'Ivy Joshua: Nobody's "Sidekick" and a Lot More, than a High-Heeled Woman', in *Women in Caribbean Politics*, edited by Cynthia Barrow-Giles, 60–66. Kingston, Jamaica: Ian Randle Publishers.

Beckles, Hilary. 1989. *Natural Rebels: Social History of Enslaved Black Women in Barbados*. New Brunswick: Rutgers University Press.

_____. 1998. 'Historicizing Slavery in West Indian Feminisms'. *Rethinking Caribbean Difference, Feminist Review* 59 (Summer): 34–56.

Blais, Melissa and Francis Dupuis-Déri. 2012. 'Masculinism and the Antifeminist Countermovement'. Social Movement Studies: *Journal of Social, Cultural and Political Protest* 11(1): 21–39.

Boyce Davies, Carol. 2008. *Left of Karl Marx: The Political Life of Black Communist Claudia Jones*. Durham, NC: Duke University Press.

Campbell, Shirley. 2014. 'Feminist/Womanist Advocacy Toward Transformational Leadership in the Anglophone Caribbean: The Interplay of Individual and Collective Agency', in *Politics, Power and Gender Justice in the Anglophone Caribbean: Women's Understandings of Politics, Experiences of Political Contestations and the Possibilities for Gender Transformation IDRC Research Report 106430-001*, by Principal Investigator Gabrielle Jamela Hosein and Lead Reasearcher Jane Parpart. Ottawa, ON Canada: International Development Research Centre.

Charles, Mary Eugenia. 1985. 'Caribbean Challenge'. Address presented to the Opening of the National Symposium on Women and Development. Bureau of Women's Affairs, Kingston, Jamaica.

Compton, John. 2002. 'Interview by Alicia Mondesire'. 2 July. Roseau, Dominica.

Cornwall, Andrea and Anne Marie Goetz. 2005. 'Democratizing Democracy: Feminist Perspectives'. *Democratization* 12(5): 783–800.

Ellis, Patricia. 2003. 'Women in Leadership and Decision Making', in *Women, Gender and Development in the Caribbean: Reflections and Projections* edited by Patricia Ellis, 49–63. Kingston, Jamaica: Ian Randle Publishers.

Enloe, Cynthia. 2004. *The Curious Feminist.* Berkeley: University of California.

Fox, Richard, and Jennifer Lawless. 2005. 'To Run or not to Run for Office: Explaining Nascent Political Ambition'. *American Journal of Politics* 49(3): 642–59.

_____. 2010. 'If Only They'd Ask: Gender, Recruitment, and Political Ambition'. *The Journal of Politics* 72(2): 310–26. http://digitalcommons.lmu.edu/cgi/viewcontent.cgi?article=1001&context=poli_fac. Accessed June 28, 2016.

Henry-Wilson, Maxine. 1989. 'The Status of the Jamaican Woman, 1962 to the Present', in *Jamaica in Independence: Essays on the Early Years,* edited by Rex Nettleford, 229–53. Kingston, Jamaica and London: Heinemann Caribbean and James Currey.

_____. 2004. 'Governance, Leadership and Decision-making: Prospects for Caribbean Women', in *Gender in the 21st Century: Caribbean Perspectives, Visions and Possibilities,* edited by Barbara Bailey and Elsa Leo-Rhynie, 585–91. Kingston, Jamaica: Ian Randle Publishers.

Jagan, Janet. 2009. 'A Bit of History about Women and the Vote'. *Stabroek News*, March 29. Accessed June 29, 2016. http://www.stabroeknews.com/2009/stories/03/29/a-bit-of-history-about-women-and-the-vote/.

Joseph, Tennyson. 2011. 'Grace Augustin: Feminist Trailblazer or Defender of Colonialism? Unravelling the Contradictions of St Lucia's First Female Legislator', in *Women in Caribbean Politics*, edited by Cynthia Barrow-Giles, 37–52. Kingston, Jamaica: Ian Randle Publishers.

Kempadoo, Kamala. 1999. *Sun, Sex and Gold: Tourism and Sex Work in the Caribbean, ed.* Oxford: Rowman and Littlefield.

Lovenduski, Joni. 2005. *Feminizing Politics.* Cambridge: Polity Press.

Massiah, Joycelin. 2003. Preface. *Gender Equality in the Caribbean: Reality or Illusion,* edited by Gemma Tang Nain and Barbara Bailey, xi–xviii. Kingston: Ian Randle, CARICOM Secretariat, UNIFEM Caribbean.

Mohammed, Patricia. 2010. 'Gender Politics and Global Democracy: Insights from the Caribbean'. Paper Summary, Conceptualising Global Democracy Project. http://www.buildingglobaldemocracy.org/sites/www.buildingglobaldemocracy.org/files/gender_politics_and_global_democracy.pdf. Accessed June 29, 2016.

Mowlah-Baksh, Sabrina. 2015. 'The Decision to Run: Experiences of Women who have Succeeded in Winning Elected Office'. MSc. Thesis, The University of the West Indies, St. Augustine Campus.

Neal, Juliette and Florence Goldson. 2011. 'Sylvia Flores: The Humble and Patient Politician', in *Women in Caribbean Politics*, edited by Cynthia Barrow-Giles, 87–91. Kingston, Jamaica: Ian Randle Publishers.

Paxton, Pamela and Melanie Hughes. 2007. *Women, Politics and Power: A Global Perspective.* SAGE Publications. http://dx.doi.org/10.4135/9781452225944. Accessed June 28, 2016.

Paxton, Pamela, Sheri Kunovich, and Melanie Hughes. 2007. 'Gender in Politics'. *Annual Review of Sociology* 33: 263–70.

Peake, Linda 2011. 'The Development and Role of Women's Political Organisations in Guyana', in *Engendering Caribbean History: Cross-Cultural Perspectives*, edited by Verene Shepherd, 642–62. Kingston, Jamaica: Ian Randle Publishers.

Pfall Effinger, Brigit. 1998. 'Gender Cultures and the Gender Arrangement – A Theoretical Framework for Cross-National Gender Research'. *Innovation: The European Journal of Social Sciences* 11(2): 147–66.

Reddock, Rhoda. 1994. *Women, Labour and Politics in Trinidad and Tobago: A History*. London: Zed Books.

———. 1998. 'Feminism and Feminist Thought', in *Gender in Caribbean Development*, edited by Patricia Mohammed and Catherine Shepherd, 53–74. Mona, Jamaica, Cave Hill, Barbados, St. Augustine, Trinidad and Tobago: The University of the West Indies.

———. 2004. 'Reflections on Gender and Democracy in the Anglophone Caribbean: Historical and Contemporary Considerations'. Lecture delivered for Amsterdam/Dakar, South-South Exchange Programme for Research on the History of Development (SEPHIS) and The Council for the Development of Social Science Research in Africa. https://www.academia.edu/3069387/Reflections_on_Gender_and_Democracy_in_the_anglophone_Caribbean_SEPHIS-CODESRIA_2004. Accessed June 29, 2016.

———. 2011a. 'The Indentureship Experience: Indian Women in Trinidad and Tobago, 1845–1917', in *Engendering Caribbean History: Cross-Cultural Perspectives*, edited by Verene A. Shepherd, 574–86. Kingston, Jamaica: Ian Randle Publishers.

———. 2011b. 'Constitutional Change and the New Nationalist Politics', in *Engendering Caribbean History: Cross-Cultural Perspectives*, edited by Verene Shepherd, 663–88. Kingston, Jamaica: Ian Randle Publishers.

Reynolds, Andrew. 1999. 'Women in the Legislatures and Executives of the World: Knocking at the Highest Glass Ceiling'. *World Politics* 51: 547–72. doi:10.1017/S0043887100009254. Accessed June 28, 2016.

Robinson, Tracy. 1999. 'Fictions of Citizenship: bodies without Sex and the Effacement of Gender in Law'. *Small Axe* 7: 1–27.

———. 2004. 'Gender, Feminism and Constitutional Reform in the Caribbean'. in *Gender in the 21st Century: Caribbean Perspectives, Visions and Possibilities*, edited by Barbara Bailey and Elsa Leo-Rhynie, 592–625. Kingston, Jamaica: Ian Randle Publishers.

Rowley, Michelle. 2004. 'Bureacratising Feminism: Charting Caribbean Women's Centrality within the Margins', in *Gender in the 21st Century: Caribbean Perspectives, Visions and Possibilities*, edited by Barbara Bailey and Elsa Leo-Rhynie, 655–86. Kingston, Jamaica: Ian Randle Publishers.

———. 2011. *Feminist Advocacy and Gender Equity in the Anglophone Caribbean: Envisioning a Politics of Coalition*. New York: Routledge.

Samuel, Camille. 2010. 'Corporate Turnaround and Gender in Trinidad: Exclusionary Practices in Corporate Turnaround Leadership'. PhD. diss., The University of the West Indies, St. Augustine Campus.

Sheller, Mimi. 2012. *Citizenship from Below: Erotic Agency and Caribbean Freedom*. Durham and London: Duke University Press.

Shirley, Beverly. 2009. 'An Examination of the Transformative Potential of Caribbean Feminisms in Trinidad, Barbados, Guyana and Jamaica in the 1970s'. PhD. diss., The University of the West Indies, Mona Campus.

Smith, Faith. 2011. *Sex and the Citizen: Interrogating the Caribbean, ed.* Charlottesville and London: University of Virginia Press.

Stevens, Anne. 2007. *Women, Power and Politics.* Basingstoke: Palgrave Macmillan.

Tadros, Mariz. 2014. *Women in Politics: Gender, Power and Development.* London and New York: Zed Books.

Vassell, Linnette. 1993. *Voices of Women in Jamaica, 1898–1939.* The University of the West Indies, Mona Campus.

Vassell, Linette. 2003. 'Women, Power and Decision-Making in CARICOM Countries: Moving Forward from a Post-Beijing Assessment', in *Gender Equality in the Caribbean*, edited by Gemma Tang Nain and Barbara Bailey, 1–38. Kingston, Jamaican: Ian Randle Publishers.

Chapter 3

Women's Political Leadership in Trinidad and Tobago

Understandings, Experiences and Negotiations

Aleah N. Ranjitsingh

I have often been the lone woman's voice in a huge sea of men. That is what I have stood out for in my political career … being the first woman to do several things. I remember clearly what drove my decisions in those days as I voted for certain bills, and as I contributed to debates in Parliament and took certain stances in the country. It was the full and complete knowledge that I was in a rare position … as one of the few female representatives of this country … it was my duty to assume the natural role of mother when it came to national issues. In that sea of men who argued and cussed each other … I knew I had to be the rare voice of fairness, nurturing, caring and love. I knew that my vote was always influenced by the thought of how those policies or stances would affect the heart, mind and bodies of the country. My maternal instincts made me choose sometimes not by my head, but my heart. But as any true mother, those instincts were never wrong. And so, I cared for the people of my constituency, my party and the nation, as a mother. I did it because of the great love of my country. I am the woman who has awoken and I will never turn back. (Prime Minister Kamla Persad-Bissessar 2007.[1])

On May 24, 2010, history was made in Trinidad and Tobago when Kamla Persad-Bissessar was elected as the country's first woman prime minister. This victory came twenty-three years after her first political post in 1987 as a local government alderman for the St. Patrick County Council; a senator in 1994; MP for the Siparia constituency since 1995; attorney general in 1995 and 2001; and minister of education in 2000. On January 24, 2010 she rivalled United National Congress (UNC) founder and former prime minister of Trinidad and Tobago Mr. Basdeo Panday to become political leader of the UNC, and led the UNC and a coalition of political parties in the national elections against the incumbent Mr. Patrick Manning and the People's National Movement (PNM) on May 24, 2010.

As a woman of East Indian descent, Ms. Persad-Bissessar – who would only serve one term as prime minister after losing the subsequent election of September 7, 2015, to Dr. Keith Rowley and the PNM – overcame the masculinist ideals of her predominantly Hindu, East Indian political party. Presenting herself as 'the woman candidate', she highlighted her femininity, womanhood and motherhood, and appealed to Indo- and Afro-Trinidadian women constituents who found the idea of a strong woman political figure attractive. She also appealed to men who were tired of the past male, somewhat authoritarian leadership, and sought a kinder, more integrative leader. Pertinent women's rights groups and feminist activists supported her, viewing her impending election as a victory for all women in Trinidad and Tobago, and as a means to push the *gender agenda* in parliament. For many, it signalled the beginning of a shift away from masculinist, male-dominated politics and the hope that a female leader would foster the creation of a more equitable society, strengthened and enhanced democracy and gender equality (IPU 2008). Many feminist scholars have, however, argued against such an expectation. In her research on southern and eastern Africa, Meintjes (2010) for example indicates that a direct correlation cannot be assumed between women's participation in politics and improved gender equality. The Inter-Parliamentary Union (IPU) in its 2009 *Equality in Politics* report also found that women's progress in parliaments was 'patchy' and gender equality was only achieved 'occasionally' or 'rarely' in parliament (IPU 2009).

Conversely, Kabeer (2003) has pointed out that one of the indicators for monitoring gender equality and women's empowerment[2] relates to the number of seats women hold in national parliaments. She notes that when gender equality is achieved in the representation of women in parliaments, 'such an achievement could, with certain qualifications ... have the most potential for transformation' for gender equality and women's empowerment. Similarly, Caribbean feminist scholar Eudine Barriteau has asserted that 'empowering women through political participation constitutes qualitative and quantitative change in Caribbean political systems and cultures'. It 'places pressure on the value systems of states' and in doing so, 'problematizes the power vacuum women still experience as citizens'. Furthermore, she argues that such an act reorders power relations to enhance gender justice. Empowering women in politics is thus not only material, but also ideological since it means 'creating more democratic, participatory and just political and economic structures' (Barriteau 1997, 11). Most importantly, the power of having a woman elected as a political leader within what has been widely seen as a masculinist political space and political culture enables feminists to see such an election as a strategy for advancing feminist goals, and, most importantly, gender justice. According to Barriteau, gender justice is defined as

A societal condition in which there are no asymmetries of access to, or allocation of, status, power and material resources in a society, 'or in the control over
and capacity to benefit from these resources'. In a gender system characterized
by gender justice there will be no hierarchies of gender identities or of the meanings society gives to masculinity and femininity. (Ibid. 3)

A just gender system is thus pivotal in reconstructing those complex systems that create and maintain the unequal access and allocation of 'status,
power and material resources within society' (Barriteau 2001, 26). Such
unequal access has permeated and infused the political sphere and the political processes. This therefore raises questions about the structural and ideological constraints that limit women's entry into politics in Trinidad and Tobago,
as well as their advancement once they gain entry. It also raises questions
about the extent of such constraints in limiting women's ability to create the
very structural and ideological transformations needed to create greater gender justice. The election of Prime Minister Persad-Bissessar is thus worthy of
a critical feminist analysis in order to examine these structural and ideological
constraints, and whether being elected a political leader and the prime minister of Trinidad and Tobago was a successful strategy for advancing women's
rights, gender equality, democratic governance, women's political participation and leadership, and gender justice.

To this end, this chapter maps the gendered political space within Trinidad
and Tobago during the leadership of Persad-Bissessar (and specifically
between 2010 and 2013) so as to determine whether the prime minister
advanced gender equality and equity in her own political party, across parties, and throughout the nation. It examines the possibilities and limitations of
female political leadership as a means to increase women's political participation and power by specifically examining Persad-Bissessar's experiences
as a woman, mother, grandmother and wife; the meanings and understandings of these experiences; and her attempts to mainstream gender in budgets,
ministerial and state-board appointments, as well as legislation, namely the
national gender policy. The chapter also closely examines the experiences
of women MPs and women in local government throughout their campaigns
and their experiences in political office. The process of political campaigning
is further interrogated to reveal the gendered climate in politics that women
navigate, and how this in turn impacts and limits their leadership and their
own understandings of politics and power.

Grounded in ethnography,[3] this chapter is a case study of women's political
leadership in Trinidad and Tobago. It employs a mixed method qualitative
approach and includes interviews, discourse analysis, content analysis and
participant and non-participant observation. Additionally, in-depth, semi-
structured interviews were conducted with participants between January and

July 2013. In order to understand women's experiences of political contestation and political life in Trinidad, heterogeneous groups of women in politics
in Trinidad were interviewed. These included women across racial and party
lines in local government, and those serving in the House of Representatives
as MPs and members of the Senate. Women in local government were much
more open to facilitating face-to-face interviews. On the other hand, women
MPs and those who hold ministerial posts were more difficult to contact and
often multiple calls and emails were required to gain an interview. Studying
up has therefore been fraught with many difficulties, specifically in terms of
accessing those with power, consequently limiting the number of face-to-face
interviews which were conducted.

THE RISE OF KAMLA PERSAD-BISSESSAR

Prior to her election on May 24, 2010, Persad-Bissessar's rise to UNC's
political leader came after her victorious election over party founder Mr.
Basdeo Panday. Persad-Bissessar won this election by a margin of 13,493
votes to Panday's 1,359 votes. The UNC internal election of 2010 was not
only the vehicle for Persad-Bissessar's rise to prime minister, but it also signalled a shift within the UNC – a party held together by a masculinist and
predominantly Hindu and Indian political culture and infused by party loyalty
to the male party founder. This election saw Persad-Bissessar challenge her
mentor and, in doing so, publicly question Panday's ability to lead the UNC
to victory against the PNM in a national election.

In the subsequent 2010 national election Persad-Bissessar and the UNC
formed a coalition political party – the People's Partnership (PP) – with the
following political parties: the Congress of the People (COP), the National
Joint Action Committee (NJAC), the Movement for Social Justice (MSJ)[4]
and the Tobago Organization of the People (TOP). The PP ran against the
incumbent prime minister, Mr. Patrick Manning, political leader of the PNM
and the New Vision Movement (NVM) – a smaller political party which contested only ten of the 41 electoral seats. Openly running as the 'woman candidate' and appearing on political platforms to the sounds of Helen Reddy's
1975 women's anthem, *I am Woman*, Persad-Bissessar reminded the nation
of her positionality as wife and mother.

The political discursive space began to shift. Images and stories that had
never before encroached on the political space emerged. This feminizing of
the political discursive space not only challenged the 'rural, Indian, working
class'[5] UNC, but also transcended what Gilkes (2010) described as the 'patricentric Hindu cultural ideas' of a Hindu woman ascending to political power
in the male-dominated Hindu political party. In running for the office of prime

minister, Persad-Bissessar also aimed to gain the acceptance of not only the large Indo-Trinidadian electorate, but the equally large Afro-Trinidadian one. As unifier and leader of the PP which comprised political parties that included a different racial, class and issue-centred electorate than the mostly Indo-Trinidadian UNC, Persad-Bissessar campaigned as the candidate to cross all racial, ethnic and religious lines whose experience as a wife, mother and grandmother, coupled with her long political career, would bring change to Trinidad and Tobago. This appealed to many Indo- and Afro-Trinidadian women, mothers and grandmothers who understood and respected the power of a strong female figure, her humble, rural upbringing in south Trinidad, and her steady upward mobility through education.

Persad-Bissessar's victory in the 2010 UNC internal election and then candidacy in the 2010 general elections was greatly applauded by political analysts, feminists and women activists in Trinidad and Tobago and the region. Social activist Hazel Brown, founding member of the Network of NGOs, publicly endorsed Persad-Bissessar, and Persad-Bissessar's campaign formed part of the Network of NGOs 'Put a Woman' project. With the slogan 'A Woman's Place Is in the House – of Parliament', the Network of NGOs' 'Put a Woman' project stemmed from its 'Engendering Local Government' project, which commenced in 1996, and the subsequent 'Women's Parliament Forum' in 1998. Its goals were to have one hundred women run in the local government elections, bring a 50:50 representation on all levels of government and have a woman elected as mayor of Port of Spain, the capital city.[6] Brown and the Network of NGOs would thus rally behind Persad-Bissessar, with Brown often publicly speaking out against Persad-Bissessar's detractors and urging the women of Trinidad and Tobago to support a woman for prime minister. James-Sebro (2010) thus described Persad-Bissessar's victory in the general election as 'Hazel Brown's everlasting "Put a Woman" campaign' bearing 'its first full fruit'.

Male stalwarts of the UNC – many of whom had campaigned against her in the 2010 UNC internal elections – also endorsed Persad-Bissessar. Dr. Roodal Moonilal, Mr. Chandresh Sharma, Dr. Rupert Griffith, Mr. Vasant Bharath and Mr. Jack Warner heavily campaigned for Persad-Bissessar. Warner especially, who had campaigned against Persad-Bissessar's slate in the 2010 UNC internal election to win the post of deputy chairman,[7] was often at her side, speaking vociferously on her behalf.

After Persad-Bissessar's victory, Gabrielle Hosein, feminist activist and lecturer at the Institute for Gender and Development Studies (IGDS) at the University of the West Indies (UWI), St. Augustine campus, commented:

> Having a female PM is highly inspiring for a younger generation of women
> and socializes younger men to grow up in a world where women's leadership

is more accepted. Having a female PM means that we may get policies that are more gender sensitive, but this is more based on the leader's politics and ideology rather than her sex or biology.[8]

Hazel Brown also continued to call on the women of Trinidad and Tobago to support the new prime minister. She expressed of Persad-Bissessar: 'Her victory is a very important milestone that has been met in this country. There has always been doubt out there, over the capacity of a woman to lead, and it is natural to doubt'.[9] Political analyst Dr. Indira Rampersad also commented on Persad-Bissessar's general election victory in 2010 stating, She will be under intense scrutiny. The focus now will be on her and her performance'.[10] Thus for many, 'woman power' had prevailed and furthermore, as stated by Rampersad, the scrutiny had intensified. However, Hosein (2010), reminded people that Persad-Bissessar 'had done something few women, and no Indian woman,[11] had ever done in politics globally. She came into power independently and on her own terms with no family connections to legitimize her name'.[12] Nevertheless, this ascension did not take place without gender negotiations and masculinist resistances characterizing the opportunities and limitations of 'woman power' for herself as well as other women politicians in Trinidad and Tobago.

WOMEN'S POLITICAL POWER – FROM CAMPAIGN TO POLITICAL OFFICE

Existing scholarship confirms that gender impacts how women enter into politics, and once there, how they present themselves and behave in the public space. This is further supported by what Barriteau (1997, 11) describes as 'the value systems of states' in the Caribbean region and society, which perpetuates unequal power and gender relations between men and women and 'contribute to maintaining inequalities that are inimical for women, children and men' (Ibid. 14). Such 'value systems' or what Barriteau (2001, 30) would term the 'ideological relations of gender', 'reveal what is appropriate or expected of the socially constructed beings of "women" and "men"', how society forms gender identities and how such gendered hierarchies create gender ideologies within a society which influence or shape women's experiences of political life.

It is in this way that the invoking of Persad-Bissessar's womanhood, femininity and motherhood proved to be not only a source of power but also a source of vulnerability for her. Persad-Bissessar, referred to as 'the lady' by her opponent Manning, was often openly criticized as being weak and unable to lead and make decisions, 'the kind of veiled sexism often directed at women' (Hosein 2010). Before her election however, Persad-Bissessar was already privy to such accusations based on her sex and gender. During the 2010 UNC internal election, as Persad-Bissessar campaigned and called for a stronger UNC, Panday centred national discussions on her character and painted her as a woman who drank heavily. Panday argued, 'She is not yet ready. She has to get rid of that serious problem she has. I empathize with her. But the leadership of your party at this time is of overriding concern'.[13] While such an accusation was not unheard of in the public realm, the accusations held more weight in this case because they were directed at a woman for whom considerations of class, religion and respectability were significant.

Women politicians however have a general understanding of the gendered constraints of political life. They understand that the type of leadership strategy they employ is highly visible, especially given that society views leadership as a masculine trait which often undermines women's effectiveness as politicians. Gendered assumptions about leadership and the challenges it poses for women become clear when a woman presents herself as a political candidate and potential leader during the campaign. Ms. Khadijah Ameen, present opposition senator, deputy chairman of the UNC and former chairman of the Tunapuna/Piarco Regional Corporation, explained the tight rope that women must walk when it comes to political campaigning. For instance, during the 2013 Chaguanas by-election campaigns, for which she was the UNC candidate, her status as a divorced mother of one entered into the campaign discourse. Campaigning, especially in its often veiled and sometimes very open sexist discourse, is a very gendered activity. For example, Ameen explained that she will not campaign in a bar because citizens view a bar as a male or masculine space. Furthermore she stated she would not publicly drink a beer, because some social, political and religious circles view a woman drinking or even holding a beer as unacceptable. The campaign experience is thus very different for male and female political candidates as the campaign trail is a gendered space. While society expects and even excuses a male political candidate for retreating to the bar after a hard day on the job or of campaigning, the same is not accepted for a woman candidate. Such an expectation or 'value system' is based on social and cultural constructs of masculinity and femininity, and the unequal allocation of power given to each.

Therefore, while the former UNC political leader labeled Persad-Bissessar as a 'drinker' during the 2010 internal election campaign, the fact that many men of the political party indulged in drinking as well was not seen as relevant. As a woman, especially a respectable Hindu East Indian woman, drinking is unacceptable. Maxie Cuffie (2012), expressed that the allegations that Persad-Bissessar is a 'heavy drinker' is further problematic due to the perception that such a problem affected her ability to lead – as seen in the November 2, 2012 march in Port of Spain against the passage of Section 34 of the Administration of Justice (Indictable Proceedings) Act 2011. The passage of Section 34, which 'provided for the acquittal of an accused "after the expiration of ten years from the date on which an offence is alleged to have been committed"',[14] sparked great outrage throughout Trinidad and Tobago as it meant that those indicted in the famed Piarco Airport corruption cases[15] would be free of all charges. According to Cuffie (2012), during this march, participants sang to the tune of calypsonian Lord Beginner's 1940 road march calypso 'Run Yuh Run', but instead replaced the lyrics with 'Drink yuh rum, Kamla, drink yuh rum' thus 'making a clear link between the Section 34 fiasco and the former Prime Minister's alleged drinking problem' and her ability to lead.

Such allegations of heavy drinking and the questioning of her leadership were so widespread that Persad-Bissessar saw it fit to publicly denounce these charges.[16] The accusations and discourse surrounding Persad-Bissessar not only clearly reveals the gendered nature of political life but also demonstrates the inherent gendered contradictions of what society believes a female and male politician can do. Alcohol consumption by men for instance is not linked to their ability to lead. Thus, while some women such as Persad-Bissessar and Ameen may enter into the political space, society still judges them by, and demands they operate within, the inherent gender ideologies which determine gender roles and power relations. These gender ideologies force women political leaders and politicians to operate within the confines of femininity and masculinity, and to defend themselves, as Persad-Bissessar did, or to avoid 'masculine activities' all together, such as drinking beer or campaigning in bars as Ameen had done, to maintain political life.

Not all women politicians, however, resign themselves to operating within the confines masculinist ideologies create for them. For example, while Ms. Sabrina Mowlah-Baksh, former deputy mayor of San Fernando (who has also written about her experiences in electoral politics (2015)), recognized the different expectations for male and female political candidates, she took a different approach to the question of gendered spaces for male and female politicians. Questioned about her first campaign experience in local government in the San Fernando West constituency, she stated:

> Now as a male, you would have been allowed to go into bars. Now that was a big thing for me because I am not a drinking person and of course it was a big thing whether I should go into bars and campaign or not. I felt that I needed to because I felt that it was a space in which I had to meet with some of the potential voters and I should not be barred from going into those places. So I would have gone in, I would have sat down, I would have drank a soft drink with some of them, old-talked with some of them.[17]

Mowlah-Baksh further explained that she suffered some backlash for this decision but she was unfazed. Her presence in bars while campaigning was thus an act of resistance to the idea of allocated male or masculine gendered spaces.

What also cannot be denied is the notion that amid masculine, 'dirty politics', women who run for office are expected to carry out 'clean campaigns'. According to Cornwall et al. (2007, 10), 'Empirical observations have been made that women less frequently take bribes, and are less often involved in shady political deals. This is explained by the idea that women are more moral than men, either because of their dominant social roles, or because of their implied intrinsic qualities'. Such understandings permeate political life in Trinidad and Tobago. They can be seen in Persad-Bissessar's boasting of a clean general election campaign in 2010. While carrying out a clean campaign (or at least boasting of one) is not new when it comes to political campaigns, Persad-Bissessar's clean campaign 'called on her identity as a politician, mother, grandmother and woman'.[18] Goetz (2008, 90) points out, 'This idea of linking notions of womanly virtue with incorruptibility is not new. It is based upon essentialist notions of women's higher moral nature and their propensity to bring their finer moral sensibilities to bear on public life, and particularly on the conduct of politics'. While an anti-corruption agenda or clean campaign is not questioned, what is implicated in such, are understandings of women in political power and the necessity to link their femininity with notions of morality.

The messy relationship between gender, morality and political power can be clearly seen in the political campaigns of the two major candidates in the Chaguanas West by-election which took place on July 29, 2013. Mr. Jack Warner and his newly founded Independent Liberal Party (ILP) emerged victorious over his closet rival Ameen and the UNC. There were marked differences in campaign tactics, party management and support. These differences reveal much as they allow one to understand the gendered experiences of political contestation and campaigning, how women and men in the political party and on the ground negotiate masculinist political ideologies, how they negotiate around dominant gender ideologies, and the inherent power relations. Given that this election was truly a fight for the UNC to remain strong and united in the upcoming 2015 general election, Persad-Bissessar campaigned heavily with Ameen, who was welcomed to the stage to songs like 'Girl on Fire' by Alicia Keys. This performance aimed to resolidify Persad-Bissessar's political might as a woman leader of the UNC and the country. She aimed to guide Ameen to victory – two women; two sisters; a mother and a daughter. Speaking during the campaign, Ameen made it a habit to state publicly that she would keep her campaign 'clean'. Her speeches, though short, were often issue-based and party-based – a vote for Khadijah Ameen meant a vote for Persad-Bissessar and the UNC, and thus the country.

However, not many supported Persad-Bissessar's strong and very public support of Ameen. Describing her as a 'child' or 'little girl' during his campaign rally in La Paille, Caroni Village on July 10, 2012, Warner publicly stated that Ameen 'only has value when she holds on to the PM's coat tails'. This raises a number of issues. First, on the campaign trail, the political discourse is a gendered one especially when one or more of the candidates are women. The implications of phrases such as 'little girl' to describe a woman are manifold.[19] First, while the term 'girl' has been somewhat contested according to Brown (2011, 108) – as many young women have reclaimed the term girl', in order 'to make distinctions of their own, within the public sphere' – what is meant here by the terms 'girl' and 'little girl' is an accusation that Ameen is not 'a mature and serious contributor to adult life', (Ibid. 108) and therefore has no place in politics or in a political race against a powerful man. Second, it raises the issue of the strategic alliance between two women – the former prime minister and Ameen – which excludes the need for male public support or patronage. For many women who aspire to politics and the political party hierarchy, there must be a negotiation with the male networks. In this way, many male allies or patrons support female politicians since these are the men who wield the most power – especially financially – within the political party.

Understanding the gendered nature of such political relationships is therefore important. Male–male patronage is less apt to elicit accusations of control, but society regards highly visible female–female patronage with concern. It is seen as problematic and the abilities of the women candidates to lead are questioned because this disturbs the common notion that political leadership is naturally masculine and best undertaken by men. Thus, the issue of female–female patronage dominated the political discursive space more than any discussions on the serious accusations of fraud and corruption levelled against Warner while he was the president of the Confederation of North, Central American and Caribbean Association Football.[20] In fact, supporters of Warner and the ILP did not see these as issues due to these gendered assumptions about masculinity, femininity, power and leadership. Warner, the male powerful leader, survived the electoral campaign unscathed.[21]

In addition to understanding patronage and leadership as male and masculine, the role women play in the gendered division of labour also permeates the political experiences and understandings of women in politics in Trinidad and Tobago. While women politicians work in the same political or public sphere as their male counterparts, this does not negate their roles in the household as mothers, daughters and caretakers, especially given the expectation that they are responsible for unpaid care work within the home. Former opposition senator Nicole Dyer-Griffith expressed her concern as a mother and a politician who had to be present during extended parliament sittings, some of which begin at 1:30 pm and go on till 5:00 am the next morning.[22]

Ameen as a councillor and chairman shared similar concerns:

So sometimes you have to go visit a project site early in the morning or go on a television or radio show very early in the morning. That means my mother would have to get [my son] ready for school.... I can't normally leave work at two o'clock or three o'clock to pick him up. His bedtime is half seven and I don't get home until nine o'clock in the night. So it's easy to not even see your child in this kind of work.... Due to the cultural expectations men expect their wives to cook for them, I was married for two years and one of the issues that my husband had was that.... I didn't cook often enough. I know some of my female colleagues have that problem, they have to go home and cook for their husbands so that prevents you from getting involved in certain meetings, participating in certain committees as well as in things that could readily advance you in politics.[23]

The word 'balance' has therefore become quite useful for women politicians to describe their lives. The prime minister herself publicly showed that 'balance' is needed, as she did not shy away from her duties as mother, wife and grandmother. Pictures of her and her grandson flooded local newspapers. For some, such a show of family and familial space is positive. For others, like former independent senator Corinne Baptiste-McKnight, this focus on family falls short. According to Baptiste-Knight, '[The Prime Minister] isn't lying, she is a mother she is a grandmother but that has absolutely nothing to do with what happens thereafter'.[24] When asked to expound, the senator replied, 'because I would be surprised to discover that she or anybody on her staff is particularly mandated to look carefully at legislation to see how it is supposed to impact families, children, et cetera, et cetera'.[25]

Such disappointment in the prime minister was also shared by the former MP for San Fernando West, minister of public administration and chairman of the COP, Ms. Carolyn Seepersad-Bachan. Ms. Seepersad-Bachan expressed her frustration with the prime minister and explained that when Persad-Bissessar was elected she was elated and hoped for great change, especially for women in positions of political power. Ms. Seepersad-Bachan pointed out that despite the former prime minister appealing to women constituents on the campaign trail, change had not happened. The reality is that Persad-Bissessar's invocation of femininity, womanhood and motherhood has not been able to transform gendered relations of power to the extent that she promised during her campaign, and which were expected by Ms. Seepersad-Bachan and other constituents. This trend continues to affect women in politics due to the ideological and structural confines of political parties, the cabinet and the continuous need for wider party and electorate support – especially for Persad-Bissessar.

In examining women's experiences from the campaign ground to political office, it is clear that gendered assumptions of leadership, and masculinity and femininity, permeate political life. These assumptions dictate the spaces in which women can campaign, their campaign strategies, their relationship with other women in politics and expectations by the general public. Dress code is also dictated. Persad-Bissessar's dress code and style of dress was very open to public scrutiny. The media especially regularly commented on her apparent change of dress since becoming prime minister of Trinidad and Tobago. Her array of pant suits made it to daily news stories in a way that the former male prime ministers' style and choice of dress did not.[26]

The privileging of men and masculine behaviour in political spaces thus impacts and limits how women in politics are able to lead, what is expected of them and what they are able to achieve. As a woman, certain expectations exist, especially of the prime minster, that she, as a mother, wife and grand-mother, would help to increase women's political participation and politi-cal leadership, create and implement policies and legislation that empower women, and change the patriarchal political landscape.

THE GENDER AGENDA

Such expectations were held by women's rights activists, academics and feminists who saw Persad-Bissessar's 2010 candidacy as 'a reflection of the times' as stated by Patricia Mohammed, professor of gender and cultural studies at the IGDS at the UWI, St. Augustine campus.[27] She further stated, 'I hope they would take up the *gender policy* and drive it home because it is something we have been pushing for some time'.[28] There was, thus, collective hope that with a woman at the helm, and one who campaigned on the platform of 'woman power', Trinidad and Tobago's National Gender Policy would manage to become official and bypass the policy evaporation it had suffered since it was laid as a green paper in the Office of the Parliament in 2009.[29] It did not. Many believed that part of the reason why the national gender policy did not gain the expected momentum was due to the constant changes in the appointment of the minister of gender, youth and child development. The ministry saw three persons appointed as minister between 2011 and 2013. Verna St. Rose, an avid supporter of the policy, advocated a national policy on gender in Trinidad and Tobago that would include a woman's right to choose, and gay/homosexual rights. She made this very clear at the ministry's gender stakeholder consultation, which was held at Cascadia Hotel, St. Ann's, Trini-dad, on May 16, 2012. Persad-Bissessar fired St. Rose in June 2012.[30] While Persad-Bissessar gave no official reason for the action, Anil Roberts, former minister of sport (2010–2014), revealed during a press conference in Decem-ber 2012 that St. Rose was fired due to her personal beliefs on same-sex and reproductive rights – rights which put her in contention with her fellow members of cabinet.[31] Ms. Marlene Coudray, former COP member and former mayor of San Fernando, replaced St. Rose. In September 2013, Coudray was reappointed to the Ministry of Local Government; Mr. Clifton De Coteau became the new minister and Ms. Raziah Ahmed was appointed the new minister of state in the Ministry of Gender, Youth and Child Development.[32] During these appointment changes, the national gender policy was presented to the cabinet, but to date, even after a number of public consultations led by Professor Patricia Mohammed and gender machinery consultant Dr. Rawwida Baksh, the policy document remains stalled.

It is clear that Persad-Bissessar's engagement with feminist issues has been quite uneven. Initially, splitting the Ministry of Planning and Gender Affairs into two separate ministries was lauded by women activists because the new Ministry of Gender, Youth and Child Development promoted the issues of gender, youth and child affairs, and women's empowerment as national issues worthy of their own budget, staff and ministerial portfolio. However, the subsequent replacement of ministers forces one to reconsider Persad-Bissessar's commitment to gender equality in Trinidad and Tobago. Furthermore, Persad-Bissessar publicly assured that the lesbian, gay, bisexual and transgender community would be protected against discrimination. However, it appeared that her cabinet and her own electorate held her captive on this issue. This resistance is structural and ideological, and therefore politics itself became a form of resistance for Persad-Bissessar in terms of championing a truly equitable and gender-just national gender policy. Such is even more pertinent given that after the 2015 general election, prime minister elect Dr. Keith Rowley did not appoint a ministry with the oversight of gender.

On International Women's Day in March 2011, however, Persad-Bissessar appointed Hazel Brown and Ms. Brenda Gopeesingh, founding member and former president of the Hindu Women's Organization (HWO) of Trinidad and Tobago, as special envoys to look at women and children's issues in the Commonwealth Caribbean. During this time, Persad-Bissessar also announced that a National Commission on the Status of Women in Trinidad and Tobago would be created. No commission has been created, though, under her administration, the number of women appointed to state boards increased. Even though Persad-Bissessar officially set a goal to have 40% female representation on all state boards in 2010, this came after interventions by Brown and the Network of NGOs. Only then did the number of women on state boards increase – 198 appointees to 79 state boards were women[33] an improvement from the prior PNM administration in which women comprised 26% of state boards (Douglas 2010).

Furthermore, in 2011 the former Prime Minister announced that the 2012 national budget would be a 'gender responsive budget' – one to 'enhance a gender-responsive national development plan to support the allocation of funding to all ministries and sectors' (Lord 2011).[34] The $58 billion 2012 budget thus included more social programmes that created grants for poor, single mothers with special-needs children, for families with children with disabilities, and other allowances for individuals with disabilities.[35] In 2013, training was provided to government ministries on gender-responsive budgeting; however, under Persad-Bissessar's leadership a truly gender-responsive budget, or even guidelines for such a budget was not developed. Thus, Persad-Bissessar's record on advancing women's rights and gender equality remains largely uneven. While her presence in the parliament as prime minster showcases her 'woman power', the negotiations and contestations which sought to limit this power persisted, especially in regard to advancing gender justice

HAS THE PATRIARCHAL LANDSCAPE CHANGED?

As stated above, Persad-Bissessar's record on promoting gender equality and women's rights has been uneven. Appointments of women to political and decision-making positions, including ministerial posts and state boards, remained low under her leadership. Under the PP, women comprised 28.6% and 19.4% of parliamentarians in the House of Representatives and the Senate respectively.[36] This can be compared to the parliamentary composition under her male successor Dr. Rowley where as of December 1, 2015, women comprised 31% and 32.3% of parliamentarians in the House of Representatives and Senate respectively (IPU 2015).

Persad-Bissessar's time in office was fraught with challenges and limitations. Accusations of corruption were rampant in the lead up to and during the 2015 general election campaign. Warner for instance described her as 'unfit to lead',[37] amid accusations of 'misconduct and misbehavior in public office'.[38] It is no secret that Persad-Bissessar's administration was plagued with many scandals, such as the appointment and then subsequent firing of Ms. Reshmi Ramnarine as director of the Security Intelligence Agency; the Section 34 fiasco as discussed above; the firing of cabinet members; and accusations of sexual misconduct against Persad-Bissessar herself.

The 2015 general election saw a type of 'Kamla vs Rowley' campaigning – borrowed from the US presidential system – where according to esteemed journalist Sunity Maharaj, the citizens saw the 're-casting of the PP in the image and likeness of Kamla'.[39] This recasting presupposed that Persad-Bissessar was the PP's strongest asset.[40] As the perceived 'strongest asset' and political leader of the UNC, she was once again the target of the Opposition – her personal life and positionality as a woman laid bare on the campaign trail. Dr. Rowley, for example, argued at a campaign meeting in Brazil

Village on March 17, 2015, that 'she could jump high, she could jump low. She could drink this, she could drink that. She could bark at my dog because I will ignore she cat'.[41] Laced with sexual innuendo, the UNC Women's Arm under the chairman Ms. Stacy Roopnarine immediately called for Dr. Rowley to apologize to Persad-Bissessar and to all the women of Trinidad and Tobago for his derogatory comment. It also called on the PNM's Women's Arm to support this call, which they refused to do. Instead they supported Rowley.[42] It must be noted however that Dr. Rowley did apologize.

Many also questioned Persad-Bissessar's power amid accusations that she was, and had not really been, in charge of her political party, her (former) cabinet and thus the country. Throughout her term, Persad-Bissessar had to address claims that there was a *cabal* or secret political faction of men within her party and that they held the true reins of power in the cabinet and in the UNC. Accusations such as these not only worked against her as political leader and prime minister, but also undermined her reputation with male UNC party stalwarts and financiers. Therefore, she had to be consistent and strong in defending her leadership, as she was on December 3, 2012, during the UNC's Monday night forum at the Tulsa Trace Hindu School in Penal. Persad-Bissessar announced:

> You have been hearing our detractors say that I am not in charge, that I am being manipulated. I want to tell you why they are pushing that kind of propaganda. They thought that as a woman, I would have succumbed to the challenges of leading this country. They said that I could not hold the Government together. The results are there for all to see.[43]

Such challenges do not only speak to Persad-Bissessar as a woman, but also as woman of East Indian descent leading a mostly male East Indian party amid deeply rooted Hindu religious and cultural ideals. Her race and ethnicity have therefore affected her experiences of political leadership as she continued to traverse UNC party politics. These intersectional factors all affected how she has been regarded in the political arena. The political terrain that Persad-Bissessar faced is much different than that faced by Basdeo Panday when he became the country's first Indo-Trinidadian and Hindu prime minster in 1995, especially given the gendered assumptions about leadership and power, and what has been described earlier as 'patricentric Hindu cultural ideas' – in other words, the idea that leadership is a masculine virtue.

Persad-Bissessar failed to be re-elected in 2015. However, without argument, the election of Persad-Bissessar proved that a woman can successfully contest national elections to become a country's leader. It also proved to women everywhere that political leadership is possible. But we are reminded that her leadership existed within a political space and through

political processes that support, and are supported by, unequal power relations between men and women. It is because of this that men have dominated the political space and have had an easier relationship with power and
politics. Furthermore, as we have seen, women's political power comes with
different experiences that are highly gendered, and, in this way, power has to
be negotiated or even challenged.

Such experiences are relevant to discourse on political leadership as they
not only reveal the role of gender in political life in Trinidad and Tobago, but
also allow us to understand the larger implications of having women in political positions of power and the possibility that this can be a means towards gender justice. However, as seen from Persad-Bissessar's experiences and those
of other women in national and local government in Trinidad and Tobago, it
appears that the inspiration that many saw in Persad-Bissessar's 2010 triumph
has not trickled down to the political parties, politics and society itself.

We are therefore reminded that in order to achieve a gender-just society,
while a 'critical mass of women in politics is necessary', it is not sufficient
(Barriteau 1997, 14). A system of governance must develop that not only
responds to the needs of women, but also allows them to better experience
and articulate power. In this way, women will understand that not only is
access to political power important, but this access empowers one to change
political systems and cultures which have created a power vacuum for women
(Barriteau 1997, 11) and which have left women out of policy. It is only
in this way that feminist goals and gender justice can be achieved, and the
masculinist, patriarchal political landscape can begin to change.

Furthermore, challenges to prevailing political processes must take place.
According to Rao and Kelleher (2005, 60), such negotiations and challenges
need to occur at the personal and social levels, as well as within formal and
informal relations before any changes to 'inequitable social systems and
institutions' can take place. This may seem unlikely for a society that relies
greatly on religious and cultural ideals about gender roles. Such changes can
not only be initiated through policies and appointments, for instance, but also
through interventions by women's and feminist NGOs to strengthen policies
and programmes that seek to advance women's rights and gender justice.
Cross-party support by women on pertinent gender issues is also necessary.
Without some sort of cooperation and with it an understanding of gender
relations and gender justice at the personal and social level, the parliament
and the cabinet cannot push forward critical legislation which affects women,
men, children and marginalized groups in society.

Therefore, while women's political leadership can be a successful strategy
to advancing democratic governance, women's rights and gender equality
in Trinidad and Tobago and in the wider Caribbean, feminist activism and
organizational advocacy must be built and strengthened in order to continue

to support those women currently in power (Baksh and Vassell 2013) so that they are able to not just be leaders, but also be transformational leaders and act to transform the very structures, bureaucracies and ideals which seek to keep them out of politics. However, as Blackstock's chapter in this edited collected reminds us, transformational leadership of this sort requires a feminist understanding and an engagement with political power for gender justice to be achieved in Trinidad and Tobago and the wider Caribbean region.

NOTES

1. Known as the 'No Woman No Cry Speech', after the famous Bob Marley song, which was played before her entrance, Persad-Bissessar delivered this speech during the UNC Alliance's election rally at Mid Centre Mall in Chaguanas on Sunday October 7, 2007.

2. As stated in Millennium Development Goal 3 (MDG 3) – Promote gender equality and empower women.

3. Ethnography is the study of social interactions, behaviors and perceptions occurring within a group, organization or community (Reeves, et. al. 2008, 512).

4. The MSJ officially withdrew from the PP on June 17, 2012.

5. Hosein, 'Looking Back at the 2010 Trinidad and Tobago General Election'.

6. After the 2010 elections, eleven out of twenty-six women were elected to parliament (five women from the PP and six from the PNM).

7. Warner was re-elected in the March 24, 2012, UNC internal election. He would later resign from this position on April 23, 2012 and found the Independent Liberal Party (ILP).

8. Karel McIntosh. 'Broken Ceilings and Woman Power in T&T'. *Outlish Magazine.* June 7, 2010, http://www.outlish.com/broken-ceilings-and-woman-power-in-tat/

9. Cecily Asson. 'Kamla's Victory: An "Important Milestone"'. *Trinidad Newsday.* May 26, 2010, http://newsday.co.tt/news/0,121413.html.

10. Peter Richards. 'First Woman PM takes the Helm in Trinidad'. *Inter Press Service News Agency.* May 25, 2010, http://www.ipsnews.net/2010/05/first-woman-pm-takes-the-helm-in-trinidad/.

11. That is, a Trinidadian woman of East Indian descent.

12. Gabrielle Hosein. 'Looking Back at the 2010 Trinidad and Tobago General Election'. *StarbroekNews.com.* May 31, 2010, http://www.stabroeknews.com/2010/features/05/31/looking-back-at-the-2010-trinidad-and-tobago-general-election/.

13. Maxie Cuffie. 'The PM's Alleged Drinking Problem – The Perception'. *Trinidad Guardian.* December 9, 2012, https://guardian.co.tt/columnist/2012-12-09/pm%E2%80%99s-alleged-drinking-problem%E2%80%94-perception.

14. Dana Seethahal. 'The Scandal of Section 34'. *Trinidad Express.* September 14, 2012, http://www.trinidadexpress.com/commentaries/The_scandal_of_Section_34-169864216.html.

15. See Khrystal Rawlins. '$11.5M bail for Piarco Airport 8'. *Trinidad and Tobago Newsday.* May 19. 2004. http://www.newsday.co.tt/news/0,18300.html.

16. Keino Swamber. 'Kamla: I Don't Have a Substance Abuse Problem'. *Trinidad Express*. December 6, 2012, http://www.trinidadexpress.com/news/Kamla-I-dont-have-a-substance--abuse-problem-182308571.html.

17. Sabrina Mowlah-Baksh, Interview, March 15, 2013.

18. Gabrielle Hosein, 'Looking Back at the 2010 Trinidad and Tobago General Election'.

19. The word 'girl' is also used describe men who seemingly do not act within the confines of society's construct of masculinity.

20. Clydeen McDonald. 'Jack Warner resigns as FIFA VP'. *Trinidad Guardian*. June 20, 2011. https://www.guardian.co.tt/news/2011/06/20/jack-warner-resigns-fifa-vp.

21. However, while reclaiming his Chaguanas West seat in this by-election, Warner and the ILP would fail to make a mark in the 2015 general election, losing all twenty-six seats that the party contested.

22. Nicole Dyer-Griffith, Interview, June 7, 2013.

23. Khadijah Ameen, Interview, March 13, 2013.

24. Corinne Baptiste-McKnight, Interview, May 11, 2013.

25. Ibid.

26. It must be noted that in April 2014, *Vanity Fair* named Persad-Bissessar as a 'top ten' best-dressed world leader. Both male and female past and present political world leaders were included in this list.

27. Carol Matroo. 'Can Women in the Election Make a Difference?' *Trinidad Newsday*. May 6, 2010, http://www.newsday.co.tt/news/0,120254.html.

28. Ibid.

29. See Deborah McFee's chapter in this edited collection.

30. Trinidad and Tobago Gazette. Monday 25 June, 2012. Vol. 51. No. 112. http://www.news.gov.tt/archive//E-Gazette/Gazette%202012/Gazette/Gazette%20No.%20112%20of%202012.pdf.

31. Anna Ramdass. 'Anil: Verna Fired for Gay/Abortion rights'. *Trinidad Express*. December 6, 2012, http://www.trinidadexpress.com/news/anil__verna_fired_for_gay_abortion_rights_-182475091.html.

32. Trinidad and Tobago Gazette. Wednesday 16 October, 2013. Vol. 52. No. 136. http://www.news.gov.tt/archive//E-Gazette/Gazette%202002/Gazette%20No.%20136%20of%202013.pdf.

33. Twenty boards were still awaiting appointments.

34. Richard Lord. 'PM: Budget to Focus on Gender Issues'. *Trinidad Guardian*. September 20, 2011, http://www.guardian.co.tt/news/2011/09/20/pm-budget-focus-gender-issues.

35. Government of the Republic of Trinidad and Tobago. *Budget Statement 2013. Stimulating Growth, Generating Prosperity*. Presented by Minister of Finance and the Economy, Larry Howai, October 1 2012. https://guardian.co.tt/sites/default/files/story/Budget-Statement-2013.pdf.

36. Inter-Parliamentary Union. *Women in National Parliaments*. January 1, 2014. http://www.ipu.org/wmn-e/arc/classif010114.htm.

37. Alexander, Gail. 'Scandal: Jack exposes more alleged corruption, PM dismisses new claims'. *Trinidad and Tobago Guardian*. June 24 2015. http://www.

guardian.co.tt/news/2015-06-23/scandal-jack-exposes-more-alleged-corruption-pm-dismisses-new-claims.

38. Ibid.

39. Maharaj, Sunity. 'The incredible shrinking campaign'. *Trinidad Express Newspapers.* August 15, 2015. http://www.trinidadexpress.com/20150815/editorial/the-incredible-shrinking-campaign.

40. Ibid.

41. *Trinidad Express Newspaper.* 'UNC women want an apology from Rowley'. March 19, 2015. http://www.trinidadexpress.com/news/UNC-women-want-an-apology-from-Rowley-296902081.html.

42. *Trinidad Express Newspapers.* 'Rowley Apologises for 'cat' Comment'. March 25, 2015. http://www.trinidadexpress.com/news/Rowley-apologises-for-cat-comment-297605571.html.

43. Speaking notes of the Honourable Kamla Persad-Bissessar, Prime Minister of Trinidad and Tobago, UNC Monday Night Forum. Tulsa Trace Hindu School, December 3, 2012. http://www.unitedvoiceblog.com/2012_12_01_archive.html.

REFERENCES

Alexander, Gail. 'Scandal: Jack exposes more alleged corruption, PM dismisses new claims'. *Trinidad and Tobago Guardian.* June 24 2015. http://www.guardian.co.tt/news/2015-06-23/scandal-jack-exposes-more-alleged-corruption-pm-dismisses-new-claims.

Asson, Cecily. 2010. 'Kamla's Victory: An "important milestone"'. *Trinidad and Tobago Newsday.* May 26, 2010. Accessed November 30, 2013. http://newsday.co.tt/news/0,121413.html.

Baksh, Rawwida and Linnette Vassell. 2013. *Women's Citizenship in the Democracies of the Americas: The English-speaking Caribbean.* Inter-American Commission of Women, OAS.

Barriteau, Eudine. 2007. '30 Years Towards Equality: How Many More? The Mandate of the Bureau of Gender Affairs in Promoting Gender Justice in the Barbadian State'. Caribbean Review of Gender Studies. Issue 1, 16p. http://sta.uwi.edu/crgs/april2007/journals/Eudine_Barriteau_Gender_Justice.pdf.

———, ed. 2003. *Confronting Power, Theorizing Gender: Interdisciplinary Perspectives in the Caribbean.* Kingston, Jamaica: University of the West Indies Press.

———. 2001. *The Political Economy of Gender in the Twentieth-Century Caribbean.* New York: Palgrave.

———. 1998. 'Engendering Local Government'. Working Paper Series No. 1. Cave Hill, Barbados Centre for Gender and Development Studies, University of the West Indies.

———. 1997. 'Engendering Local Government in the Commonwealth Caribbean'. Regional Background Paper for the Commonwealth Caribbean Regional Symposium on Engendering Local Government. St. Lucia.

Brown, Hazel. 2007. 'Put a Woman'. Paper presented at First Annual Commonwealth Caribbean/Parliamentary Workshop, January 10–11, 2007, University of West Indies, St. Augustine.

Brown, M. 2011. 'The Sad, the Mad and the Bad: Co-Existing Discourses of Girlhood'. *Child and Youth Care Forum*, 40(2): 107–20.

Corey, Connelly. 2010. 'PM stands by PP state board appointments'. *Trinidad Express*. October 17, 2010. http://www.newsday.co.tt/news/0,129247.html.

Cornwall, Andrea, Elizabeth Harrison, and Ann Whitehead. 2007. 'Gender Myths and Feminist Fables: The Struggle for Interpretive Power in Gender and Development'. *Development and Change* 38(1): 1–20.

Cuffie, Maxie. 2012 'The PM's Alleged Drinking Problem – The Perception'. *Trinidad and Tobago Guardian*. December 9, 2012. Accessed December 3, 2013. http://guardian.co.tt/columnist/201212-09/pm%E2%80%99s-alleged-drinking-problem%E2%80%94-perception.

Doughty, Melissa. 2013. 'Activist: Budget not Sensitive to Gender'. *Trinidad and Tobago Guardian*. September 13, 2013, Accessed December 6, 2013. http://guardian.co.tt/news/2013-09-13/activist-budget-not-sensitive-gender.

Douglas, Sean. 2012. 'Verna Backs Gay-Rights, Abortion in Gender Policy'. *Trinidad and Tobago Newsday*. May 17, 2012. Accessed December 5, 2013. http://newsday.co.tt/politics/0,160230.html.

———. 2010. 'King: 198 Women on State Boards'. *Trinidad and Tobago Newsday*. November 30, 2010. December 15, 2013. http://newsday.co.tt/news/0,131674.html.

Gilkes, Corey. 2010. 'Well a Woman is Almost There. So What Bout the Politics Now?' *Trinicenter.com*. March, 2, 2010. Accessed December 15, 2013. http://www.trinicenter.com/Gilkes/2010/0203.htm.

Goetz, Ann Marie. 2008. 'Political Cleaners: Women as the New Anti-Corruption Force?' in *Gender Myths and Feminist Fables: The Struggle for Interpretive Power in Gender and Development*. Edited by Andrea Cornwall, Elizabeth Harrison and Ann Whitehead, 85–104. Massachusetts: Blackwell Publishing.

Government of the Republic of Trinidad and Tobago. 'Budget Statement 2013. Stimulating Growth, Generating Prosperity'. Presented by Minister of Finance and the Economy, Larry Howai, October 1, 2012. https://guardian.co.tt/sites/default/files/story/BudgetStatement-2013.pdf.

Honourable Kamla Persad-Bissessar, Prime Minister of Trinidad and Tobago, UNC Monday Night Forum. Tulsa Trace Hindu School, December 3, 2012. http://www.unitedvoiceblog.com/2012_12_01_archive.html.

Hosein, Gabrielle. 'Looking Back at the 2010 Trinidad and Tobago General Election'. StarbroekNews.com. May 31, 2010. Accessed December 10, 2013. http://www.stabroeknews.com/2010/features/05/31/looking-back-at-the-2010-trinidadand-tobago-general-election/.

Inter-Parliamentary Union. 'Women in National Parliaments'. January 1, 2014. http://www.ipu.org/wmn-e/arc/classif010114.htm.

Inter-Parliamentary Union. 'Equality in Politics. A Survey of Women and Men in Parliaments. An Overview of Key Findings'. 2009. http://www.ipu.org/PDF/publications/equality08-overview-e.pdf.

Inter-Parliamentary Union. Summary Report of Proceedings, 52nd Session of the UN Commission on the Status of Women, New York. February, 2008.

Inter-Parliamentary Union, Women in National Parliaments. December 31, 2007. http://www.ipu.org/wmn-e/arc/classif311207.htm.

James-Sebro, Meryl. 2010. 'Woman Power and Leadership Styles: Lessons from Trinidad and Tobago'. *Caribbean Political Economy*, normangirvan.info. June 24, 2010. Accessed February 1, 2014. http://www.normangirvan.info/james-sebro-woman-power/.

Kabeer, Naila. 2003. 'Gender Equality, Poverty Eradication, and the Millennium Development Goals: Promoting Women's Capabilities and Participation'. Economic and Social Commission for Asia and the Pacific. Gender and Development. Discussion Paper Series. No 13. December 2003. http://www.unescap.org/sdd/publications/gender/gender_dp_13.pdf.

Lord, Richard. 2011. 'PM: Budget to Focus on Gender Issues'. *Trinidad and Tobago Guardian*. September 20, 2011. Accessed December 14, 2013. http://www.guardian.co.tt/news/2011/09/20/pm-budget-focus-gender-issues.

Maharaj, Sunity. 'The incredible shrinking campaign'. *Trinidad Express*. August 15, 2015. http://www.trinidadexpress.com/20150815/editorial/the-incredible-shrinking-campaign.

Matroo, Carol. 2010. 'Can Women in the Election Make a Difference?' *Trinidad and Tobago Newsday*. May 6, 2010, Accessed December 15, 2013. http://www.newsday.co.tt/news/0,120254.html.

McDonald, Clydeen. 2011. 'Jack Warner resigns as FIFA VP'. *Trinidad and Tobago Guardian*. June 20, 2011. https://www.guardian.co.tt/news/2011/06/20/jack-warner-resigns-fifa-vp.

McIntosh, Karel. 2010. 'Broken Ceilings and Woman Power in T&T'. *Outlish Magazine*. June 7, 2010. Accessed December 14, 2013. http://www.outlish.com/broken-ceilings-and-womanpower-in-tat/.

Meintjes, Sheila. 2010. 'Gender Governance and Democracy: Southern and Eastern Africa'. Report prepared for DFID and the IDRC. http://idlbnc.idrc.ca/dspace/bitstream/10625/43870/1/130392.pdf.

Mowlah-Baksh, Sabrina. 2015. *The decision to run: Experiences of women who have succeeded in winning elected public office*. St. Augustine, Trinidad and Tobago Institute for Gender and Development Studies, the University of the West Indies. 89 p. Thesis for the Degree of Master of Science in Gender and Development Studies.

Rambally, Rhonda Krystal. 2012. 'Gender Policy Not Just for Women Only'. *Trinidad and Tobago Guardian*. May 20, 2012. Accessed February 20, 2014. http://guardian.co.tt/news/2012-05-20/genderpolicy-not-just-women-only.

Ramdass, Anna. 2012. 'Anil: Verna Fired for Gay/Abortion Rights'. *Trinidad Express*. December 6, 2012. Accessed December 12, 2013. http://www.trinidadexpress.com/news/anil__verna_fired_for_gay_abortion_rights_-182475091.html.

———. 2011. 'Kamla Appoints Hazel Brown as Special Envoy'. *Trinidad Express*. March 10, 2011. Accessed December 13, 2013. http://www.trinidadexpress.com/news/Kamla_appoints_Hazel_Brown_as_special_envoy-117777653.html.

Rao, Aruna and David Kelleher. 2005. 'Is There Life After Gender Mainstreaming?' *Gender and Development*, (13)2: 57–69.

Rawlins, Khrystal. 2004. '$11.5M bail for Piarco Airport 8'. 2004. *Trinidad and Tobago Newsday*. May 19. http://www.newsday.co.tt/news/0,18300.html.

Reeves, Scott, Ayelet Kuper and Brian David Hodges. 2008. 'Qualitative Research Qualitative Research Methodologies: Ethnography'. *BMJ*, 37: 512–14.

Richards, Peter. 2013. 'First Woman PM Takes the Helm in Trinidad'. 2010. *Inter Press Service News Agency*. May 25, 2010. Accessed December 11, 2013. http://www.ipsnews.net/2010/05/first-woman-pm-takes-the-helm-in-trinidad/.

Roopnarine, Stacy. 2015. 'UNC women want an apology from Rowley'. Trinidad Express. March 19, 2015. http://www.trinidadexpress.com/news/UNC-women-want-an-apology-from-Rowley-296902081.html.

Seethahal, Dana. 2012. 'The Scandal of Section 34'. *Trinidad Express*. September 14, 2012.Accessed December 16, 2013. http://www.trinidadexpress.com/commentaries/The_scandal_of_Section_34-169864216.html.

Swamber, Keino. 2012. 'Kamla: I Don't Have a Substance Abuse Problem'. *Trinidad Express*. December 6, 2012. Accessed December 8, 2013. http://www.trinidadexpress.com/news/Kamla-I-dont-have-a-substance--abuse-problem182308571.html.

Trinidad Express Newspapers. 'Rowley Apologises for 'cat' Comment'. March 25, 2015. http://www.trinidadexpress.com/news/Rowley-apologises-for-cat-comment-297605571.html.

Trinidad Express Newspapers. '…Group Calls for More Female Representation'. October 8, 2012. http://www.trinidadexpress.com/news/___Group_calls_for_more_female_representation-104616639.html.

Trinidad and Tobago Gazette. Wednesday 16 October, 2013. Vol. 52. No. 136. http://www.news.gov.tt/archive//EGazette/Gazette%202002/Gazette%20No.%20136%20of%202013.pdf.

Trinidad and Tobago Gazette. Thursday 15, August 2013. Vol. 52. No. 103. http://www.news.gov.tt/archive//EGazette/Gazette%202013/Gazette/Gazette%20No.%20103%20of%202013.pdf.

Trinidad and Tobago Gazette. Monday 25 June, 2012. Vol. 51. No. 112. http://www.news.gov.tt/archive//EGazette/Gazette%202012/Gazette/Gazette%20No.%20112%20of%202012.pdf.

Trinidad and Tobago Gazette. Wednesday 13 July, 2011. Vol. 50. No. 89. http://www.news.gov.tt/archive//EGazette/Gazette%202011/Gazette/Gazette%20No.%2089%20of%202011.pdf.

Wilson, Sascha. 2012. 'Kamla: Panday Can't Win another Election'. *Trinidad Guardian*. January 9, 2010. Accessed November 3, 2013. http://www.guardian.co.tt/archives/news/politics/2010/01/09/kamla-panday-can-t-winanother-election.

Chapter 4

Arriving at 33%

Guyana's Road to Quota Adoption

Natalie Persadie

GUYANA'S QUOTA SYSTEM

Guyana presents an interesting case study for quota adoption.[1] Guyana's adoption of the gender quota was a function of key national and international developments: Beijing; mobilization of the local women's movement; and extensive constitutional reform. While it is accepted that experiences in neighbouring countries can influence a nation to press for domestic quota reform, this does not hold true for Guyana. The wave of quota adoption across Latin America had absolutely no bearing whatsoever on Guyana's decision to adopt its legislative quota.[2] Discussions at the Beijing Conference and Guyana's unique sociopolitical history lay the foundation for quota adoption. From 1964–1992, Guyana experienced a period of non-democratic governance. Guyana falls into that category of countries that have only now been able to shape a democratic framework, having emerged from a period of non-democratic governance. The consolidation of a democratic framework and the recognition that women represented a group that had to be addressed specifically explain the early adoption of the quota in Guyana's return to democracy, and its first round of constitutional reform in this new era of 'inclusive governance'.

ORGANIZATION OF CHAPTER: ONTOLOGY; METHODOLOGY

This chapter examines the establishment of the electoral gender quota system in Guyana, the only country in the Anglophone Caribbean to have adopted such a measure. The focus here is specific to the *process* involved *prior* to the establishment of the quota system, particularly the struggles and masculinist resistances in getting to 'yes'. It provides the framework for presenting data on Guyana,[3] including a review of the sociopolitical background that preceded the adoption of the quota system, the country's electoral system, the choice of quota system types and the lessons learnt.

The chapter combines two main approaches: feminist legal theory and feminist critical theory. Combining feminist legal theory, which exposes the male bias of law, with feminist critical theory, which offers a space in which women can 'emancipate' themselves, allows a comprehensive process of reflection *and* emancipation. These two theories are also useful in the examination of rights issues. They can 'rescue' the idea of women's rights by exposing biased normative assumptions and politicized knowledge claims (Persadie 2012, 2–3). The establishment of a gender quota is a means of bestowing specific political rights onto a disadvantaged sex, hence the idea of rescuing rights.[4]

The methodology employed in this chapter relies on a largely qualitative approach and focuses on a case-study research method, which is 'an empirical inquiry that investigates a contemporary phenomenon within its real-life context; when the boundaries between phenomenon and context are not clearly evident; and in which multiple sources of evidence are used' (Yin 2009, 23). As such, this chapter uses primary and secondary sources of information. Primary data was gathered from semi-structured interviews with approximately twelve to fifteen people from government, the judiciary, academia and civil society in Guyana, as well as parliamentary documents, constitutional and legislative provisions and newspaper articles. Secondary sources of data included journal articles, textbooks, websites and reports.

THE INTERNATIONAL AND REGIONAL FRAMEWORK FOR QUOTA SYSTEMS

While a number of international and regional law instruments have recognized women's underprivileged political status, the Fourth World Conference on Women in Beijing, which again called for political equality between the sexes, restated and emphasized the need for women's full participation in the decision-making process and access to political power (UN Women 1995). Overall, the Beijing Declaration represented a turning point for many women's groups globally in their pursuit of political access and equality, as it legitimized affirmative action measures for including more women in politics. The proliferation of quota systems across the globe occurred in the post-Beijing era after women's groups were invigorated to pursue more political access, representation and equality for women, as occurred in Guyana. Regional instruments (CARICOM 1997) addressing political and civil rights of women seem to have had little influence.

WHAT ARE GENDER QUOTAS IN POLITICS?

Gender quotas represent practical means for achieving the democratic ideal of inclusion (Kittilson 2005, 644), but what are they? They are a feminist strategy to increase women's political participation. More specifically, they are legal or voluntary mechanisms that identify a minimum number or percentage of women that must constitute the membership of a named political institution. For the purposes of this chapter, such membership refers to electoral candidate lists, parliament, or political parties (Dahlerup 2009). The percentage for gender quotas seems to range from 30 to 50%. Sometimes, bodies adopt or promote the 60/40 rule, where no gender should have more than 60% or less than 40% representation. Regardless of its range, gender quotas are seen as an 'effective mechanism for improving women's numerical representation', (Kittilson 2005, 638) as 'they represent a shared agreement that women have often received short shrift in the nomination process, and an admission that a concerted effort should be made to get more women elected' (Ibid. 2005, 638–39).

The under-representation of women in parliaments around the world symbolizes a serious 'democratic deficit' (Phillips 1998, 228). On average, only about 23% of women hold seats in lower houses of parliament around the world (Inter-Parliamentary Union 2015). Electoral gender quotas, meant to correct this deficit, are inherently controversial. Nevertheless, approximately 59 countries around the world have adopted gender quotas over the last twenty years (Dahlerup 2008; Dahlerup 2009), with Argentina leading the way in 1991 (Araújo and García 2006, 83; and Pande and Ford 2011, 9).

While quota systems represent a means to an end – women's political empowerment – both the means and the end differ according to the sociopolitical contexts of the country involved.

CANDIDATE QUOTAS

Quotas are often classified as voluntary party quotas, legislative quotas and reserved seats. Candidate quotas fall under the second type. They require political parties to ensure that a minimum number of female candidates are included on the electoral list, as in the case of Guyana. Fifty-three countries have adopted candidate quotas (International IDEA 2015), the highest number of any quota type at the national level. However, many of these countries exploit a loophole in this quota system, ensuring that parties meet the requisite minimum number of women on their candidate lists, but not guaranteeing that even a minimum number will make it into parliament. To overcome this obstacle, more attention must be paid to the 'minutiae' (Krook 2009, 204) of instances when countries effectively implement quotas to ensure that a percentage of women on political party candidate lists actually get elected. Many parties will place women at the bottom of the nomination list,[5] in unwinnable seats (or in unsecure seats in majority-voting systems), for instance, unless the law is drafted in such a way as to ensure nomination *and* election. Even sanctions for non-compliance do not provide the necessary impetus to ensure compliance, as exemplified in France (Kittilson 2005, 639; Sineau 2005, 128). Placement mandates, or 'double quotas' (Dahlerup 2009),[6] could be a feature of the quota law to ensure enforceability (Dahlerup 2005, 150). Iraq and Argentina, for example, have placement mandates as part of their quota laws (Ibid. 151), which specifically prescribe the ranking of women with respect to men. In some instances, rank-order rules, such as the 'zipper system', ensure that every other name is a woman's (Larserud and Taphorn 2007, 8). In other cases, parties may use ceilings to ensure that a minimum number of women candidates feature on the upper part of the nomination list.

POLITICAL GENDER QUOTAS IN THE CARIBBEAN

Compared to Latin America, gender quotas have not quite made their way to the Anglophone Caribbean, presumably as those countries do not share a

Table 4.1 Women's Representation in National Parliaments in the Independent Anglophone Caribbean

World Rank	Country	Lower or Single House			Upper House or Senate			TOTAL % Both Houses
		Seats*	Women	% Women	Seats*	Women	% Women	
26	Grenada	15	5	33.3	13	2	15.4	25
34	Trinidad and Tobago	42	13	31	31	10	32.3	31.5
37	Guyana	69	21	30.4	—	—	—	30.4
60	Dominica	32	7	21.9	—	—	—	21.9
85	Barbados	30	5	16.6	21	5	23.8	19.6
85	Saint Lucia	18	3	16.7	11	3	27.3	20.6
98	Saint Kitts and Nevis	15	2	13.3	—	—	—	13.3
99	Bahamas	38	5	13.2	16	4	25.0	16.6
100	Saint Vincent and the Grenadines	23	3	13	—	—	—	13
102	Jamaica	63	8	12.7	21	6	28.6	16.6
109	Antigua and Barbuda	18	2	11.1	17	7	41.2	25.7
134	Belize	32	1	3.1	13	5	38.5	13.3

* *Figures correspond to the number of seats filled in country parliaments on November 01, 2015.[7]* (Inter-Parliamentary Union, 2015).

history of intense liberation struggles. The number of female parliamentarian representatives is slim in the region. Table 4.1 illustrates that apart from Trinidad and Tobago, Grenada, and Guyana – the only English-speaking country in the Caribbean that has instituted a gender quota – figures fall between 22% to as low as 3.1% in the lower house of parliament. Even when both houses are taken into account, figures still generally fall below 22%.

Jamaica, the Bahamas and Belize have considered introducing a quota system, but to no legal effect. Even though Jamaica's and Trinidad and Tobago's previous prime ministers are female, this achievement does not seem to have advanced women's political power or representation in these countries or measures to attempt to do so, such as instituting gender quotas.

GETTING TO ONE-THIRD? THE QUOTA SYSTEM IN GUYANA

Guyana is geophysically a part of South America, but identifies culturally with the Anglophone Caribbean. It has a brutal political history – 'an interrupted democratic period' (Dow 2012) – but now enjoys political freedoms associated with newly democratic countries. A period of extensive constitutional reform in the late 1990s–early 2000s included the adoption of a gender quota system, for which an electoral law provides specificity. Out of the May 2015 election, Guyana boasts 30.4% women in its National Assembly (Inter-Parliamentary Union 2015), just 3% shy of the law's requirements. This section briefly reviews the electoral system in Guyana, and the need for constitutional reform; examines the process undertaken and influences in moving towards quota adoption, including the sociopolitical context at the time of the quota adoption; and examines the actual legislative framework parliament established to institute the quota.

THE ELECTORAL SYSTEM IN GUYANA

In 1964, Guyana's electoral system switched to a List Proportional Representation which, many agree, offers more favourable conditions for electing women than majoritarian electoral systems (Mansbridge 2005; Matland 2005; Nanivadekar 2006; Trembley, 2006; Krook 2007; Larserud and Taphorn 2007; Tremblay 2008). Under List PR, each party presents a list of candidates for a multi-member electoral district, voters vote for a party, and parties receive seats in proportion to their overall share of the vote (Larserud and Taphorn 2007, 23). The National Assembly, a unicameral legislature, comprises sixty-five directly elected members (Guyana Elections Commission n.d.).[8] Along with geographical considerations, the list must consider gender, ethnicity, religion and age to ensure a proper balance of candidates (Teixeira 2012).[9] While List PR systems can be open or closed, Guyana's is closed. Ordinarily, in a closed List PR system, the party predetermines the ranking of candidates on the list and voters elect candidates in the order in which they appear so they have an idea about the individual for whom they vote. In Guyana, however, parties' lists do not rank their candidates, but simply list them alphabetically (*Stabroek News* 2012, 3).[10] Therefore, the electorate selects a party without knowing which candidates the party will select to hold seats in parliament.

CONSTITUTIONAL REFORM: TOWARDS THE ADOPTION OF A LEGISLATIVE GENDER QUOTA

Adoption of the gender quota in Guyana resulted from key national and international developments, specifically the 1995 Fourth World Conference on Women in Beijing, mobilization of the local women's movement, and extensive constitutional reform. Krook (2006, 114) notes that other country quota campaigns also reference international commitments and experiences in neighbouring countries as contributors to domestic quota reforms. Interestingly, while Krook (2009, 27) points out geographic patterns with respect to the types and timing of quota adoption, Guyana does not follow such patterns. Its attendance and participation at the 1995 Beijing Conference, however, seemed to be a significant influence, especially with respect to the suggestion of quotas as a politico-legal mechanism to increase women's participation and representation.[11]

The imperative to adopt a gender quota in Guyana lies in the country's political history and the very rights-oriented mindset of those affected during the period. Initial interviews in Guyana revealed people with a very strong sense of rights, stemming from what many claim was a 28-year period of non-democratic rule in the country between 1964–1992. This sentiment was further confirmed during subsequent interviews. Some argue, however, that democracy was always present in Guyana. When the elements of democracy are considered – free and fair elections, active participation of citizens in politics and civic life, protection of all citizens' human rights, and equality before the law (Diamond 2004) – they certainly bring into question whether this was in fact the case in Guyana.

Accounts of Guyana's political history suggest that during the period 1964–1992, violent and deadly expressions of difference replaced peaceful public expressions, and citizens experienced great difficulty participating in free and fair elections, which was evidenced by repeated allegations of vote-rigging and voter intimidation. Free and fair elections and the rule of law must exist to support the right to vote. Otherwise, that right is violated. This 28-year period was thus a time during which democracy was perverted or interrupted, and where a charade of democracy underpinned authoritarian rule.

Similar to other countries transitioning to democracy that have experienced intense liberation struggles, such as South Africa, Rwanda, Uganda and many Latin American countries, Guyana witnessed the role of women entering politics because of political experiences and tragedies (Teixeira 2012). The struggle became more than getting women into politics; it became about getting women to undertake a role as significant actors in the changes and dynamics of these political environments. Moreover, viewing the adoption of a gender quota as merely a woman's issue loses the rationale for why these changes continue to take place in many countries. Guyana, having emerged from a period of non-democratic governance, falls into the category of countries that are only now able to shape a democratic framework. The consolidation of a democratic framework and the recognition that this was a group that had to be addressed specifically explain the early adoption of the quota in terms of Guyana's return to democracy and its first round of constitutional reform in this new era of 'inclusive governance' (James 2006, 32).[12]

THE SOCIOPOLITICAL CONTEXT OF CHANGE IN GUYANA

Violence during campaigns, elections and post-elections has consistently marred free elections in Guyana. Emerging out of the violence and claims of electoral fraud in the 1997 elections, the need for serious constitutional reform became increasingly apparent. CARICOM intervened to quell the situation and eventually brokered an agreement between the two main political parties: the Herdmanston Accord. This agreement specifically called for a legally established Constitution Reform Commission (CRC)[13] with a wide mandate and broad-based membership, which would be required to consult with civil society at large over an eighteen-month period (Caribbean Community 1998). The CRC spent the next 18 months reforming the 1980 Constitution, since it concentrated power in an executive president, bestowing on him 'virtual imperial powers' (Spencer 2007, 51), and ensuring the then president's control over the People's National Congress (PNC) and, in turn, the party's control over the people (Merrill 1992). Consequently, in 1992, all political parties unanimously agreed to the need to reform this extremely controversial document (George 2012),[14] but it took some eight years before it was actually realized. The 1997 elections, therefore, were held under the 1980 Constitution (Ibid.).

Unfortunately, after dutifully signing the Herdmanston Accord,[15] tensions between the PNC and the People's Progressive Party (PPP), which won the

1997 elections, arose again. Leaders of both parties met in St. Lucia to hold
discussions on the matter where they signed the St. Lucia Agreement (George
2012),[16] which essentially reiterated the Herdmanston analysis and measures.
Despite lost time, the CRC was finally appointed in January 1999 (Parris
2003, 71)[17] and had only had six months to complete all the tasks that the
two agreements outlined to meet the legislative deadline of July 18, 1999.
It was within this restructured framework, on the heels of Beijing, that the
gender quota was introduced into Guyana. It is generally held that countries
undergoing major constitutional and legal reform have a greater window of
opportunity to introduce quota laws than in established regimes (Peters and
Suter 2009, 178). The very strong rights-oriented mindset of the political
actors in Guyana at the time also provided support for this move. Red Thread,
a local, grassroots women's NGO, recognized the 'unparalleled opportunity'
presented by the constitutional reform process and ensured that its concerns
related to the lack of women's political participation were heard (Red Thread
1997, 2).[18] Gender quotas were viewed as a legitimizing tool in the eyes of
the international community, as 'the inclusion of women ... bec[a]me a sign
of democracy and modernity' (Dahlerup 2008, 323) especially since being
introduced at Beijing (Sacchet 2008, 340). On this new-found path to democracy, Guyana deemed it important, therefore, to include such measures in
its general governance restructuring. This was even more so due to a strong
Guyanese presence at Beijing, which preceded the constitutional reform
activity by only a couple of years. The issue of women's representation was,
therefore, very alive in the minds of those who attended.

SITES OF RESISTANCE: THE CRC

Only three women held seats on the twenty-member CRC, but even achieving this level of representation was a hard-won struggle. The mandate of
one woman – Anande Trotman-Joseph – in particular was to ensure that
amendments considered by the CRC for recommendation for adoption by
the National Assembly addressed a wide spectrum of women's rights, which
would become justiciable and enforceable (Trotman-Joseph 2012). Although
Trotman-Joseph's mandate was to lobby for a 50:50 ratio of men to women,
most commissioners resisted her suggestion. In fact, all political parties
argued against the 50:50 recommendation because Guyana already had
existing legislation that protected women. Some proposed a constitutional
provision of a ratio of 60:40 men to women or vice versa. The majority of
CRC commissioners did not view this favourably either, and a four-member
subcommittee report stated, 'I have indicated my firm objection to any such
course of action [60:40 gender ratio].... The entrenchment of quotas or ratios

in a constitution is not found in any part of the world. *Such institutionalised reverse discrimination will be a forensic nightmare'* (Persaud 1999, 8).[19]

Trotman-Joseph reported this to the women's movement, which then decided on a more incremental strategy to advance a structural approach to quota recommendations. Professor Kathleen Mahoney, coming from a similar exercise in South Africa and whose specializations included gender equality, constitutional law and international human rights, held a briefing session with various individual commissioners. The response was polite, but not necessarily well received, which made her presentations that much more important to ensure that experiences and lessons learnt from other countries' constitutional reforms, as they related to the inclusion of women's rights, were understood. Unsurprisingly, a network of women in Guyana also helped promote the quota issue. However, this 'network' was really a select few, and, overall, there was little solidarity among Guyanese women on the issue. The general public was not involved in the process (Andaiye 2012). The overall consensus was that the average voter did not care about how many women were on political party candidate lists, and that the issue really only mattered to middle-class and politically active working-class women (Dow 2012). While the major political parties each had their own women's arms, this network comprised a 'very informal, ad hoc cross-party caucus that shared an interest in having more women officially included in political leadership' (George 2012). Despite various attempts, no formal cross-party caucus or inter-party committee to address gender issues was ever formed.[20] Unofficial cross-party networks did develop, however, to promote the gender quota.

Once Trotman-Joseph notified the network that she was making a submission for a gender quota to the CRC, in 1999, the women's network in Guyana offered their support in various ways and facilitated public hearings on varying women's issues, including the gender quota, throughout Guyana to raise awareness of the issue and to obtain feedback. The CRC, as mandated, invited public comments through advertisements in the media (Backer 2012). The network capitalized on this offer and made formal written and oral submissions about gender equality (Trotman-Joseph 2012). These submissions were very important to ensure that the issues of gender equality and quotas were taken into consideration, as this was the only chance the public had to incorporate their views. The CRC even scheduled eight special public hearings to facilitate further submissions on gender equality outside the formal period (Parris 2003, 52).

Eventually, the CRC prioritized the quota issue and voted to determine whether they should forward the issue to parliament. Seventeen of the twenty commissioners voted in favour of the 50:50 quota recommendation (Persaud 1999, 8).[21] The CRC wrote up its report, containing approximately 174 recommendations, including the call for a 50:50 gender quota (Roopnaraine

2012). The report represented a distillation of some 4,601 recommendations the CRC received during the public hearing period (Parris 2003, 52).[22]

SITES OF RESISTANCE: PARLIAMENT

Parliament represented the second site of resistance against the gender quota in Guyana. The CRC presented their report to the National Assembly, which convened a Parliamentary Special Select Committee to filter the recommendations, and an Oversight Committee to turn the CRC report language into constitutional language. During the process, some recommendations were diluted and the 'struggle over words violated the recommendations' (Ibid. 74). The issue of tokenism arose, especially when women already had everything they needed in law (Trotman-Joseph 2012). At the time, the Commonwealth position was that women should hold 30% of parliament seats; therefore, the recommendation of a 50:50 ratio was idealistic in the context of Guyanese politics. Nevertheless, political parties' strong women's arms and the high visibility of politically and academically minded women did not allow the issue to disappear.

During an oral submission to the PSSC, women advocates focused on the wording of the one-third provision,[23] lobbying that it *created a floor and not a ceiling* for women's representation in parliament. They also focused on the fact that political party candidate lists are alphabetized (unranked); that the proportion of women candidates needed to increase from one-third to 50% by the year 2010 (this did not materialize); and that ensuring one-third of candidates were women on party lists did not guarantee their placement in parliament (Submission by the Delegation 2000, 2). The delegation further urged the OC to be faithful to the CRC's recommendations, which recognized that women must be adequately represented in parliament (Ibid. 3). This presentation was necessary mainly because the OC did not like the wording by the CRC's drafters. Women advocates brought international data to illustrate that ensuring women's equal representation in politics was an international standard and Guyana should not allow itself to fall behind these standards. After the presentation, certain OC members questioned how one could be sure competent women would be elected, which outraged women about the presumed competence of men who enter politics. This second round of resistance resulted in Hazel Halley Burnett mobilizing women to 'descend onto the parliament',[24] and sit in the parliament public gallery to offer moral support to the women delegates attempting to advance the 50:50 quota law. The action restrained male parliamentarians' urge to resist. Burnett also briefly lobbied the OC to honour Guyana's international commitments and take into account the Platform for Action that resulted from the 1995 Women's Conference in Beijing, which promoted the adoption of quota systems.

One view was that OC members held consultations because their agency and donors required them (Andaiye 2012), and they did not want to simply dismiss well-known people coming before them. Despite this assessment, Rupert Roopnaraine – political leader of the Working People's Alliance (WPA), member of the OC and supporter of the gender quota – indicated that the presentation was very well received. An unprecedented representation of women's organizations argued that the OC ensured that women are extracted off the electoral lists to reflect adequate seats in the National Assembly (Roopnaraine 2000). As one activist noted, 'Why would we have wasted our time, effort and intelligence to only have women put on the list? That is not what was intended. The point of it is that from the list you get into the House' (Radzik 2012). Ultimately, the OC ensured that one-third of the candidates placed on the electoral list were women, but did not include a placement mandate to ensure their inclusion in the National Assembly. Despite this, the role of a unified women's movement and the physical presence of women lobbying the quota cause proved crucial to this partial success. 'At every step of the way, if there were no women to speak about women's issues, they would have gotten lost' (George 2012).

SITES OF RESISTANCE: CULTURE AND RACE

The ideologies that permeated the CRC and parliament are important to note when discussing sites of resistance to the adoption of the gender quota in Guyana. Overall, 'no public view' existed on the quota issue (Andaiye 2012). The intersection of gender with class and ethnicity/race determines the manner and impact of women's political participation, mirroring a process of exclusion experienced by other marginalized groups (Kudva 2003, 447). Moreover, 'race trumps gender, sometimes even trumps class' (Andaiye 2012). Many of the interviewees agreed that election issues were based on race and party politics and little else. According to McCormack (2012), 'The electoral system is based on ethnic manipulation'.

The cultural arguments surrounding the quota debate seem to have been based on the racial divide. The PPP (whose members and representatives are largely of Indian descent, and who epitomize deeply rooted patriarchal attitudes), for example, argued that in their communities women were reluctant to come forward and do political work (Roopnaraine 2012). Moreover, PPP women politicians were reluctant to offer support in the public gallery when women's groups were making presentations about the quota. 'Indian women had to persuade their men to let them come out' (Pollard 2012). 'While Black women are accustomed to working and fighting for certain rights and putting their spouses out, Indian men saw Indian women as child-bearers and carers with no place in politics' (Halley Burnett 2012). Further, 'creeping conservatism pervading religious communities' affected the extent of freedom and independence women perceived they had (McCormack 2012). Beyond perception, conservatism favoured patriarchy in practice. Then president Cheddi Jagan thought that women's role was to look after the children, not be the backbone of the party (Halley Burnett 2012). Nevertheless, he eventually pledged his support for the quota.

At the CRC level, masculinist resistances, in the guise of religious and cultural ideologies, also presented a strong front against the gender quota. As mentioned above, 17 of 20 commissioners voted for the 50:50 quota recommendations. One of three commissioners who voted against it represented the Hindu community, and did so because he felt women already had everything they needed in law (Trotman-Joseph 2012), a sentiment that seemed largely based on religious and cultural conservative beliefs that prevail throughout the Hindu community. Indeed, even at community meetings, Indian women, whether Hindu or Muslim, were conspicuously absent (Lagan 2012) due to these deeply rooted patriarchal beliefs.

THE RECOMMENDATIONS THAT WENT FORWARD

As mentioned above, the CRC received approximately 4,601 recommendations during the public hearing period (Parris 2003, 52). Among the 43 recommendations it received relating to women's rights were suggestions for changes to constitutional provisions, including a mandatory provision to ensure and encourage women's participation in decision making at all levels. The recommendations stated that the provision should provide for (a) a one-third ratio of inclusion of women or (b) a 60:40 ratio of women to men (Report of Subcommittee n.d., 12). While the CRC report submitted to the National Assembly recognized these concerns, the section of the report that outlined specific recommendations only made general, discretionary statements concerning women's participation in public decision making and the inclusion of gender representativeness in the electoral system (Constitution Reform Commission 1999, 194). The recommendations stated:

> 3) There should be an enshrined general principle which encourages women's participation in public decision-making so that national decisions which affect women significantly can be informed by them. Parliament should be required to take measures designed to increase women's participation in the various processes and fora of decision-making in society, including the National Assembly itself, to a level that takes into account the proportion that women form of the

society.... 4) The Constitutional provisions on the electoral systems, including electoral lists, should be informed by the inclusion of requirements for gender, as well as geographical, representativeness. (Ibid.)

The final OC report included similar non-specific language (Oversight Committee 2000, 14–15). The recommendations of one-third or 60:40 were not ultimately put forward in any specific terms. 'The Commission was not persuaded that specific percentages should be set as targets but felt that as more women are exposed to public life, the greater would be their participation' (*Stabroek News* 1999, 16). This raises the question as to how women could be exposed to public life. Moreover, the decision to use such non-committal language contradicts the rationale for including recommendations concerning gender equality in the first place, which is to address systemic and widespread gender inequality and discrimination (Parris 2003, 182).

THE LEGISLATIVE FRAMEWORK FOR THE GENDER QUOTA SYSTEM

Section 29 of the Constitution enshrines the notion of equality of the sexes in all spheres of political, economic and social life.[25] Yet, specific measures should still be taken to ensure that de facto equality matches the de jure provisions for political participation. In this regard, the revised Constitution contains enabling provisions in section 160(3) that address three main issues related to women's representation: extraction of women's names from the political party lists; the minimum proportion of female candidates to be placed on a party's list; and the maximum proportion of geographical constituencies in which a party may contest if its lists have no female candidates. Parliament passed the Elections Laws (Amendment) Act, No 15 of 2000 to provide specificity to these provisions. It is through this piece of legislation that Guyana adopted a candidate quota in 2000 to ensure that a minimum of one-third female candidates would be included on each electoral list.

Sections 11B(5) and (6) of the Elections Laws (Amendment) Act mandate a minimum of one-third women on all lists. Subsection (7) mandates that a party cannot contest in more than 20% of geographical constituencies if its lists have no female candidates. Subsection (8) deals with the contentious issue of extraction. It is crafted in such a way that the extraction of one-third women off the list is discretionary and not mandatory, despite the use of mandatory language. Therefore, the latter provides no guarantee that women will hold one-third of the seats in parliament.[26] To compound the matter, the representative of the list has full and unfettered power of extraction pursuant to subsection (9) with no reference to gender.

Guyana, has the only legal quota system in the English-speaking Caribbean. It ensures that all parties nominate one-third female candidates – which
is sanctioned by sections 14(1) and 17(1) that address 'defective' lists (lists
not meeting the one-third requirement must be revised to be accepted, as
evidenced in the 2015 election). Parliament, however, has no obligation to
translate that one-third into representation. This presents a technical loophole,
which can be, and is, exploited.[27]

LESSONS LEARNT

Now that the quota has been legislated, the issue of extraction of women off the
list remains. While one-third women are named on each list, there is no guarantee that one-third women will be appointed to serve, as it is not mandated by
law. Currently, the system operates on the basis of asking individual parties to
honour the intent of the law – not just placing one-third women on the electoral
list, but extracting at least one-third as well. This system has worked relatively
well, with only the PPP/C not properly adhering to the honour system. It is nevertheless a significant improvement over the pre-constitutional reform elections
held in the new democratic era and aligns with the explanation about countries
with similar political histories catapulting women into leadership positions.

   This list must be prioritized to ensure that women will be chosen from the
list using some manner of rank-order system, such as the 'zipper system' or
a ceiling to ensure that a minimum number of women candidates features on
the upper part of the list. While the quota law includes a recommendation for
the implementation of a rank-order system, no party acquiesced, as they were
not 'comfortable' with such a move (Backer 2012). In fact, four elections have
passed since the adoption of the quota law with no extraction requirement, and
no one has moved to address the issue, which suggests a lack of political will to
change the status quo of a limited number of women holding seats in parliament.

CONCLUSION: WHAT NEXT?

Quota adoption and implementation is not a case of one size fits all; what has
worked in one country may not work in another. The success of any quota
system is highly contextual. While one-third may represent a concessionary
tactic and downward compromise from ensuring 60:40 percentages or parity,
it is only one step forward. The struggle falls to the women's movement and
usually requires the support of at least one (or more) well-placed elite man to
promote the cause (Krook 2007, 370; Krook 2009, 22), as well as the political will to move the issue forward.

In the case of Guyana, there were two main drivers behind the adoption of the quota system: the country's attendance and participation at the Beijing Conference, where quota systems were presented as a politico-legal mechanism to increase women's participation and representation; and the opportunity presented by the subsequent comprehensive constitutional reform process to introduce a quota. These events were further complemented by the very strong rights-oriented mindset of the key actors in Guyana, emerging out of a period of non-democratic governance to ensure that various rights issues were included during the constitutional reform process. Interestingly, quota adoption did not spread throughout the Anglophone Caribbean; however, *only* Guyana has experienced such a brutal political history, as have its Latin American neighbours, and therefore only Guyana truly appreciates the concept of rights. The rest of the Anglophone Caribbean does not share this history, which could account for the failure to push for gender quotas, despite the gender injustice that persists in politics in the region.

This is not to say that regional conversations around gender equality were non-existent. CARICOM's introduction of a package of Model Legislation in six critical areas related to women's issues between 1989 and 1991 (CARICOM 1997) provided the foundation for similar legislation subsequently enacted in Guyana, a clear attempt to address gender injustice and proof of regional conversations on gender equality.

While only a partial success, the disillusionment on the issue of extraction must be replaced with celebration: the feminization of the party lists is a critical step towards the feminization of parliament. Moving the extraction issue forward entails reinvigorating the movement or passing the baton on to younger women. The latter will need strong role models to emulate and to help them understand the importance of the battle they must wage. Women have to be prepared to fight and stand up for themselves; the veterans must also be prepared to nurture the young ones (Chanderpal 2012). The Guyana's Women's Leadership Institute, as well as other organizations, plays a critical role in this process, which is supplemented by the activities of the Women's Affairs Bureau. Indeed, it is important to remember that

> the extent of women's formal participation in politics is an important marker for women's empowerment. The premise is that increasing women's participation in political processes, as both voters and candidates, will change the nature and functioning of public institutions, which will ultimately influence future development decisions and create a more equitable, gender-responsive and humane society. (Kudva 2003, 446)

That goal remains key to the future of gender equality in the Anglophone Caribbean.

Chapter 4

APPENDIX A

Constitution of the Cooperative Republic of Guyana, Cap. 1:01.

29. (1) Women and men have equal rights and the same legal status in all spheres of political, economic and social life. All forms of discrimination against women on the basis of their sex are illegal.

160. (3) Subject to the provisions of this Constitution, Parliament may make provision –

(a)(ii) for the manner in which lists of candidates shall be prepared, including the provision in a list of the names of a sufficient number of candidates to enable any vacancies to be filled under subparagraph (vii), and which manner shall allow voters to be sure which individuals they are electing to the National Assembly.

(v) for the extraction from the lists and declaration of names of the candidates who have been elected, and for such provision for extraction to take into account the proportion that women form of the electorate;

(b) (iii) for the minimum number or proportion of female candidates on a party's list for geographical constituencies taken individually or together;

(iv) for the maximum percentage or the number of geographical constituencies a party can contest in which its lists contain no female candidate.

Representation of the People Act, Cap. 1:03, amended by Elections Laws (Amendment) Act, No 15 of 2000

11. B (5) The total number of females on each party's national top-up list shall be at least one-third of the total number of persons on that list.

(6) The total number of females on any party's lists for geographical constituencies, taken together, shall be at least one-third of the total number of persons on those lists taken together for the geographical constituencies in which that party is contesting.

(7) There shall be no more than twenty percent of the number of geographical constituencies in which a party is contesting for which the party's geographical constituency list contains no female.

(8) In the extraction from the list declaration of names of the candidates who have been elected account shall be taken –

(i) of the total number of females on each party's national top-up lists and the lists for geographical constituencies, taken together, being at least one-third of the number of persons on those lists as mentioned in paragraphs (5), (6) and (7); and

(ii) of the proportion that women formed of the electorate.

(9) The order in which a party states the names of candidates on its lists shall be as the party deems fits.

14. (1) If it appears to the Commission that a list of candidates is defective, that is to say, that its list or its submission does not comply in all respects with the requirements of section 11(1), (2), (3), (4), (5) or section 11B ... the Chief Election Officer shall so inform the representative and the deputy representative of the list, specifying the defects.

15. The representative and the deputy representative of a list of candidates, or either of them, may ... submit to the Chief Election Officer corrections of any defects in the list.

17. (1) no list of candidates shall be valid unless it has been approved by the Commission.

NOTES

1. For a fuller account, see Natalie Persadie, (2014), 'Getting to One-Third? Creating Legislative Access for Women to Political Space in Guyana', in *Politics, Power and Gender Justice in the Anglophone Caribbean: Women's Understandings of Politics, Experiences of Political Contestation and the Possibilities for Gender Trans-formation IDRC Research Report 106430-001*, by Principal Investigator Gabrielle Jamela Hosein and Lead Researcher, Jane Parpart (Ottawa: International Development Research Centre 2014).

2. It was very plainly stated by various interviewees that this was not the case for Guyana.

3. Very little information, if any, is available via written record; most of the data on Guyana for this chapter was obtained through personal interviews. Overall, the gender quota system did not seem to garner public debate.

4. While the gender quota laws in Guyana are inherently biased against women, honour systems seem to somewhat mitigate against this challenge.

5. This refers to countries with electoral systems based on proportional representation.

6. 'The ... "double quota" ... not only requires a certain percentage of *women* on the electoral list, but also prevents ... women candidates ... just [being] placed on the bottom of the list with little chance to be elected.... "Placement mandates" or rules about the rank order of candidates, especially at the top of the list, are other terms for the same phenomena'.

7. The last column was added by the author.

8. There is an 'overhang' provision that allows for one extra member in the event of a special situation arising that affects proportionality. For further details on Guyana's electoral system, see full paper by Persadie (2014).

9. By way of example, Amerindians account for 10% of the population; they had 6 members, of a total of 65, in Parliament.

10. The alphabetical listing was introduced in 1968. It should be noted that s 160(3)(a)(ii) of the revised constitution now contains an enabling provision to mandate prioritized lists, which would give voters an idea of who they are voting for.

This, however, depends largely on the political will of those in power to legislate. As expected, this matter came to the fore in the 2011 elections. See Appendix A for the full text of this provision.

11. This was made emphatically clear by all respondents.

12. The PPP/C Party equated inclusive governance with democracy. This is specifically attributed to then president Bharath Jagdeo.

13. Established through the Constitution Reform Commission Act, Cap. 1:14.

14. It has been stated that, despite the extensive reform process, many of the disliked provisions remain.

15. Signed in Guyana on January 17, 1998.

16. Signed in Castries on July 2, 1998. It is interesting to note that neither the Herdmanston Accord nor the St. Lucia Agreement mentioned women with respect to how either should unfold. The accord, however, particularly referred to other groups, such as 'the youth and other social partners', but did not specifically mention women as one such partner.

17. Similar exercises conducted in South Africa, Uganda and Papua New Guinea took three years to complete.

18. The NGO was actually permitted to make a special oral presentation to the CRC.

19. Emphasis added.

20. Regarding why the cross-party caucus never materialized, it is safe to surmise that the answer lies in parliamentary politics and the need to maintain solidarity on positions adopted by parties.

21. Two of the persons who voted against it were legal practitioners. One was the head of the bar association, and the other represented the Hindu community. The third opponent was a member of the opposition, who was influenced by the opposing member of the Hindu community. He argued that religious and cultural concerns were involved, and tried to argue that women had everything they needed in law (See Persaud's statement above).

22. It should be noted that recommendations were counted individually, even where the contributor repeated it. Moreover, not all public submissions received a sufficient level of attention (Parris 2003, 74).

23. See below for text of recommendations (3) and (4).

24. This is very similar to the Argentinian account.

25. See Appendix A for the full text of the provisions cited in this section.

26. See Appendix A.

27. Mexico has adopted a creative way of avoiding adherence to the quota system by holding 'primaries' where parties that chose their candidates via 'direct election' are exempt from the gender quota. See Baldez (2006), 106–7 and Krook (2008), 116.

REFERENCES

Araújo, Clara and Ana Isabel García. 2006. 'Latin America: The Experience and the Impact of Quotas in Latin America', in *Women, Quotas and Politics*, edited by Drude Dahlerup, 83–111. London: Routledge.

Baldez, Lisa. 2006. 'The Pros and Cons of Gender Quota Laws: What Happens When You Kick Men Out and Let Women In?' *Politics and Gender* 2(1): 102–9.

Ballington, Julie and Azza Karam. 2005. *Women in Parliament: Beyond Numbers.* Stockholm: International Institute for Democracy and Electoral Assistance.

Caribbean Community Mission to Guyana. 1998. 'Herdmanston Accord'. Signed in Guyana January 17, 1998. Accessed March 2, 2012. http://www.caricom.org/jsp/ secretariat/legal_instruments/herdmanston_accord.pdf.

CARICOM Secretariat. 1997. 'Charter for Civil Society for the Caribbean Community'. Accessed September 2012. http://www.caricom.org/jsp/secretariat/ legal_instruments/chartercivilsociety.jsp#Political Rights.

_____. 1997. 'Model Legislation on Issues affecting Women', Retrieved 11 December 2012. http://www.caricom.org/jsp/secretariat/legal_instruments/model_ legislation_women_issues.jsp.

Constitution of the Cooperative Republic of Guyana, Cap. 1:01 (Laws of Guyana).

Constitution Reform Commission Act, Cap. 1:14 (Laws of Guyana).

Constitution Reform Commission. 1999. 'Report of the Constitution Reform Commission to the National Assembly of Guyana'. Georgetown, Guyana.

Dahlerup, Drude. 2009. 'About Quotas'. *Quota Project: Global Database of Quotas for Women*. International IDEA and Stockholm University. Accessed February 20, 2012. http://www.quotaproject.org/aboutQuotas.cfm.

_____. 2008. 'Gender Quotas – Controversial But Trendy'. *International Feminist Journal of Politics* 10(3): 322–28.

_____. 2005. 'Increasing Women's Political Representation: New Trends in Gender Quotas', in *Women in Parliament: Beyond Numbers*, edited by Julie Ballington and Azza Karam, 141–53.

_____. ed. 2006. *Women, Quotas and Politics*. London: Routledge.

Diamond, Larry. 2004. 'What is Democracy?' Lecture at Hilla University for Humanistic Studies. January 21. Accessed December 11, 2012. http://www.stanford.edu/~ldiamond/iraq/WhaIsDemocracy012004.htm.

Elections Laws (Amendment) Act, No 15 of 2000 (Laws of Guyana).

George, Roxane. 2000. 'Observations on Gender Rights – Recommendation 9.5.3 (4)'. [Letter to the chairman of the Oversight Committee]. [Copy with author.]

Guyana Elections Commission, n.d. 'About Guyana'. Accessed March 2, 2012. http:// www.gecom.org.gy/guyana.html.

International Institute for Democracy and Electoral Assistance (IDEA). 2003. *The Implementation of Quotas: Latin American Experiences*. Stockholm: International Institute for Democracy and Electoral Assistance.

_____. 2015. 'Global Database of Quotas for Women'. http://www.quotaproject.org/ uid/search.cfm#.

_____. 'Unified Database. 2015, May 18. Country View: Trinidad and Tobago'. Accessed January 12, 2016. http://www.idea.int/uid/countryview.cfm?id=224.

Inter-Parliamentary Union. 2015, November 1. 'Women in National Parliaments'. Accessed January 12, 2016. http://www.ipu.org/wmn-e/world.htm.

James, R.W. 2006. *The Constitution of Guyana – A Study of its Dysfunctional Application*. Turkeyen, Guyana: Institute of Development Studies and Faculty of Social Sciences, University of Guyana.

Kittilson, Miki Caul. 2005. 'In Support of Gender Quotas: Setting New Standards, Bringing Visible Gains'. *Politics & Gender* 1(4): 638–45.

Krook, Mona Lena. 2007. 'Candidate Gender Quotas: A Framework for Analysis'. *European Journal of Political Research* 46(3): 367–94.

_____. 2009. 'Gender Quotas in Parliament: A Global View'. *Al-Raida* 126–27: 8–17.

_____. 2006. 'Gender Quotas, Norms, and Politics'. *Politics & Gender* 2(1): 110–18.

_____. 2009. *Quotas for Women in Politics: Gender and Candidate Selection Reform Worldwide.* Oxford: Oxford University Press.

Kudva, Neema. 2003. 'Engineering Elections: The Experiences of Women in *Panchayati Raj* in Karnataka, India'. *International Journal of Politics, Culture and Society* 16(3): 445–63.

Larserud, Stina and Rita Taphorn. 2007. *Designing for Equality: Best-fit, Medium-fit and Non-favourable Combinations of Electoral Systems and Gender Quotas.* Stockholm: International Institute for Democracy and Electoral Assistance.

Mansbridge, Jane. 2005. 'Quota Problems: Combating the Dangers of Essentialism'. *Politics & Gender* 1(4): 622–38.

Matland, Richard. 2005. 'Enhancing Women's Political Participation: Legislative Recruitment and Electoral Systems', in *Women in Parliament: Beyond Numbers,* edited by Julie Ballington and Azza Karam, 93–111.

McClain, Linda and Joanna Grossman, ed. 2009. *Gender Equality: Dimensions of Women's Equal Citizenship.* Cambridge: Cambridge University Press.

Merrill, Tim. 1992. *Guyana: A Country Study.* Washington: GPO for the Library of Congress. Accessed October 21, 2012. http://countrystudies.us/guyana/.

Nanivadekar, Medha. 2006. 'Are Quotas a Good Idea? The Indian Experience with Reserved Seats for Women'. *Politics & Gender* 2(1): 119–28.

Oversight Committee. 2000. 'Final Report of the Oversight Committee on Constitutional Reform'. Resolution No. 33 of 1999, August 2000. Georgetown, Guyana.

Pande, Rohini, and Deanna Ford. 2011, April. 'Gender Quotas and Female Leadership: A Review'. Background Paper for the World Development Report on Gender. Available from http://scholar.harvard.edu/files/rpande/files/gender_quotas_-_april_2011.pdf.

Parris, Haslyn. 2003. *An Annotated Handbook of the 17, July 1999 Report of the Constitution Reform Commission, Guyana.* British Columbia: Trafford Publishing.

Persadie, Natalie. 2012. *A Critical Analysis of the Efficacy of Law as a Tool to Achieve Gender Equality.* Lanham, MD: University Press of America.

Persaud, Vidyanand. 1999. 'Addendum to the Report of the Sub-Committee No. 5'. June 15, 1999.

Peters, Anne, and Stefan Suter. 2009. 'Representation, Discrimination, and Democracy: A Legal Assessment of Gender Quotas in Politics', in *Gender Equality: Dimensions of Women's Equal Citizenship* edited by Linda McClain and Joanna Grossman, 174–200. Cambridge: Cambridge University Press.

Phillips, Anne. 1998. *Feminism and Politics.* Oxford: Oxford University Press.

Presentation by Ms Hazel Halley-Burnett, Administrator, Women's Affairs Bureau to the Oversight Committee of the Constitution Reform Commissions. n.d. [Copy with author.]

Red Thread. 1997. 'Advance Notes on Oral Presentation by Red Thread Women's Development Programme'. Submitted to the Special Select Committee, July 30, 1997.

Report of Subcommittee on the Topic of Women's Rights. n.d. [Copy with author.]

Representation of the People Act, Cap. 1:03 (Laws of Guyana).

Roopnaraine, Rupert. 2000. 'National Assembly Debates'. Proceedings and Debates of the National Assembly of the First Session (1998–2000) of the Seventh Parliament of Guyana under the Constitution of the Co-operative Republic of Guyana. 58th Sitting, 23 November 2000.

Sacchet, Teresa. 2008. 'Beyond Numbers: The Impact of Gender Quotas in Latin America'. *International Feminist Journal of Politics* 10(3): 369–86.

Sineau, Mariette. 2005. 'The French Experience: Institutionalizing Parity', in *Women in Parliament: Beyond Numbers,* edited by Julie Ballington and Azza Karam, 122–31.

Spencer, Stephen. 2007. *A Dream Deferred: Guyanese Identity and the Shadow of Colonialism.* London: Hansib Publications.

Stabroek News. 1999. 'Bolstered Women's Input in Decision Making Recommended'. *Stabroek News*, July 19, 16.

_____. 2012. 'Voters Should Know Likely MPs Before Polls – Commonwealth Observers'. *Sunday Stabroek*, 26, no. 8. January 8, 3.

'Submission by the Delegation of Women's Organisations to the Oversight Committee on Constitutional Reform'. July 1, 2000. [Copy with author.]

Tremblay, Manon. 2006. 'Substantive Representation of Women and PR: Some Reflections on the Role of Surrogate Representation and Critical Mass', *Politics & Gender* 2(4): 502–11.

_____. 2008. *Women and Legislative Representation: Electoral Systems, Political Parties, and Sex Quotas.* Hampshire, UK: Palgrave Macmillan.

UN Women. 1995. The Fourth World Conference on Women. 2012. 'Beijing Platform for Action'. September 1995. Accessed 27, February 2012. http://www.un.org/womenwatch/daw/beijing/pdf/BDPfA%20E.pdf.

Yin, Robert. 2009. *Case Study Research: Design and Methods.* Newbury Park, CA: Sage Publications.

INTERVIEWS

Andaiye. 2012. (Co-founder of Red Thread). Interview with author, January 5 and 8 2012, Georgetown, Guyana.

Backer, Deborah. 2012. (Attorney at law, acting chief whip of the PNC, deputy speaker of the House). Interview with author January 6, 2012, Georgetown, Guyana.

Chanderpal, Indranie. 2012. (Member of parliament; chair of the Woman and Gender Equality Commission). Interview with author January 10, 2012, Georgetown, Guyana.

Dow, Jocelyn. 2012. (Co-founder Red Thread; former President WEDO). Interview with author, January 9, 2012, Georgetown, Guyana.

George, Roxanne. 2012. (Puisne Judge). Interview with author January 7 and 21 September 2012, Georgetown, Guyana.

Halley Burnett, Hazel. 2012. (Former Head of the Women's Affairs Bureau). Interview with author January 9, 2012, Georgetown, Guyana.

Lagan, Hymawattie. 2012. (Administrator, Women's Affairs Bureau; Member, Women and Gender Equality Commission). Interview with author September 24, 2012, Georgetown, Guyana.

McCormack, Mike. 2012. (Co-president of the Guyana Human Rights Association). Interview with author, January 10, 2012, Georgetown, Guyana.

Pollard, Magda. 2012. (Member, Women and Gender Equality Commission). Interview with author January 9, 2012, Georgetown, Guyana.

Radzik, Vanda, 2012. (Co-founder, Red Thread; Member, Woman and Gender Equality Commission). Interview with author January 10, 2012, Georgetown, Guyana.

Roopnaraine, Rupert. 2012. (Leader of the WPA; vice chairman of the APNU). Interview with author on January 10, 2012 in Georgetown, Guyana.

Teixeira, Gail. 2012. (Presidential Advisor on Governance). Interview with author on September 21, 2012 in Georgetown, Guyana.

Trotman-Joseph, Anande. 2012. (Former Commissioner). Interview with author on January 28, 2012.

Chapter 5

Inclusion without Influence

Women, Power and the Quota System in Guyana

Iman Khan

INTRODUCTION

A series of constitutional reforms in 1998 and 1999, resulting predominantly from the mobilization of Guyana's feminist movement and influences from the 1995 Beijing Conference on Women, gave birth to the establishment of an electoral quota system, making Guyana, in 2001, the first country in the Anglophone Caribbean to legally and systematically promote higher representation of women within the political sphere. The quota law stipulates that the total number of women on each party's national top-up list be at least one third of the total number. However, there is no mandatory law about the number of women to be selected to the National Assembly, and political parties are allowed to allocate their parliamentary seats as they wish. Nonetheless, while the constitution does not require 33% women to actually be extracted from the list and placed in the National Assembly, it is strongly recommended that women are represented 'in and around' the one-third benchmark of the total number of parliamentarians. In fact, the Carter Centre on its most recent visit to Guyana expressed concern that while the Representation of the People Act mandates that one-third of the lists of candidates on the national top-up list be female, there is no requirement imposed on the parties to do the same for the National Assembly (*Kaieteur News* 2015).

Guyana's quota system has indeed acted as a catalyst for the representation and inclusion of women in politics at the level of parliament as well as in other levels of government. But while the quota system has been successful in increasing the visibility and descriptive representation of women, and certainly creating space for some women, it has not managed to bridge the distance between women and patriarchal norms, patriarchal state processes and patriarchal state structures. Nor has it translated into substantive increased representation of women in leadership roles outside parliament or increased representation of women's issues within parliament. Women's participation and involvement in the decision-making process and in top-level management has traditionally been terribly skewed, and Guyana's quota system has had little effect on translating the gains related to participation and empowerment of women in politics to other spaces, such as arenas where women have traditionally been marginalized like on state boards and in the country's corporate world.

One of the central reasons that Guyana's quota system has had little impact on translating the gains related to participation and involvement of women in politics to other arenas such as state boards, commissions, and in corporate Guyana is because the quota system is grounded in a feminist framework that seeks justice by focusing on women's empowerment. The problem however is that it seeks justice in a national context where the struggle for women's empowerment has already been delegitimized by the destructive effects of male privilege and a pervasive myth of male marginalization that positions men as the disempowered victims of women. Thus quotas, which seek to ensure a mere 33% of women in parliament end up reinforcing an overall view that women do not need access to more power because they already have enough, further making invisible and reducing the significance of male power, even when the numbers tell a different story of women's continuing inequality. This is an example of how the discourse on women's rights and empowerment becomes systemically undermined ideologically and materially. It has therefore been counterproductive in Guyana's case as it places women as the main category of analysis in a masculine and traditionally male-dominated and controlled space. As a result, patriarchy prevails and feminism is policed (Khan 2014). While Guyana can boast legislation such as the Peoples Representation Act, with a 'high' number of women in parliament, along with women's bureaus and commissions, the country continues to misunderstand gender, gender inequality and the role, responsibility and capacity of these structures to deal with inequality and the advancing of gender justice. Eudine Barriteau argues that 'we can achieve conditions of "equality" and still have an "unjust" outcome' (Barriteau 2007) and to an extent this is what appears to be the problem in Guyana, with an attractive-looking electoral quota that does not translate to equality in reality. While the country may have policies, systems and politicians who talk a good talk, Guyana still suffers from an unbalanced distribution of power, access and material gains between men and women, with men predominating. For some, equality appears to be alive and well, but as Barriteau points out, there is often a tendency to focus on the concept of gender equality rather than delving into an analysis of gender justice. Oftentimes, like in Guyana, the vision for equality and the targets that are set out, differ from implementation, norms and practices on the ground. While women may have the right to participate in various activities and positions of power, the gender prejudices and injustices that inhibit women from effectively and equally participating retain their power and cannot be ignored.

The following chapter therefore analyses the resistances, limitations and challenges of Guyana's quota system for effectively creating greater numbers of women representatives, advancing gender justice and placing gender issues as a central obligation of the government of Guyana. It also examines the ability of women in parliament to challenge patriarchy, as well as engage and negotiate with state hierarchy for policies, legislations, projects and reforms aimed at advancing the status and conditions of not only women within the parliament, but women across Guyana, as well as transforming dominant masculinities, building gender consciousness and feminist allies among men, and promoting equitable gender relations through gender mainstreaming. This chapter is situated within major global debates on: (1) quota provisions as empowerment; as creating critical mass and further allowing women to transform or, in any way, shape politics; and (2) quota provisions as merely artificially symbolic, and with limited significance as a feminist strategy for advancing gender justice. The research used to build this chapter predominantly examines women in parliament under the former PPP administration and their effectiveness in advancing gender justice, negotiating masculinist space, and redistributing rights and power to women, but the chapter will also pay some attention to women in parliament under the new administration. It also focuses on the number of women elected to parliament and other state boards, the treatment of women, and the role of women and gender relations under the current administration.

The months leading up to the 2015 May 11th general election remain particularly curious with regard to politics and women in Guyana as the two major political parties, the PPP and A Partnership for National Unity/ Alliance for Change (APNU/AFC) coalition battled it out for the female vote, with female political leaders and new female recruits playing a more prominent role on the campaign trail, speaking more frequently at rallies and appearing more visible on banners and flyers. Prior to the May 11 election, the PPP government, in power for twenty-three years, came under intense criticism by women's rights groups and advocates for its failure to properly address women's priorities. In fact, the former administration had been criticized for ill-treating and sidelining women in and out of politics, and in the lead-up to the 2015 elections, the PPP was heavily scrutinized for its poor record of treatment of women, with examples ranging from personal issues, such as accusations of ministers and presidents mistreating and abusing their wives, to the shuffling of female ministers, to taxation on items that poor mothers need for daily subsistence (*Kaieteur News* 2015). To make matters worse, the former administration was accused of normalizing misogynistic attitudes towards women after former minister of health and current MP Bheri Ramsaran, under the PPP, threatened a female activist, saying that he would have 'his' women slap and strip her (*Kaieteur News* 2015).

The refusal of PPP women to condemn Ramsaran and the prolonged silence from the former administration on the matter worked to the advantage of the coalition. Large APNU+AFC campaign billboards were erected around the country proclaiming 'Guyana, It Is Time for Our Women', suggesting that a vote for the coalition would translate into the advancement of women in Guyana, both in and out of parliament. The APNU/AFC government campaigned relentlessly against the abuse of women at the hands of the PPP administration, advocating for change for Guyana's girls and women. On the campaign trail, Sita Nagamootoo, the wife of Guyana's honourable prime minister Moses Nagamootoo, proclaimed, 'My sisters, I urge you to vote for the APNU+AFC.... We know what to expect if (President Donald) Ramotar is reelected, "more slapping and stripping of our women". It is a shame that Ramotar is sorry for Bheri, his Minister: the abuser, and not the woman victim, Sherlina Nageer' (Enough is Enough, *Kaieteur News* May 6, 2015). The incumbent's campaign was predominantly focused on gender justice and the advancement of Guyana's women with promises of a better life for them.

However, interestingly, although the APNU/AFC promised to put gender equality and equal opportunity with regard to the nation building process as a key agenda, the coalition still initially failed to meet the legal requirement for the number of women on its list of candidates for the May 11 general and regional elections. When the coalition submitted its list of candidates only 14 out of the 75-person list were women on Nomination Day, April 7. Due to rules and regulations of Guyana's quota system as outlined in the Representation of the People Act, the coalition was forced to resubmit its list with an additional 11 women, to meet the requirement. This hinted that while female politicians and new recruits were playing a more visible role and were being featured more heavily on the campaign trail than in previous years, the election battle was still being run by men, and for men, and women were still being sidelined.

What is even more curious is that since the ascendency of the coalition, scholars, activists, individuals on social media, and various organizations have expressed outrage and disappointment at the lack of women on boards and in ministerial positions. With reference to the representation of women on government boards, Dr. Alissa Trotz (2015) wrote, 'There has been a robust and outraged response by individuals and various organizations (SASOD, Citizens Against Rape, Help & Shelter, GRPA, Red Thread, Child-Link Inc., GAWL) to the abysmal lack of gender representation on the newly formed boards. The Guyana Human Rights Association issued a statement in which they drew public attention to the fact that "although the Government has only announced the full membership of 20 out of the 32 boards thus far, only 18% are females which represents 22 persons out of a possible 125; and of that figure, one woman serves on three boards and another on two. Both women are employees of the Ministry of Finance'" (*Stabroek News* 2015). Melissa Ifill, a women's rights activist and lecturer at the University of Guyana (2015), recently wrote,

> Anyone who believes that women are in the ascendancy and taking over in Guyana needs only look at recent political and administrative appointments to clearly understand the true status of women in Guyana and how they are viewed by the present political directorate. While we agree that quotas may not be the best way to ensure fair gender representation, in the present climate they may be the best way to proceed in the face of the almost total invisibility of women in formal leadership positions. Based on gazetted appointments to state boards, the GHRA has analysed that only 3 (9.4%) of chairpersons to 32 of these boards are women. Even worse are the revelations that of the 125 state-board members, only 22 or 18% are women and two of these women are to sit on more than one board. To add insult to injury, four commissions have not a single woman representative, while eight boards have only one, seven two and one three.

In her article, Ifill questions whether it is a deliberate intention on the part of the APNU+AFC government to minimize the role and visibility of women in Guyana, but asserts that it 'is shocking, embarrassing, illegal and reflects badly on the new administration's commitment to gender equality and equity in governance'. (*Kaieteur News* 2015). In the aftermath of an election season that held the APNU/AFC coalition as an agent of national change, healing and reconciliation for Guyana, with particular attention to the treatment of women, the promotion and development of national gender policies, and the advancement of women's rights and needs, women and women's rights activists across the country are demanding that the government of Guyana stop its discrimination against women and move immediately to equitable participation of women on all state boards and commissions and in all other areas. Activists are further suggesting that an independent body with adequate gender and diversity representation be set up to assist with the recruitment of suitably qualified women for Guyana's boards and commissions. The frustration, outrage and criticism from civil society of the former government's misogynistic treatment of women in the lead-up to elections and the current government's alarming discrimination of women has been high, but unfortunately not high enough to challenge masculinist structures and ideologies and create more space for women in areas where they continue to be underrepresented and marginalized. From a policy outlook, women in Guyana are afforded equal rights and privileges but if we evaluate qualitative conditions we find that the very policies and amendments that have been made to help address the issue of women's exclusion do not even begin to function adequately. Prior to the 2011 election, when women's rights activist Stella Ramroop asked presidential candidates about their views on gender equality in leadership and how they would translate into policies once elected, President Granger responded by saying,

> The answer is very simple, equality means equality. Five equals five. Ten equals ten. It's like I say – not trying to be vulgar – equality is like virginity, it is absolute. You cannot be partial. You cannot be partially equal. In 1976, our party [the PNC], which was then the government, introduced a white paper on the equality of women – and that was 35 years ago. We were the party to describe, or to lay down the guidelines, for women's equality and I believe it must be fulfilled to the letter. I believe women must be given equal status, not semi-equal status. Equal/equal. Fifty/fifty. Right now, our party [the PNC] is the only party in the National Assembly that has exact equality in the members. I am committed to equality for women. And as I said, equality means equality. (*Stabroek News* 2011)

Yet, in the lead-up to the 2015 election, the list was rejected because it did not meet the one-third representation of women as stipulated in the quota law. Even after the appointment to parliament there have been concerns about the under-representation of women. This is no doubt one of the biggest problems in Guyana – the striking gap between the vision and plan for gender equality and the reality of gender justice.

GUYANA'S QUOTA SYSTEM

Guyana's quota system was realized as a result of extensive networking and solidarity among Guyanese women. While a formal cross-party parliamentary caucus never materialized in Guyana, women within various political parties built informal cross-party networks to advance their collective interests and needs (Khan 2014). The early 1990s represented an interesting policy shift for Guyana as the conversation around the rights and needs of women put pressure on the state to concede to plans, policies and legislations focused at women and gender equality. Women of Guyana saw big strides during the fight for the Medical Termination of Pregnancy Bill, which was passed in 1995, and the Domestic Violence Act, which was passed in 1996 (Desouza, Interview 2013). A few years after these victories, the informal mobilizing of political partywomen, combined with strong support from Red

Thread, an energetic grassroots women's organization, and other civil society actors, played a significant role in the development and implementation of the Representation of the Peoples Act in November 2000.

Subsection 11B (8) has been criticized for containing a major loophole with serious implications for the actual extraction and translation of women off the list and into parliament. While it is mandatory for women to comprise one-third of the party list, the language does not make it mandatory for one-third of the total number of parliamentary seats to be allocated to women (Guyana Model of Quota System for Female Representation in Parliament 2012; Persadie 2012; Interview, Karen Desouza 2013). Despite this loophole, however, women's rights advocates have been active and persistent in ensuring that the gender electoral quota system achieves its true purpose and intent. Sections 14 and 17 of the Representation of the Peoples Act legally ensure that of all candidates, all parties nominate at least 33% female candidates to their party lists. These subsections which address defective lists' and 'approval of lists' state that lists which do not comply with all respects and requirements of section 11(1), (2), (3), (4), (5) or section 11B must be corrected or will otherwise be refused. And while there is nothing that mandatorily stipulates that one-third is translated into representation in parliament, women's rights advocates, and the Women and Gender Equality Commission have worked feverishly during elections, scrutinizing political party manifestos, to ensure that they have policies and programs aimed at empowering and advancing the needs and interests of Guyanese women. The commission has also been vocal in advocating that various political parties go beyond the minimum requirement and increase the number of 'competent' women on their party lists (Interview, Indra Chandarpal 2013; also see: *Stabroek News* Women and Gender Equality Commission, June 8, 2011). Many female parliamentarians whom I have interviewed, including the chair of the Women and Gender Equality Commission Indra Chandarpal, the late PNC parliamentarian Faith Harding and the late parliamentarian Deborah Backer, have argued that selection should also be based on competency not gender and on quality not quantity, suggesting that we need to make sure that the women selected are qualified for the post. I will revisit the implications of this kind of thinking below.

Guyana's quota system has been lauded by the regional and international community as an outstanding contribution and development for Guyanese women (Global Status of Women in Parliament Report 2010; Inter-Parliamentary Union, Women in National Parliaments 2011; T Shirley, UN Rep lauds outstanding achievements of Guyanese women, Guyana Chronicle 2011). Regionally, Guyana's quota system was upheld as a model for female representation in parliament at the Regional Commonwealth Women's Parliamentary Meeting 2012, in Jamaica. Internationally, Guyana earned a high ranking at the 2010 Global Status of Women in Parliament where it placed 25th out of 186 countries around the world with regard to its high percentage of women in parliament. The quota system has resulted in a steady increase in the number of women occupying seats in Guyana's parliament as well as women in the cabinet and other top-level parliamentary positions. The new electoral amendments regarding the electoral quota system for women came into effect for the 2006 general elections and saw a jump in the percentage of women in parliament to 30.7 from 20% in the 2001 general elections. After the November 2011 general elections, women held 32% of Guyana's parliamentary seats (Commonwealth Secretariat, Report of Commonwealth Observer Group: Guyana National and Regional Elections Report 2011; Regional Commonwealth Women's Parliamentary Meeting 2012).

Now we know that the quota exists and that it has increased numerical representation of women in parliament in Guyana. However, to determine what this really means for women and gender relations, this chapter will apply gender justice as a major conceptual framework to address questions such as: Does the quota system have any impact on increasing women's empowerment, protection from employment and wage discrimination, or overall socio-economic conditions? Have women in parliament managed to redistribute empowerment, access and power? Does the increase in the presence of women in Guyana's parliament translate into a more gender-conscious or feminist parliament? Does the increase in the presence of women translate into a more gender-conscious or feminist society? Has it in any way shaped or transformed the people, space, processes and structures within various parties and within the state? This introduction has highlighted crucial questions concerning women's political representation in Guyana. In the following sections I will outline my methodology for investigating these questions. Next, I will also look at the theoretical perspectives for analysing the lived reality of Guyana's quota system, paying close attention to its limitations and challenges. Finally, I will conclude by arguing that the quota system on its own has not managed to necessarily increase women's voice, capacity, or bring about equal opportunity and gender justice.

METHODOLOGY

The research is based on various elements of qualitative analysis and is grounded particularly in the case-study approach which allows researchers to study complex phenomena within their contexts using a variety of data sources to ensure that the phenomena are not being explored through one lens (Baxter and Jack 2008). The research also relies on content analysis, which is useful for gathering, sorting, and analysing secondary literature such as journal articles, textbooks, websites and other relevant reports such as television interviews relating to the research-question themes. This approach allows the researcher to collect and organize information in a standardized format that enables the researcher to make inferences about the meaning of written and/ or recorded material (Krippendorff 2004). ATLAS.ti is the coding software used in the research design to systematically analyse the collected data. Primary data was collected from semi-structured interviews with 32 people, predominantly women, from political parties, government, women's rights groups, retired politicians and observers within Guyana. The researcher also combed through parliamentary Hansards, constitutional and legislative documents, as well as newspaper articles. The coding process involved converting the collected content into a suitable format for analysis. 'Coding entails the interpreting of the phenomenon under study and stating the observations in the formal terms of an analysis' (Krippendorff 2004, 126). Through the use of ATLAS.ti, the content was recorded in an analysable form. The researcher also developed a written codebook as a guide to code the variables under investigation and ensure consistency and stability. Final coding focused on three broad categories: opportunities, resistances to women's effective participation and limitations. Subcategories included: (1) impact and effectiveness on social processes and policy and legislative outcomes for women outside of parliament, (2) impact and effectiveness on equality with regards to political processes among men and women in parliament, (3) possibilities for critical mass and caucusing, (4) possibilities for gender transformation, (5) limitations of gender transformation, (6) empowerment, and (7) disempowerment.

THEORETICAL FRAMEWORK – GENDER JUSTICE

Gender justice is the central theoretical framework guiding this research. Gender justice is defined by Eudine Barriteau as 'a societal condition in which there are no asymmetries of access to, or allocation of, status, power, and material resources in a society, or in the control over and capacity to benefit from these resources' (Barriteau 2003, 327). Barriteau further states that in a gender system characterized by gender justice there will be no hierarchies of gender identities or of the meanings society gives to masculinity and femininity. She further argues, 'Conversely, in an unjust gender system, there is unequal distribution of and access to material resources and power'. The concept of gender justice therefore becomes more useful because it includes working towards gender equality and equity but 'it moves beyond the measures of achievement to evaluating qualitative conditions' (Barriteau 2003). If we use the concept of gender justice to analyse the results and impact of Guyana's gender quota, we can move beyond the simple existence of the law with a conceptual framework and methodologies that addresses certain questions such as the follows: Why do women continue to experience discrimination in politics and in business? Why do women continue to be mistreated and abused in a patriarchal society? Why is there such resistance to women's political leadership? What are the factors that continue to fuel the perpetuation of male domination and female subordination in postcolonial Guyana? Although realities will differ, if we analyse the ideological dimensions of gender justice we can see more clearly what it means to be a man or woman in society. Barriteau argues that the concept of gender justice allows us to look at both the material and ideological dimensions that will further permit us to determine whether we are challenging and removing inequalities. In the context of Guyana, when we isolate dimensions and examine gender ideologies and the unbalanced distribution of resources of power, status and material means, we see that the state continues to function through an unjust gender system. We could agree with Barriteau that it is possible to achieve conditions of 'equality' and still have an unjust outcome (Barriteau 2003). Barriteau explains that this occurs because the measures and indicators that are used to indicate that gender equality exists are outlined in societal rights and are reflected in statements such as 'women are already afforded with all sorts of rights'. To be more specific, she argues that when women and men are given the 'right' to participate in a given societal activity, that participation is reflected or captured in a measurement. However, that measurement does not indicate intricate dynamics that include gender issues and prejudices which affect the participation and fair involvement of women (Barriteau 2003).

This chapter reflects the combination of qualitative findings and the application of gender justice as a framework to examine: (1) the electoral gender quota system in Guyana, and (2) parliamentarians' roles in advancing gender justice and redressing gender inequality, as well as in reproducing and reinforcing gender inequality. It relies on qualitative methods to determine to what extent the quota has managed to confront and negotiate hierarchies.

QUALITATIVE CONDITIONS

The quota system has to some extent challenged barriers to exclusion, discrimination and numerical under-representation of women interested in pursuing political paths in Guyana. There is also no doubt that it has led to a steady increase in the number of women participating in parliamentary politics in Guyana (Khan 2014). One female parliamentarian stated that without the quota system, women's representation in parliament would be much less substantial. As mentioned, another clear example is that in the most recent general election, the APNU+AFC coalition (now current administration), failed to meet the legal requirement which stipulates that female candidates represent at least one third of the list. When the original list was submitted only eighteen of the seventy-five candidates were female. However, the Guyana Elections Commission forced the party to resubmit the list with at least two additional females in order for the party to be in compliance. Therefore, it is clear that without the presence of the quota law, even fewer women would have been selected as list representatives. This is one example of how the presence of the quota places pressure on those in control of the recruitment process to recruit more women. However, the media coverage around the failure to comply also implied that politicians are oftentimes elected because of their gender and not because of their qualifications, with more qualified candidates being pushed aside.

The core idea behind the quota system is to recruit women into political positions and to ensure that women are not marginalized or discriminated against in political life. Guyana's quota law aims to increase women's representation because of traditional under-representation of women in politics. But how effective has the quota been in transforming female representation?

Most female parliamentarians and women's rights activists I interviewed felt that the opportunities for advancing gender justice, brought about by the implementation of the quota system, were generally limiting and disappointing (Khan 2014). While all of the respondents agreed that the quota system has indeed provided better access and higher numbers of women in parliament, most did not feel that higher representation strengthened political processes as they relate to women in any way. Many respondents believed that some of the reasons for this are that many female parliamentarians themselves lacked sufficient gender consciousness and the intent required to push forward and represent a women's agenda. In fact, one interviewee mentioned that during her time in parliament (post quota implementation), she the presence of women made little difference with regards to issues that dealt with women and children (C. Haynes, Interview 2013). Most of the respondents interviewed, with a few exceptions, agreed that support, solidarity and gender consciousness among women in parliament were generally lacking. Respondents also felt that party discipline and loyalty often prevented women from advancing a women's agenda. This is extremely important because political parties are essentially the gatekeepers when it comes to the election and nomination of women to political positions. These gatekeepers regard party loyalty as a major component of partisanship and advancement. Therefore, women occupying seats in parliament tend to demonstrate most of their loyalty and focus on advancing the agendas of their respective parties, rather than pursuing gender justice. Party discipline is also viewed as a major constraint that may prevent women from pursuing policy reforms relating to women or from caucusing or building relationships with other political women outside of their respective parties. This has raised suspicions about women who come in under the quota system as being selected based on their blind loyalty to their often male party seniors, above their personal views, agendas or independence.

Volda Lawrence also agreed that 'the sad thing about parliament is that you are there on a party card ... so even if you are inclined to push a particular issue, it is always the party that comes first' (V. Lawrence, Interview). Karen Desouza of Red Thread also highlighted that party loyalty is key to admission into the inner circles of party workings, arguing that women in parliament are not serving anyone but their respective parties. Desouza further stated that 'the politics are very bound up in party domination and women in parliament are essentially subject to the party so ... they as far as I am aware they certainly do not appear to hold any agenda which is at the service of women or grassroots women. I am trying to think, I mean the last the very last organizing of women in parliament I think was 1996; this is to get the Domestic Violence Act passed. I don't know that women have, in parliament have organized together ... um ... since then' (Desouza, Interview).

She argued that while the quota system has ensured higher numbers of women in parliament, meaningful representation of women as a group has not been achieved. Disappointed with the outcome, Desouza said that grassroots women have been let down by their female parliamentarians, who simply do not act in the interest of women and are unwilling to engage with civil society groups. Red Thread has tried tirelessly to engage the government on issues relating to grassroots women. In 2012, Red Thread activists staged a protest in front of Guyana's Parliament Building calling for more accountability from female parliamentarians. According to *Kaieteur News*, a statement issued by Red Thread said that 'women parliamentarians have forgotten their background.... The problem is that the women in Parliament account to their parties, not to all the women outside. And what do the parties offer us? So far, empty promises made during the election campaign to get our votes. We have had enough. We demand better' (*Kaieteur News* 2012).

An example of how party loyalty often forces women to ignore private injustices, particularly those relating to women, was recently seen by the nation when Bheri Ramsaran, former minister of health under the PPP administration (current PPP parliamentarian), publicly threatened to slap and strip a popular women's rights activist Sherlina Nageer. The issue occurred when Nageer approached the former minister to ask why he was wasting time on a protest line when he has more important issues to attend to such a maternal health. In response, the former minister shouted, 'Shut your mouth and get out my face'. The exchange continued between Nageer and Ramsaran, and the activist pointed out that 'we have children and women dying under your watch and what are you doing here wasting time. You have a responsibility to the People of Guyana and their health.... This is a waste of taxpayers' dollars, my money is paying your salary'. The former minister responded by shouting, 'Get the hell out my face! Please ... I am having a private discussion. Please, please, I am having a private discussion ... I am a candidate of the PPP ... F-off ... little piece of shit'. Ramsaran further boasted that he would very well 'slap her ass, you know, just for the fun.... No, no, no, just for the fun ... I can have some of my women strip her here' (*Stabroek News* 2015).

Even more shocking, media outlets contacted members of the party including Indra Chandarpal, former chairperson of the Women and Gender Equality Commission, who was incapable of responding. Red Thread almost immediately released a statement claiming that

> while the PPP has been purporting to be a party that upholds the rights of women and is sincerely interested in women empowerment, evidence suggests otherwise. We have this caring Government that on the one hand has spent money launching the Task Force on Sexual Offences at least four times between 2010 and 2014. Nothing else has happened. This Government that cares so much about women has paid a consultant to draft a National Plan of Action that is supposed to be done by the Task Force.... We even have a new Prime Ministerial candidate, Elisabeth Harper, who we are told will ensure that all of these things happen. And we are told that this new Prime Ministerial candidate will not debate the coalition's Prime Ministerial candidate Moses Nagamootoo because he was disrespectful to her and the ruling party will not under any circumstances tolerate any disrespect of women. Let us for the moment set aside Attorney-General Anil Nandlall's attempt, in the most disrespectful terms, to solicit the sexual services of a young female reporter for his uncle. Let us for the moment say okay that was terrible, but the PPP was not campaigning then, they were not electioneering, and had not recommitted to addressing these issues of sexual and domestic violence and other questions relating to women and children. But now that they have done all of this, what are we to make of the exchange between the dishonourable Minister of Health Bheri Ramsaran, when asked by a concerned citizen who has repeatedly attempted to address the issue of maternal and infant mortality, how he had the time to appear in a protest in Berbice in the face of the continuing inadequate care offered by the medical institutions that are his responsibility?

For days, not one woman from the party condemned Ramsaran's actions. In fact, Ramsaran and the former president released statements apologizing but at the same time excusing Ramsaran's actions, with the president saying that he feels sorry for him (Ramsaran): 'It is very clear that he was provoked' (*Stabroek News* 2015). For two weeks individuals and civil society groups led protests demanding Ramsaran be fired. Eventually, the president reluc-tantly responded by temporarily relieving Ramsaran from his ministerial duties. Nonetheless, Ramsaran returned to parliament as a PPP parliamentar-ian despite cries by women around the country to have him disqualified. In July, Red Thread activist Karen Desouza returned to the picket line saying 'Ramsaran and [Anil] Nandlall have demonstrated that they are abusers of power and I don't understand how they are putting abusers of women into parliament' (Paul 2015).

The fact that these men continue to occupy seats in parliament despite their misogynistic and sexist actions, demonstrate a tendency within patriar-chal Guyana to dismiss women's cries for justice. This also reinforces how the state continues to act as the key purveyor of patriarchy and disrespect to women. The result is that masculinity and power appear to be premised on anti-feminism, manipulation, aggression and the vulnerability of women in and out of parliament. It shows that despite feminist strategies, efforts are limited and curtailed by patriarchal norms. This reproduces masculinist hege-mony in the broader Guyanese society and creates obstacles for the advance-ment of gender justice in daily life. It further highlights how misogyny is reinforced and perpetuated at the institutional level and how political leaders continually reinforce patriarchal authority at the risk of patriarchal mirroring in a society which already suffers from rampant domestic violence, gender inequality and gender stereotypes.

Former parliamentarian Vanessa Kissoon spoke to me about the lack of respect and regard she received at the institutional level from police and government officials, and how the disrespect was mirrored by citizens. She spoke of one incident when she was harassed and abused by the police dur-ing a protest in Linden during her term as an MP. 'When I think of how I was treated during the Linden protest, and how I was harassed by the police, I really feel disrespected. In other countries parliamentarians are treated with respect. Now I don't want people to go around praising me, but if you're not driving a fancy vehicle, sometimes you even have a problem getting into the parliament compound itself' (Kissoon, Interview).

Respondents also believed that deeply entrenched masculinism and patriarchy in party structures, hierarchy and leadership, combined with partywomen's own lack of gender consciousness as well as their party loy-alty make it difficult for women to negotiate for gender justice. Patriarchy and male-centeredness remain extremely prevalent and visible in Guyana's parliament and the effects are often felt through the over-representation of men in parliament, through the control and policing of feminism, through the perpetuation of patriarchal norms and dominance and through unequal respect and power in parliament. According to female parliamentarians, the quota has not done much to challenge patriarchal norms. Volda Lawrence, who has been serving in parliament since 1997, even prior to the enactment of the quota system, said, 'I don't think it has brought much change, I think it depends on how a woman asserts herself in parliament. It is still very much a male-dominated field, but change will depend on the strength of the women because you can go in there to make up the number and just be another number' (V. Lawrence, Interview). Lawrence mentioned that there are many female parliamentarians who have been in parliament for years, but have never brought a motion, never been vocal, never introduced a bill. According to Lawrence, 'You can be there, you can be present but unless you are assertive you can be used like a pack of cards, they shuffle you around, they tell you what to talk about and all of that…. It's a sad thing when you have women who are placed there to represent us, but they just allow themselves to be trampled on' (V. Lawrence, Interview).

Indeed, the shuffling of female parliamentarians down the party hierarchy has raised eyebrows among women's rights activists and observers in Guyana. When former APNU parliamentarian Vanessa Kissoon was unexpectedly demoted to the last row without notice, PPP parliamentarian and former minister of education Priya Manickchand stood up in parliament during a debate on the Recording of Court Proceedings Bill and said, 'For persons who are myopically saying that I should concern myself with this side of the House, I want to suggest that the cause of women in Guyana, the cause of women across the world, still has to be a united front … every little demotion like that seen here really dents our progress' (Chabrol 2014). Shortly after Ms. Kissoon's demotion, letters appeared in popular newspapers denouncing the move. In a letter titled 'Vanessa Kissoon Was Treated with Disrespect by the Decision-Makers in APNU', the writer wrote, 'What I have is a profound difficulty with the way young Member of Parliament Vanessa Kissoon was treated at the last sitting of parliament. Ms. Vanessa Kissoon is a sitting member of the National Executive Committee of the Guyana Youth and Student Movement (GYSM), youth arm of the People's National Congress and a Member of Parliament of seven years of distinguished service. Thus by virtue or her office she should have been granted at the minimum, the common courtesy of a notification of the change in her seating arrangements' (Currie 2014). Despite the public shock at her sudden demotion and despite the solidarity and empathy expressed by fellow female parliamentarians, Kissoon only stated: 'Where I sit does not matter. I have been elected to serve the Guyanese people … and in particular the people of Region Ten … and that's what matters' (Chabrol 2014). The circumstances surrounding her sudden demotion remain unclear, but it is clear that party leaders in the APNU demonstrated an intentional act of disrespect against Kissoon by failing to even inform her of her demotion prior to her arrival at the House. Regardless of whether or not her demotion was based on party discipline or on administrative purposes, it highlights the powerlessness that Kissoon was forced to confront. During a *Guyana Times* interview, Ms. Kissoon did admit that she was 'not sure about the protocols that would govern reassignments of seats in the APNU coalition and that she was not aware either whether it was a decision that should have been communicated formally' (*Guyana Times* 2014). In the most recent election, Ms. Kissoon was completely omitted from the list and newspaper headlines suggested that the failure to include Ms. Kissoon reinforced former APNU parliamentarian Africo Selman's whistle-blowing that 'there is no place for women in the APNU unless you accept that your place is to be barefoot and pregnant'. In a shocking 2015 interview with the *Guyana Times* newspaper, Selman accused her former party, the APNU/PNC, of seriously abusing women in the party, adding that women do not grow unless they are like Amna Ali (current minister of social cohesion and government) 'who revel in their lapdog, doormat role'. She further stated, 'The proof of the subservience is in the roles women were allocated in the PNC. President or Presidential Candidate? None. PM?? None. Debra Backa was dropped like a hot potato after filling the "security portfolio" the moment Felix came aboard. The PNC has never "walked the walk" when it comes to females. Barefoot and pregnant is the best a PNC woman can aspire to' (*Guyana Times* 2015).

Similarly, eyebrows were raised when Jennifer Webster, a former minister within the PPP administration with a background in finance and accounting, was shuffled from her junior ministerial position within the Ministry of Finance to the Ministry of Human Service and Social Security (*Stabroek News* 2011). Perhaps Volda Lawrence's words can be taken literally: 'You can be used like a pack of cards, they shuffle you around' (Lawrence, Interview).

CONCLUSION

Despite the presence of the quota system, and a vision for gender equality and women's empowerment, women in Guyana and their issues are still not treated with priority or represented sufficiently. Female parliamentarians are forced to act more in the interest of their respective parties than in the interest of each other. They remain loyal to party ideologies. No direct correlation exists between Guyana's quota system and the presence of women at the top of state hierarchy or as opposition leader and the quota system also has not changed the climate of gender relations and hierarchies in Guyanese politics. Guyana's first female president, the late Janet Jagan, served the country after the passing of her husband from 1997 to 1999 (before the realization of the quota). It is important to note that since the implementation of the quota,

Guyana has never had a female president or vice president. In fact, since then, only one female has entered into the presidential candidacy race. She was the late Faith Harding, who entered the PNC race in 2011. Unfortunately, Faith complained that she was cheated of her true number of votes, that she received no support both from men and women within the party, and that she was sidelined because she was a woman (*Stabroek News* 2012).

While there are a higher number of female parliamentarians in Guyana as compared to other Caribbean states, gender imbalance in Guyana's parliament as well as on state boards, despite the recommended one-third, and despite promises to make the gender ratio 50:50, remain pervasive. Recently, the Guyana Human Rights Commission flayed the government for its failure to ensure that there is fair gender representation. Part of the statement released by the commission stated, 'All Government functionaries responsible should feel ashamed over today's announcement that only three (9.4%) of the new Chairs of the 32 State Boards in the Finance Sector are females' (*Guyana Times* 2015). When journalist Stella Ramsroop asked political candidates in 2011 (all of which were male) their views on gender equality in leadership, former president Ramotar responded by saying:

> Yes, I would like to promote women in various institutions. Right now, it is also getting easier because if you look at our institutions, particularly the University of Guyana, you will see a lot more women graduating than men. Clearly I would like to see people in positions where they can make a contribution and they are not discriminated against, on the basis of sex. I would like to see – as far as that is possible – that it should be in our society as a whole, particularly in public institutions. (*Stabroek News* 2011)

However, although more women than men are graduating from the University of Guyana and despite the tremendous pool of qualified and competent women, they are terribly outnumbered by men in leadership positions in both state and corporate sectors. Additionally, despite Ramotar's vision for women, the PPP party has not managed to ensure that one-third of their thirty-two seats are occupied by women. Women continue to be significantly under-represented in top-level private sector positions in the county, and work mostly in very low-paying jobs. The commendable statistics of women in parliament in the country has therefore not translated outside of the legislature. Female politicians have not been able to transform and create more spaces for women in other areas in which they are marginalized. An implication of this is the perception that women have only been able to advance in politics due to special treatment, and not based on competency or any real or tangible ideological shifts about women's political roles. This research, therefore has not found any direct correlations between numerical representation and Guyanese female parliamentarians' substantive representation. In fact, this research reveals that the emphasis of the quota system deals with numbers rather than challenging or transforming masculinist structures and ideologies of gender power relations.

At its core, the quota system emerges as a feminist strategy aimed at creating space for women and promoting feminist transformations within the political sphere. The tragedy in Guyana is that men still control most of the resources required to implement women's claims for justice and there continues to be an increased war between masculinities and femininities, as well as between party expectations and expectations from women's rights activists (Khan 2014). Despite attempts at creating space for women, Guyana's gendered institutions and social structures contribute to the inclusion and privileging of men and the disproportionate exclusion of women from positions of power, wealth and authority. Masculinism is deeply entrenched in party structures, hierarchy and leadership, and women have not effectively been able to negotiate it for various reasons, including lack of personal gender consciousness, fear of jeopardizing their positions, and lack of a strong women's movement. Activist Bonita Harris said, 'We don't have a women's rights movement. A women's rights movement involves women rising up as a body and moving. We don't have that. We have some organizations and persons speaking out on cross-cutting issues, but we have not been able to organize women as women' (Harris, Interview). Harris believes that the only way to move forward and change the culture is to instil gender consciousness in children, while activist Karen Desouza argues that change will only come with organizing and mobilizing people who are passionate and focused on challenging patriarchal and masculinist structures. Female parliamentarians cannot, on their own, change Guyana's discourses of gender and power. Real change can only occur if Guyana's representatives in parliament engage and are constantly being engaged by members of autonomous, but united, women's organizations in civil society. Female parliamentarians and male parliamentarians, along with civil society groups, need to collectively and powerfully negotiate with political parties and hierarchies in order to push for gender justice. More importantly, policymakers need to consider equality not just as something descriptive, but as a system that facilitates equal opportunity. Guyana's attempts towards achieving gender equality have failed to substantially materialize, and a stark gap between formal commitments to the equal rights and responsibilities of men and women and against discrimination and subordination based on sex and gendered realities continues to exist in Guyanese women's daily lives. For gender equality to translate into gender justice in Guyana, the country will need to ensure that the rights and endowments outlined in the constitution, in policies and in national documents are translated into the accumulation of opportunities for women across Guyana – and that these opportunities are further translated into norms that foster gender equality and justice. Additionally, parliamentarians and policymakers will need to go beyond the unrealistic notions of equality and look towards fair opportunity. This could perhaps be a first step towards alleviating gender injustice in Guyana.

REFERENCES

Barriteau, Eudine. 2003. 'Issues and Challenges of Caribbean Feminism'. Agenda. Empowering Women for Gender Equity. 17, Issue 58: 37–44. Special issue of African Feminisms III.

Barriteau, Eudine. 2003. 'Theorizing Ruptures in Gender Systems and the Project of Modernity in the Twentieth Century Caribbean', in *The Culture of Gender and Sexuality in the Caribbean*, ed. Linden Lewis. Gainsville, University Press of Florida.

Barriteau, Eudine. 2007. '30 years towards Equality - How many More? The Mandate of the Bureau of Gender Affairs in Promoting Gender Justice in the Barbadian State'. *Caribbean Review of Gender Studies*, Issue 1, p. 15.

Baxter, Pamela and Susan Jack. 2008. 'Qualitative Case Study Methodology: Study Design and Implementation for Novice Researchers'. *The Qualitative Report* 13(4): 544–59

Chabrol, Scott. 2014. 'APNU Demotes Vanessa Kissoon Down the Back Bench'. *Demerara Waves*. February 10, 2014. http://www.caribnewsdesk.com/news/7423-apnu-demotes-vanessakissoon-down-the-back-bench.

Constitution of the Republic of Guyana (Laws of Guyana). 1980–1986. Accessed from: http://gina.gov.gy/wp/?page_id=134.

Constitution Reform Commission Act (Laws of Guyana). 1996. Accessed from: http://gina.gov.gy/wp/?page_id=134.

Ifill, Melissa. 2015. 'The Invisibility of Women' *Kaieteur News* August 1st 2015 Accessed from http://www.kaieteurnewsonline.com/2015/08/01/the-invisibility-of-women/.

Kaieteur News. 2015. 'Gender Must be Central in the Formulation of Policies'. August 2015. Accessed from: http://www.kaieteurnewsonline.com/2015/08/29/gender-must-be-central-in-the-formulation-of-policies-sita-nagamootoo/.

Kaieteur News. 2015. 'Minister Ramsaran Verbally Abuses, Threatens to Slap Activist'. April 22, 2015 Accessed from http://www.kaieteurnewsonline.com/2015/04/22/minister-ramsaran-verbally-abuses-threatens-to-slap-female-activist/.

Khan, Iman. 2014. 'Advancing Gender Justice? The Opportunities, Resistances, and Limitations of Guyana's Quota System'. IDRC Research Report 106430-001. Ottawa, ON Canada: International Development Research Centre.

Krippendorff, Klaus. 2004. *Content Analysis: An Introduction to its Methodology.* (2nd ed.). Thousand Oaks, CA: Sage.

Paul, Jomo. 'Activists Protest against Jagdeo, Nandlall and Ramsaran being Parliamentarians'. Inewsguyana.com. http://www.inewsguyana.com/activists-protest-against-jagdeo-nandlall-ramsaran-being-parliamentarians/. (Accessed November 25, 2016).

Persadie, Natalie. 2012. *A Critical Analysis of the Efficacy of Law as a Tool to Achieve Gender Equality*. Lanham, MA: University Press of America.

Ramroop, Stella. 2011. 'Are Guyana's Political Parties Scared of Gender Equality?' Stabroek News. June 10, 2011. Accessed from: http://www.kaieteurnewsonline.com/2011/06/10/are-guyana%E2%80%99s-politicalparties-afraid-of-gender-equality/.

Ramroop, Stella 2011. 'What Does your Candidate Think about Gender Equality in Leadership?' July 2, 2011 Accessed from http://www.stabroeknews.com/2011/features/07/02/135989/.

Stabroek News. 2012. 'Red Thread Urges Women MPs to be More Accountable to Press for Livable Income'. March 16, 2012. Accessed from: http://www.stabroeknews.com/2012/news/stories/03/16/red-thread-urges-womenmps-to-press-for-livable-income/2011.

Stabroek News. 2015. 'After Contentious Apology, Ramsaran calls Activist Miscreant'. April 24, 2015 Accessed from http://www.stabroeknews.com/2015/news/stories/04/24/after-contentious-apology-ramsaran-calls-activist-miscreant/.

Stabroek News. 2012. 'PNCR sidelined me, says Harding'. February 19, 2012 Accessed from http://www.stabroeknews.com/2012/news/stories/02/19/pncr-sidelined-me-says-harding/.

Trotz, Alissa. 2015. 'Where are the Women on Boards?' In the Diaspora Column, *Stabroek News* August 10, 2015 Accessed from http://www.stabroeknews.com/2015/features/in-the-diaspora/08/10/where-are-the-women-for-all-these-boards-heh/.

LIST OF INTERVIEWS

Backer, Deborah (Attorney at law; acting chief whip of the PNC; deputy speaker of the House). Interview, June 6, 2013.

Desouza, Karen (Co-founder of Red Thread). Interview, March 19, 2013.

Harding, Faith (PNC 2011 presidential candidate; Minister of Public Service, 1989–1992). Interview, March 21, 2013.

Haynes, Chantalle (Former AFC parliamentarian). Interview, May 28, 2013.

Hughes, Cathy (AFC parliamentarian). Interview, May 20, 2013.

Kissoon, Vanessa (AFC parliamentarian). Interview, May 22, 2013.

Lawrence, Volda (APNU parliamentarian). Interview June 18, 2013.

Chapter 6

Narratives, the State and National Gender Policies in the Anglophone Caribbean

Dominica and Trinidad and Tobago

Deborah McFee

After the 1995 Beijing World Conference on Women, a number of territories in the Anglophone Caribbean committed themselves to the development of National Gender Policies (NGPs). These NGPs are multisectoral plans located in the technical language of public policy and the state, developed to provide a plan for the pursuit of gender equity and equality throughout the respective territories. The experience regionally has not been uniform. As different states initiate these national plans, the results and processes have been as varied and as complex as the Caribbean region itself. The diversity of outcomes, the various narratives attached to the NGPs' development, and the sources of resistance within, and external to, the state, provide invaluable insights into how regional populations interface with, understand, create and articulate meanings around public policy as it relates to women and Gender and Development (GAD).

This chapter seeks to rethink the relationship between policy implementation, policy design and the politics of policymaking (Mosse 2004, Parpart, Exploring the Transformative Potential of Gender Mainstreaming Limits and Possibilities 2014). Diverting from traditional measuring of the success of policy science, policymaking, bureaucracy and public management measured through the efficiency of implementation (Lodge and Hood 2003, Hood and Lodge 2004, Howlett 2010), this investigation prioritizes broader societal contexts and actors as determinants of outcomes in the politics of policymaking. The intent is to facilitate the application of a feminist critical perspective that questions the dominant intellectual traditions explaining policymaking (Ackelsberg 1992). This is achieved by analysing the process of policymaking and the content of the policy narratives, through which positions within and external to the policy process become apparent. Policy narratives represent spaces where ideologies are owned and rearticulated internal to the state, and are then co-opted by external actors to become public discourses. These public discourses provide a context-specific understanding of the ways in which women, and GAD gain or lose traction through the presence or absence of a broader population-based buy-in to the policy process.

REGIONAL OVERVIEW AND CRITICAL JUNCTURES

In the Anglophone Caribbean, the Cayman Islands, Trinidad and Tobago, Dominica, British Virgin Islands, Jamaica, the Bahamas and Belize have all publicly committed to drafting at least one NGP. Belize is the only territory which has embarked upon two policy cycles. In some territories, NGPs have proven particularly vulnerable to policy termination at any given stage of development or implementation, while in other territories, they have moved easily from drafting to implementation. The critical junctures – from the consultant's report being accepted by the gender bureau through to the approval of the document for implementation – are pivotal sites when the possibility of termination or the likelihood of passage becomes more apparent. It is at these junctures that the politics of policymaking becomes public. Shifts in the policy audiences and the introduction of new voices and interests in the policy process reveal how policy narratives are being interpreted and negotiated. (See Table 6.1 for a regional overview pf critical junctures in the NGP experience.)

These critical junctures emerge as important landmarks in the policy process only in retrospect. At the onset of the process, the public consultations, the identification of priority areas for policy intervention and the production of a draft policy are pivotal junctures. It is only in reviewing the entire regional NGP experience from 2000 to 2013 that the importance of these junctures has become increasingly apparent. They are the points when the policy narratives are more likely to take unforeseen shifts and turns, thereby creating significant moments and a common regional frame for exploring and understanding the narratives of the NGP experience in the region.

Although there are minimal bureaucratic differences within the region, the common critical junctures experienced have been:

- Consultant document accepted. (This is the product of the consultative and research phase of policy development. Actors mainly include the gender and development personnel of the government machinery, the gender and development expert contracted to guide the development of the document, NGO and community-based organization (CBO) partners and some stakeholders in other government ministries)
- Cabinet approval
- Plan of Action approved for implementation. (For implementation to become a reality, the Plan of Action should be deliberated upon and funds

Table 6.1 Overview of the Status of Caribbean National Gender Policies up to July 2012

Country	Consultant Document Accepted	Cabinet Approval Secured	Implementation Approved and on the Way	Implementation Responsibility	Year Initiated	Year Implemented	Comment
Cayman Islands	✓	✓	✓		2000	2004	Implementation aborted post Hurricane Ivan Process restarted in 2011
Trinidad & Tobago					2002		
Dominica	✓	✓	✓	BWA	2004	2006	
Belize, 2002	✓	✓	✓	BWA & NWC		2002	Implementation completed, new policy cycle identified.
Belize, 2013				NWC & BWA		2013	Sent to Cabinet in 2009 approved 2013.
Jamaica	✓	✓	✓	BWA & GAC	2004	2010	
BVI				BWA & TCG	2010	2012	
Bahamas	✓	✓					Reported to the 52nd session of the CEDAW the 1057th and 1058th Meeting on July 20th 2012 the intention of the Government of Bahamas to lay before the Cabinet the National Gender Policy in 3 months.

BWA, Women's Affairs Bureau; NWC, National Women's Commission; GAC, Gender Advisory Committee; TCG, Technical Committee on Gender.

assigned to the policy process. The actors at this stage are the representatives of the gender ministry and the political hierarchy.)
- Implementation accepted and responsibility allocated. (These critical
  junctures are important markers for framing diverse regional experiences
  around NGPs. It should be noted that the likeness in markers are not the
  only commonalities shared by these documents and processes. Similarities[1]
  are also influenced by factors such as common governmental institutional
  arrangements, like the 2003 CARICOM commitment to use Trinidad and
  Tobago's draft document.)

Dominica and Trinidad and Tobago

Although regional territories sign on to drafting NGPs, the NGP is a public
policy conundrum. For regional states, the NGP represents a post-Beijing
modernization strategy, building on a Women in Development (WID)–
derived legacy of legal equality and economic autonomy attributed to
Caribbean Women (Barriteau 1998). The NGP provides a multisectoral road
map for gender-conscious national development within a gender-neutral state
apparatus. Lastly, in its commitment to advance gender equity and equality
through the state, the NGP epitomizes the conflict between the ideological
and material dimensions of gender systems as experienced in the English-
speaking Caribbean (Ibid). This conflict exemplifies the slippage, bending
and contorting of gender to meet the needs of contending and converging
interests of state and non-state actors in the public policy process (Sardenburg
2007, Dugdale 1998). The chapter maps this conflict within the politics of
policymaking in two Anglophone Caribbean territories, the Republic of
Trinidad and Tobago (Trinidad and Tobago) and the Commonwealth of
Dominica (Dominica).

The messiness of the NGP process is a theoretical opportunity for
Caribbean feminist political thought and policy construction. It provides an
intimate terrain to evaluate the political costs and advancements consistent
with shifting from WID to GAD. We are afforded a lens into regional social
relations of gender, through which men and women gain differentiated access
to power, status and resources (Barriteau 2003). The complexity of these
relations also facilitates understanding of how this differentiated gendered
access is reflected in both state and public discourses around public policy on
women and GAD.

Translating the NGP into a nationally recognized, multisectoral development tool provides a productive space that reinforces the distinct practices,
but common origins and goals, of regional feminist scholarship, feminist

activism and feminist practitioners. Concurrently, it creates opportunities to engage in the art of the possible across disciplinary and political silos (Tinker 1990, Sardenburg 2007). Lastly, this complex conceptual messiness destabilizes the perceived homogenous construct of the public policy mainstream in the Anglophone Caribbean.

THE ART OF THE POSSIBLE: HARMONY OUT OF DIFFERENT RHYTHMS?

Dominica embarked on the NGP process immediately after Trinidad and Tobago. Both share the same international and regional commitments in the area of women and GAD, and also share similar governmental structures and the same NGP lead consultant. Despite these similarities, Dominica started its policy development in 2004 and received cabinet approval in 2006. Trinidad and Tobago embarked on its policy in 2002 and by the end of 2015, had yet to secure cabinet approval. These different outcomes emerged from the convergence of many multidimensional factors. Building on the regional impact of the stalled Trinidad and Tobago NGP experience, Dominica produced a model of policymaking which saw a managed, measured filtering of the policy narrative within the state and to the populace. The drafters of Trinidad and Tobago's NGP process never achieved control over the policy narrative. This begs the question: to what extent is controlling the policy narrative a plausible goal where public participation is seen as fundamental to good policymaking? In this inquiry, the question is not what makes good or implementable policy. Rather it is what is involved in the politics of negotiating competing voices and how does the convergence and splintering of conceptualizations of gender affect policymaking?

The policy narrative is an amalgamation of diverse group discourses (Boswell, Geddes and Schollen 2011). Competing narratives are involved in a power struggle that shapes the policy process. The most powerful narrative becomes the basis of public perception of the given public policy initiative. Both NGPs are products of the power struggle among narratives. Trinidad and Tobago's NGP provides a view into competing group narratives around gender, interfacing with societal perceptions of policymaking around women and gender, which can distort understandings of gender and fashion powerful narratives and discourses resistant to gender equality within society. The DNGP produced a model of narrative building which secured interests in a manner that pre-empted possible powerful pockets of resistances within policymaking. This model produced a packaging of GAD that was digestible to the national palette. In the case of Trinidad and Tobago, the NGP remains crippled.

DOMINICA: PRODUCTIVE CONVERGENCE
OR GENDER WITHOUT RUPTURE?

From its inception the core driver of the DNGP process was the Technical Support Committee. Although the consultant was responsible for compiling the situational analysis, completing the gender analysis of the data sets informing the policy document and drafting the final Plan of Action, the Technical Support Committee functioned as a research and oversight arm of the policy process. Every government ministry was represented and non-state actors in the areas of religion, media and culture were members of the committee. In the main, these persons formed a core group to guide research, priority areas and public engagement with the policy process. The committee created a strong sense of national ownership from the design phase of the NGP.

Beyond the committee's role as the local policy hub, the membership was instrumental in convincing Dominicans that their ideological constructs of gender were being *appropriately* negotiated within the NGP process. Three NGOs, which formed part of the Steering Committee, were pivotal to this national buy-in and ultimately central to producing a palatable national policy product.

They include:

- The Dominica National Council of Women (DNCW);
- The Dominica Association of Catholic Men (DACAMEN) and
- The Catholic Archdiocese of Roseau.

The presence of these three organizations on this committee created a collective buy-in to the NGP process from diverse pockets within Dominican society. All were NGOs, and two were faith-based. Although their constituencies varied, they all played a key part in creating a nationally owned narrative about Dominica's NGP.

The DNCW was a long-time partner of the then Bureau of Women's Affairs (BWA). One of its primary NGP-related roles, dating back to 1999, was encouraging preliminary community sensitization initiatives. This pre-2005[2] work was community-based and had a two-fold output. First, the work of the DNCW focused on empowering women about their legal and economic rights, their health and the need to end violence against women and children. Secondly, the DNCW advanced the policy process by partnering to develop a concept paper on the status of women in Dominica. This paper fed into the larger NGP process. It became a tool for data collection, informing the situational analysis of NGP, and it was also a means of sensitizing the population to the goals of the impending NGP. In undertaking its substantive work and developing the concept paper, the DNCW targeted churches to build awareness of women's rights and the NGP. One such encounter was described as follows:

> Generally, I would go to the churches, make arrangements to have permission just to share at the end of the service with the congregation. There were pockets of resistance to the policy at first. A few voices here and there, but they were pockets, they were not influential. In Dominica, 38% of the households are single female-headed households. *When men talking about 'who is the head?'* That does not make any sense in Dominica. (President and Vice President DNCW, Interview, July 2011)

In exploring the work of the DNCW further, the policy implications of the fallout from the shift from WID to GAD can be unpacked. This example reveals the need to interrogate the difficulties that may arise from the methodological shift from WID to GAD (Barriteau 1998). Interestingly, in 2004, almost ten years after the Beijing World Conference on Women, Dominica was one of the few regional territories maintaining a BWA.[3] In spite of this, the bureau was working with its partners to build awareness of and commitment to an NGP. When questioned about its awareness-building strategies for the NGP, the DNCW spoke about its initiative to capitalize on the public perception of the shift from women to gender translating into the inclusion of men. Recalling a popular cry from the population at that time, the DNCW pointed out that

> we needed the men because people always asking if you're talking gender and it's only women, women, women. (President of the DNCW, Interview, July 2011)

The conceptual shift from WID to GAD in the Caribbean (Barriteau 2003, Bannon and Correia 2006) provided a critical narrative-building opportunity for the work of the DNCW within the DNGP process. By developing an NGP, the BWA partnering with the DNCW, employed a policy strategy operating somewhere between the use of gender as a development buzzword (Palmer Cooper and van der Vorst 1997, Cornwall and Brock 2005, Buscher and Mutimukuru 2007), thereby depoliticizing the regional feminist agenda (Mukhopadhyay 2004, Cornwall, Harrison and Whitehead 2007, Squires 2007), and maximizing the elasticity of gender in policymaking, while paying homage to the feminist politics which birthed the call for an NGP (Mohammed 2011). It is easy to relegate such a policy document to the annals of another depoliticized technical document, a victim of the shift and the inevitable 'smoothing out of more radical undertones' associated with gender (Sardenburg 2007). Although the smoothing was undeniable, it was coupled with a decoding or the gender jargon that advanced local ownership of the policy.

The narrative around the DNGP always presented the document as a public good. Like the 2004 version of the Trinidad and Tobago document, it called for revisiting the laws around women's rights to safe abortions and the traditional heteronormative legal frameworks which marginalize some groups. Lastly, gender was similarly defined. In spite of the presence of these clauses, unlike the Trinidad and Tobago case, Dominica's document was approved. The narrative was a process of negotiated voices. One such voice was that of Dominican masculinity. The approval and passage of the DNGP required a specific narrative, one that ensured that neither masculinity nor the Church was marginalized.

The NGP process opened a space for a very public engagement with men. The perceived need for a non-governmental male voice led to the inclusion of the DACAMEN in the DNGP formulation process. Its association to the Church was a strategic bonus. At the time of the data collection in 2011 DACAMEN was not as active as it had been in 2004/2005. Yet their representatives were convinced of the essential need for DACAMEN's voice in the NGP process. They believed that their legitimacy in the process emanated from a number of places, including the fact that they were one of the only NGOs organized around men's issues at the time. This legitimacy was bolstered by the fact that they were representing the interest of Catholic men in the process.

The entitlement of place assumed by DACAMEN is one of the novel products of the Anglophone Caribbean's gender system's convergence with public policy. In the shift from women to gender in development, the Anglophone Caribbean drew on the male marginalization school of thought as a valid policy space. In other geographies, the 'slipping away' to gender (Cornwall, Harrison and Whitehead 2007) did not produce a vocal cadre of, at times, 'vulnerable' males laying claim to the policy space originally carved out through the work of feminist activists, scholars and practitioners. Dominica's was the first NGP process that courted this masculinist narrative in the region. The details and negotiations of this process, particularly the masculinist voice, are discussed in greater depth in the chapter on the DNGP. Fundamentally, the negotiation has been about the transition to gender, understood as synonymous with the inclusion of men (Barriteau 1998). Reconciling the extent to which DACAMEN's presence produced a publicly necessary male discourse, and the value of that voice, is pivotal to framing public meanings of the mechanics of men and masculinities in the NGP processes and all other regional policies. Similarly this issue also extended to the Dominican relationship with its third NGO, the Catholic Archdiocese of Roseau.

The third NGO narrative-defining presence in the NGP process was the Catholic Archdiocese of Roseau. Represented by Sister Lorraine Rogier, the archdiocese leveraged its way onto the committee. According to the representative of the diocese, Rogier was part of the committee phase to ensure that the policy did not come in direct conflict with the teachings of the Church. She believed the goals of the NGP did not oppose the work of the Church in Dominica. Even where conflicts might have been anticipated, she believed the interest of the Church would be best served by her participation in the process rather than her remaining on its periphery. Building on her long-standing relationship with the BWA and the DNCW she stated:

> I was always active in the DNCW; before the Women's Bureau I was on the advisory committee to the Bureau for a number of years, and I was asked to do things as a resource person. When they started with the policy Ms. Brown asked me if I wanted to be a part. I just said okay. Now you know I have to represent the Church and its teachings on birth control etc., but I had a history of working with the DNCW and I decided to be a part of it. (Sister Lorraine Rogier, Interview, July 2011)

Men, the Catholic Church and feminist organizing – how did these interests combine to produce a nationally accepted NGP narrative that made gender decidedly non-threatening? How did this policy narrative emerge from an intervention where people brokered their vested interests without derailing the process? The answers depend on where you look. The history of relations and societal contexts provides important markers. I doubt the terms of engagement in the development of the DNGP were perpetually cordial and without tensions or contentious issues. However, some factors did contribute to producing a public narrative around the NGP which did not overtly disrupt traditional notions of gender.

The resistances within the wider population created no measurable political fallout of merit. Consequently, the NGP remained a largely technical activity. Although the document had to be owned by the minster responsible for taking it to the cabinet, the centrality of this individual to the process was never obvious. The technical efficiency over political ownership raises a question of whether the NGP formulation failed to influence large pockets of the Dominican 'mainstream', ensuring that male bias and gender inequity remain stubbornly intact (Woodford-Berger 2007). Questions also arise about the compatibility of a largely public service–staffed Technical Support Committee guiding the NGP drafting, and the goals of the feminist agenda to promote fairness and gender justice (Barriteau 2003). To what extent are the goals and means of these constituencies reconcilable? Such questions need to be explored, informed by a cognizance of the historic reliance of the BWA on partnering with other organizations to fulfil its mandate, thereby fostering a collective ownership of the organization and its work.

Historically, the smallness of the technical staff was seen as a factor pushing the Dominican BWA to work closely with and through a number of partner organizations. As noted earlier, the bureau is a product of NGO advocacy, and sustains such partnerships. These partner organizations, mainly non-governmental bodies, were fundamental to the NGP process. The relationship forged with these groups over time located the work of the BWA intimately within communities constantly engaging with actors other than itself and those exclusive to the field of GAD. It should be noted that this was not planned. It was a result of limited economic and human resources, and the history of feminist organizing in Dominica. Clearly, advocates played a pivotal role in the politics of policymaking in Dominica, particularly with regard to advancing the gender equity and equality work of the government. The NGP was not the first experience of groups with conflicting interests working to advance the gender equity and equality mission, According to a representative of the bureau:

> Well the thing is, yes, we've had participation from other institutions that impact families (in the development of the policy). So for example there is a group NANGO (National Association of Non-Government Organizations), they were involved. We also have Dominica Planned Parenthood Association; we worked very closely with them. We had the Social Centre, the Social Centre is actually an offshoot of the Catholic Church where they started off with the Social League for Women. (Acting director of the Women's Affairs Bureau of Dominica, Interview, July 2011)

This experience of the Church collaborating with women's organizations in the Anglophone Caribbean is not new. Dominica appears to have retained this collaborative activity over a more protracted period than other regional territories. Although these partnerships were integral to the ultimate approval of the NGP, the deliberate unpacking of the policy document and distribution to the population in the form of short pamphlets based on the various policy areas also played a central role.

TRANSLATING THE POLICY, BUILDING NATIONAL OWNERSHIP

The office of the DNCW in Dominica found the pamphlets titled 'The National Gender Policy Made Simple' very useful. These pamphlets were compiled by the BWA and widely distributed with its partner organizations after the minister of women's affairs accepted the consultant's draft document, but prior to final cabinet approval for implementation. They were in fact an accessible and easily understood version of the various sections of policy produced for the general public. The actual translation of the information and the printing of the pamphlets was funded and led by UNIFEM. In talking with persons involved in the NGP process, it became apparent that by printing and distributing the 'NGP Made Simple' series prior to securing the cabinet's approval, the policy stakeholders took the narrative beyond themselves. The distribution process, led by the BWA, served to heighten expectations within the community at large around the passage of the policy. Additionally, the information within the public space specific to the content of the NGP was shaped by the BWA.

Ultimately, the DNGP appears to have moved seamlessly from formulation to cabinet approval. Looking back at the process, this formal 'ease' of passage provides an ideal space for further theorizing. The internal, intimate working of the Steering Committee, the place of the BWA as the torchbearer of the policy and the public discourse emerging out of the pamphlets are all spaces that this research was unable to access. What is clear is that this NGP was a product of both national and regional factors that offer insights into regional gender systems as determinants of public policy outcomes.

Undeniably, the DNGP benefited from fortuitous timing. The process was undertaken immediately after the first NGP attempt in Trinidad and Tobago. Learning from the difficulties faced during the Trinidad and Tobago NGP formulation, possible outliers and 'derailers' were identified early in the Dominican process. Converting these possible derailers into partners shifted the possible public national narrative to a privately negotiated discourse among stakeholders. The employment of the lead Trinidad and Tobago policy drafter as the lead consultant on the DNGP provided continuity and other necessary insights into a previous policy process fraught with tensions and contradictions among stakeholders. Nationally, Dominica's drafters had a history of working collaboratively with the BWA. Additionally, the homage paid to masculinist discourses and the public approval accorded to the process by the presence of the Catholic Church contributed to fashioning a nationally accepted NGP narrative. My inquiry into the DNGP centred on the governmental and non-governmental building of a public discourse facilitative of the advancement of the NGP towards cabinet approval. The model of narrative creation experienced in Dominica contrasted sharply with Trinidad and Tobago's NGP process. In particular, feminist activism around the NGP in Trinidad and Tobago did not enjoy the broad-based acceptance experienced by feminists and their allies in Dominica. The NGP process was embarked upon as an academic initiative, its drafters unaware of the seditious narratives that can emerge when gender is misunderstood.

TRINIDAD AND TOBAGO

Like Dominica, I start my examination of the Trinidad and Tobago NGP process through NGO eyes. Public policy is officially controlled by the State. Yet

in both NGPs my data collection started with the NGO voice towards privileging the unofficial overview of the process. Specific to the Trinidad and Tobago
experience, engaging the NGO voice is particularly pertinent because governmental control of the policy process has been very strong, notably, not by the
bureaucracy, but by the political position of the relevant minister. Therefore,
unlike Dominica, where the BWA director acted as the principal governmental
face of the NGP process, in Trinidad and Tobago, which had since the early-to-
mid 1990's institutionalized the most well-staffed division of Women's Affairs
regionally,[4] ministerial ownership and visible guidance was an imperative to
the NGP process. This contributed to the belief that, in terms of economic and
human resources, Trinidad and Tobago was equipped to undertake the successful formulation of an NGP. Dominican interviewees constructed a more
immediate history. Trinidad and Tobago's history is longer, with intervals of
acrimony and détente between the NGO community and the government. Yet
there is a persistent belief, expressed by the local NGO community, that with
the right political will the government could have funded the development of
its own NGP. Interestingly, within the government the need for an NGP is
reflected in the number of attempts by sitting administrations to write NGPs. In
spite of a common stated resolve of the NGOs and the government, since June
2009, Trinidad and Tobago's policy has been a parliamentary green paper,[*]
indefinitely out for public review. Most recently, in November 2011, the cabinet appointed a committee to review the document, and a technical committee
to rewrite it where necessary. Currently, Trinidad and Tobago sits on three
possible NGPs: a 2004 document, a 2009 green paper and the 2011 document.

BACKGROUND TO THE TRINIDAD AND TOBAGO NGP

The Early Years of Women

Trinidad and Tobago's NGP narrative is an old one. Its age, its predisposition
to sporadically appear and disappear as a government priority, the fact that it
was originally embarked upon as a position paper on women, which became
an NGP, all combine to produce a very personalized discourse with a number
of unstable, combative postures shaping relations and expectations around
the NGP. In the government, the NGP activity straddled ministers from 1988
to 2011. Internationally, post-1995, Trinidad and Tobago's commitment to
Beijing and the Convention on the Elimination of All Forms of Discrimination against Women (CEDAW) requirements provided international impetus.
Interestingly, the need for an NGP has very rarely been taken on as a publicly

---

* A parliamentary green paper represents a proposed course of action by government. It does not
represent approved public policy

owned discussion, and calls for an NGP have remained largely between the government and feminist activists.

The original call for a policy emerged in the wake of the United Nations Decade for Women (1976–1985). Influenced by the international momentum of the decade, the government of Trinidad and Tobago felt compelled to express its own commitment to expanding its work on women beyond social welfare. These initiatives included a policy statement on women, the 1987 re-establishment of a Women's Bureau in the Ministry of Health, Welfare and Status of Women and the setting up of an Inter-ministerial Committee on Women in the same year (GAD 2010).

Feminist advocates such as Hazel Brown, members of the Housewives' Association and the Trinidad and Tobago Family Planning Association's Grace Talma, challenged the government's Policy Statement on Women, developed in 1988 and approved by cabinet in 1989. They were convinced of the need for a more thorough description of the status of women in Trinidad and Tobago in the introduction, especially their contributions to the social and economic development of the country. They called for greater detail in outlining policy provisions, and demanded inclusion of specific issues such as violence against women, communications, media, culture and peace. They expressed concerns about the structure of the national machinery, including staffing (GAD 2010). Most importantly, the women's NGOs objected to the document because they believed it was not sufficiently consultative. In response, Brown and her colleagues embarked on the development of a National Paper on the Status of Women based on their own consultations throughout Trinidad and Tobago. According to Brown it was imperative that feminist organizing responded to the government with a comprehensive document reflecting the complexities of the lives of the country's women.

> What we did when we left there[5] was to go back and say 'you know what? We have to take a different track to this business of this policy'. So we had our own consultation. What we did was a series of … go talk to people, what they should do … all the women's organizations that we knew about but mostly it was Network membership because by that time the Network had been formed. … This is one of the original copies of it. (Reading) 'Trinidad on the State of Women, Comments of Non-Governmental Organizations of Trinidad and Tobago'. (Hazel Brown, Interview, May 2012)

By 1990 the NGOs completed their position paper. Although it was sufficiently consultative, the capacity of this document to influence national policy was minimal. It was not a National Policy on Women (NPW), but neither was it taken on board by the government as a draft document that could contribute to an NPW. By this time, it became increasingly apparent to the NGOs that a policy would exist only through state ownership of the process.

The regional and national build-up to the 1995 Beijing Conference on Women provided another window of opportunity for an NPW. In preparing for Beijing, the government of Trinidad and Tobago, in collaboration with NGOs such as the Network of NGOs, community-based organizations such as the Federation of Women's Institutes, and scholar activists, compiled a comprehensive, sufficiently consultative document on the status of women (GAD 2010). Additionally, the then minister of women's affairs claimed the women's portfolio as her own and committed resources to the Beijing lead-up. The Beijing document on the status of women was earmarked by the then minister as the basis of an NPW post Beijing. An early election was called in 1996 and the sitting government was removed from office. The minister changed. Between 1996 and 2002, the most profound shift in the state's position on women and gender was the change of name from women's affairs to gender affairs. No NGP-related activity was undertaken.

The Beijing moment was a critical juncture in narrative building around the issues of women in Trinidad and Tobago and regionally. In a 2011 interview, Rhoda Reddock reflected on the pre-Beijing process as a defining moment. Reddock signalled the consultations, the work undertaken among regional and national practitioners, scholars and activists in Beijing House as creating a national consciousness around the issues of women. That collective ownership was never experienced again in the Trinidad and Tobago NGP/NPW process.

ADVOCATES, PRACTITIONERS, ACADEMICS, THE PUBLIC AND POLITICIANS IN THE GENDER POLICY SPACE – 2002 ONWARDS

In 2002 Joan Yuille-Williams returned to office as minister of community development, culture and gender affairs and the unfinished business of the NGP was on the lips of feminist activists. Nationally, by 2002, Hazel Brown's Network of NGOs, the Hindu Women's Organization, Working Women for Social Progress and newer groups such as Advocates for Safe Parenthood: Improving Reproductive Equity (ASPIRE) were all part of the constituency advocating an NGP. Internationally, harsh feedback from the CEDAW expert panel commenting on Trinidad and Tobago's presentation of its first, second and third periodic report provided a critical voice. In January 2002, this expert committee repeatedly called for the government of Trinidad and Tobago to develop an NGP. The vice-chair of the CEDAW Dr. Hanna Beate Schopp-Schiling was relentless in her call for the Trinidad and Tobago government to develop a culturally specific NGP document.

When the delegation returned from the CEDAW reporting, the government convened a feedback meeting for stakeholders and NGO partners. At this session, the committee's call for an NGP formed an instrumental component of the deliberations. After this session, the United Nations Development Fund (UNDP) and Canadian International Development Agency (CIDA) agreed to partner with the government and fund components of the NGP's development. In July/August 2002 the NGP process was launched and overseen by Minister Joan Yuille-Williams. Feminist scholars from the Centre for Gender and Development Studies (CGDS) at the UWI were selected as lead consultants on the NGP. The process was supposed to include extensive consultations, both among special interest groups and community organizations throughout Trinidad and Tobago, supported by gender-sensitive sector studies. The studies and consultation outcomes were to form the basis of the sector-related policy recommendations, all of which were to be compiled by the CGDS.

THE OUTLIERS AND THE UNFORESEEN

The Gender Affairs Division, the consultants and partner organizations attempted to ensure that the voices of the widest cross-section of the population were heard. For the first time within the context of NPW/NGP formulation, the gender ministry was on the same page as most of its long-time NGO partners working in the field of women and GAD. While some of these long-term partners agreed with the process, a number of outlier groups[6] entered the process after the tabling of the first draft document in cabinet. Their reaction effectively derailed the policy. The source of contention was recommendation No. 100 of the 2004 document, which called for a review of the laws pertaining to abortion, and the call to extend the definition gender in the glossary to include sexual orientation (CGDS 2004).

The most visible groups opposing the NGP were the Lawyers for Jesus,[7] the Emmanuel Community[8] and Divine Encounter Fellowship. Other voices also engaged in advocacy against the policy behind the glare of the media, making it difficult to determine the policy narratives which were supported by silent but powerful voices influencing the process. The Hindu, Orisha and Muslim religious communities were concerned with the recommendations around the legal standardization of the age of consent, as the various marriage acts allowed for marriage before the age of consent. Within the feminist and gender organizing fraternity, actors such as members of ASPIRE and Coalition Advocating for Inclusion of Sexual Orientation (CAISO) wanted the language to go further in advancing gender justice. The bureaucracy, the policy drafters and the politicians at the helm of the process were faced with the challenge of mediating these competing interests through a very public vilification of the NGP. All of this happened at a time when the religious marginalization[9] of the draft document was being advanced by powerful voices, and gaining ground with the then prime minister and increasingly with the population at large.

Although the Trinidad and Tobago NGP began as a gender-sensitive, academically guided, data-driven, broadly consultative exercise, it has been unable to produce a nationally palatable NGP narrative. This failure provides our first regional policy encounter with the conceptual shift from an NPW to an NGP. It is a view into *the methodological implications* and the perceived expanding constituencies consistent with the use of the term gender (Barriteau 2003). Added to these complexities, the NGP drafters revealed their own cognitive shortcuts (Hutchings 2008) for explaining gender. The most compelling, oppositional, narrative-forming sentiment was expressed by the then Prime Minister Mr. Patrick Manning. His decision to publicly distance himself and his cabinet from the document locked the NGP in political abeyance. Prior to his intervention, the NGP passage was regarded as largely a technical and scholarly process. The prime minister's public opposition to the document secured its character as a political hot potato whose approval was seen as politically costly. As a result of this possible political fallout, since 2004, no politician has been willing to move the document towards approval.

The decision of the then prime minister to publicly break the relationship with the work of his gender minister compounded an already embattled policy narrative. A technically appropriate response would have seen the prime minister constructing his policy narrative in consultation with, and to some extent through, his minister of gender. However, his decision to be vocal in his dissent spoke to the power of the voices of resistance and the ease with which the personal becomes political in the politics of policymaking in the area of women and gender. The prime minister's personal and political need to ally himself with the outcry from the Catholic Church, evangelical churches, and other anti-NGP voices speaks to the power of these voices. It also raises questions around reconciling expectations between society's interpretation of the goals of GAD and the goals of feminist activism. In the words of one feminist scholar, the policy process was seen as largely administrative. The entrance and the power wielded by the outlier voices clearly indicate that the process was always political. The NGP is one of the pillars of gender mainstreaming and part of feminists' efforts to shift their activism from the margins of development practice into the centre of government programming (Mukhopadhyay 2004). Gender mainstreaming promised to negotiate new spaces for the practice of gender and policymaking (Walby 2005). The efforts to shift such work from the margins, as exemplified by policy recommendation 100 and the definition of gender in the Trinidad context, foregrounds tensions between the plausible language of GAD and the socio-historical means by which diverse actors in a given society construct and internalize meaning around language (Morgan and Youssef 2006). These identical spaces challenge the work of feminist activism, scholars and practitioners to engineer spaces of solidarity where traditional conceptualizations around gender and women may be destabilized through public policy. Additionally, the readiness of the political gatekeepers to manage the political fallout consistent with such change is another question. The Trinidad and Tobago experience demonstrates the difficulties that arise with passing an NGP when politicians in power deem political fallout too costly.

CONCLUSION

The NGP is the definitive statement of government intent around gender justice in any territory. It is not just a meta plan for one ministry; it establishes an overarching mechanism detailing how governments' machinery is to work in tandem with non-governmental actors towards a goal of gender equity and equality. In the democratic states of the Anglophone Caribbean, the process of formulating a broadly consultative NGP is a yardstick. It measures the power of drivers and drafters of the NGP to process these documents through the crucible of public opinion and the populations' personal gender ideologies in order to produce palatable narratives and policy documents.

Dominica's and Trinidad and Tobago's NGP processes are components of a broader Anglophone Caribbean moment. The technocratic-managed model of the Dominican experience may be incongruous with the emancipatory aspirations of regional critical feminist organizing. Yet the government has committed to a plan.

While Trinidad and Tobago does not have a government-approved plan, its policymaking efforts around the NGP reveal the power of competing narratives in the politics of policymaking. Although the Cayman Islands' NGP preceded the Trinidad and Tobago experience, coming immediately after the Beijing meeting, it reflected a WID paradigm-informed national consciousness which never threatened traditional gender norms. Trinidad and Tobago was the first NGP that publicly interrogated the need to place the NGP process within a popularly anticipated expanded policy constituency beyond what women thought to be consistent with the use of the term gender. As the first NGP to walk the road of gender, Trinidad and Tobago inadvertently took on a national consciousness wary of the implications of shifting to gender and increasingly vigilant in its policing of women's bodies. Neither the drafters nor the drivers foresaw the possible fallout from their attempts to introduce a broader conception of gender into the policy narrative.

The region continues to grapple with the conceptual shift from WID to GAD, and our various NGP experiences are germane to the current contestations, confusion and mismanaged gender policy narratives across the region. In 1998 when governments started changing bureau names from women to gender, starting with Trinidad and Tobago, reactions were mixed. Some feminist activists were convinced the shift from women to gender would produce a lost decade around regional work on women and GAD. Eroding the pre-Beijing fervour and resulting in a murkiness of purpose, regional development work would become rudderless as it tried to establish a constituency for the word gender. Practitioners were divided. Some regional development agencies opposed the term gender. International representatives were largely convinced that resistance was futile. In some way, the shift provided a necessary veneer of an olive branch between feminist activism, the state and the population. The post-Beijing regional governmental narrative on women/gender affairs was heavily influenced by the assertion that 'Caribbean masculinity has been rendered vulnerable'. Women's affairs needed to become a gender affairs division because men were now an obvious constituency. In the context of policy papers on how a concern with women had become a concern with gender and NGPs, Dominica and Trinidad and Tobago provide important insights into the fact that rupturing of the policy process produced as a by-product of change is never experienced in an identical fashion.

Trinidad and Tobago established a novel policy space. Every NGP after the Trinidad and Tobago experience of abeyance has been forced to court by both masculinity and religion. Brokering these elements has become a rite of passage. The 2004 NGP started as scholar activists researching and engaging in a scholarly exercise that would have produced a relevant policy document. The content of the document remains one of the most comprehensive overviews of GAD in Trinidad and Tobago. While Trinidad and Tobago's NGP floundered, it has remained the blueprint for attempts to establish NGPs that address gender inequality and gender's central role in the allocation of political and economic power. Simultaneously, the failure of the policy reminds us that public policymaking is a political process, requiring support from both legislatures and people in a given community. Thus an ideal NGP cannot be based on an idealized notion of an imagined gender equality, but rather has to contend with the limits and internal debates specific to gender in particular societies. In a region as complex and diverse as the Anglophone Caribbean, gender policies consequently face considerable challenges. The battles between ideals and socially acceptable policies remain central to understanding the politics of policymaking around gender in the region.

NOTES

1. Here the similarities speak to the structure and approach to policy design and development; the actual policy priorities and areas for action are all determined by the peculiar national context-based perspectives on development priorities.

2. 2005 was the official launch of the NGP process.

3. In 2009 the name was changed to Gender Affairs.

4. On Jan 12, 1987, following the election of a new political administration – the National Alliance for Reconstruction – a Women's Bureau was established in the newly configured Ministry of Health, Social Welfare and the Status of Women. The Women's Bureau came under the portfolio of Margaret Hector, parliamentary secretary in the same ministry. After a reshuffling of ministries the following year, the Women's Bureau was relocated to the Ministry of Community Development, Welfare and the Status of Women, with Gloria Henry as minister responsible for the bureau's affairs.

5. 'There' refers to a meeting with the then minister of women's affairs, Ms. Gloria Henry, on the government's policy statement on women.

6. These outlier groups were never thought of as very pertinent to the policy process during the formulation stage. Many of them were religious groups and their concerns were thought to have been picked up in the consultations with the respective religious groups.

7. Lawyers for Jesus is a Christian fundamentalist group of lawyers and other practitioners in the legal fraternity

8. A Catholic organization committed to safeguarding the life of the child ... Offering counselling, and providing alternatives to abortion (Pickard-Gordon, Lara. 2008 'Emmanuel Community continues pro-life work'. Trinidad & Tobago Newsday, November 9.)

9. This marginalization was demonstrated by a very vocal distancing of leading public figures from the content of the NGP. The distancing at its most extreme, included the then Prime Minister, Patrick Manning, taking time from a cabinet meeting to make a statement to the nation that the then draft policy document was in no way a government document.

REFERENCES

Ackelsberg, Martha. 1992. 'Feminist Analysis of Public Policy'. *Comparative Politics* 24(4): 477–93.

Baksh-Soodeen, Rawwida. 1998. 'Issues of Difference in Contemporary Caribbean Feminism'. *Feminist Review* 59: 74–85.

Bannon, Ian and Maria C. Correia. 2006. *The Other Half of Gender: Men's Issues in Development.* Washington: The World Bank.

Barriteau, Eudine. 1995. 'Postmodernist Feminist Theorizing and Development Policy and Practice in the Anglophone Caribbean: The Barbados Case', In *Feminism/Postmodernism/Development*, edited by Marianne, H. Marchand and Jane Parpart, 142–58. New York: Routledge.

———. 1998. 'Theorizing Gender Systems and the Project of Modernity'. *Feminist Review* 59: 186–210.

———. 2003. 'Theorizing the Shift from Women to Gender', In *Confronting Power, Theorizing Gender: Interdisciplinary Perspectives in the Caribbean*, edited by Eudine Barriteau, 27–45. Kingston: University of the West Indies Press.

Boswell, Christina, Andrew Geddes, and Peter Schollen. 2011. 'The Role of Narratives in Migration Policy-Making: A Research Framework'. *The British Journal of Politics and International Relations* 13: 1–11.

Buscher, Bram E. and Tendayi Mutimukuru. 2007. 'Buzzing too far? The Ideological Echo of Global Governance Concepts'. *Development Southern Africa* 26(7): 1043–60.

CGDS. 2004. *Draft Situational Analysis and National Gender Policy and Plan of Action for the Republic of Trinidad and Tobago.* Policy Draft, Port of Spain: Centre for Gender and Development Studies.

CGEF. 2005. *A Study of Gender Mainstreaming in the Caribbean.* Georgetown Guyana: Canadian International Development Agency.

CIDA. 2005. *Report on the Technical Meeting of the National Machineries for Women.* Kingstown: ECLAC-CDCC/CIDA.

Cornwall, Andrea and Karen Brock. 2005. 'What do Buzzwords do for Development Policy? A Critical Look at "Participation", "Empowerment" and "Poverty Reduction"'. *Third World Quarterly* 26: 1043–60.

Cornwall, Andrea, Elizabeth Harrison, and Ann Whitehead. 2007. *Feminisms in Development: Contradictions, Contestations and Challenges.* London: Zed Books.

Cuales, Sonia M. 1998. 'In Search of Our Memory: Gender in the Netherlands Antilles'. *Feminist Review* 59: 86–100.

Dugdale, Paul. 1998. 'The Art of Insider Activism: Policy Activism and the Governance of Health', in *Activism and the Policy Process*, edited by Anna Yeatman, 104–21. Sydney: Allen and Unwin.

Ely, Robin J. and Debra Meyerson. 2000. 'Maintaining a Gender Narrative Advancing Gender Equity in Organizations: The Challenge and Importance of Maintaining a Gender Narrative'. *Development in Practice* 7(4): 589–608.

Flax, Jane. 1987. 'Postmodernism and Gender Relations in Feminist Theory'. *Signs* 12(4): 621–43.

GAD. 2010. *History of the Development of the Gender Affairs Division.* Port of Spain: Government of Trinidad and Tobago Gender Affairs Division.

Howlett, Michael. 2010. 'Governance Modes, Policy Regimes and Operational Plans: A Multi-Level Nested Model of Policy Instrument Choice and Policy Design'. *Policy Sciences* 42(1): 73–89.

Hutchings, Kim. 2008. 'Cognitive Shortcuts', in *Rethinking the Man Question*, edited by M. Zaleweski and J. Parpart, 23–46. London: Zed Books.

Keddie, Amanda. 2009. 'National Gender Equity and Schooling Policy in Australia: Struggles for Non-Identitarian Feminist Politics'. *The Australian Educational Researcher* 36(2): 21–37.

Li, Tania. 2007. *The Will to Improve: Governmentality, Development and the Practice of Politics.* Durham: Duke University Press.

Lodge, Martin and Christopher Hood. 2003. 'Competency and Bureaucracy: Diffusion Application and Appropriate Response?' *Western European Politics* 26(3): 131–52.

Mohammed, Patricia. 'Gender Politics and Global Democracy: Insights from the Caribbean'. *Building Global Democracy (BGD) Programme Conceptualising Global Democracy Project.* 2011. http://www.BuildingGlobalDemocracy.org (accessed November 21, 2015).

Mollyneux, Maxine and Shahra Razavi. 2003. 'Gender Justice, Development and Rights'. *Democracy, Governance and Human Rights Programme Paper No. 10.* Geneva: United Nations Research Institute for Social Development, January.

Mosse, David. 2004. 'Is Good Policy Unimplementable? Reflections on the Ethnography of Aid and Policy Practice'. *Development and Change* 35(4): 639–71.

Mukhopadhyay, Maitrayee. 2004. 'Mainstreaming Gender or Streaming Gender Away: Feminists Marooned in the Development Business'. *IDS Bulletin* 35: 95–103.

Nurse, Keith. 2004. 'Masculinities in Transition: Gender and the Global Problematique', in *Interrogating Caribbean Masculinities: Theoretical and Empirical Analyses*, edited by Rhoda Reddock, 3–37. Kingston, Jamaica: The University of the West Indies Press.

Office of the Status of Women. 2000. 'National Policy Framework for Women's Empowerment and Equality 2000'. Government of South Africa, Office of the Presidency.

Palmer, Jason, Ian Cooper and Rita van der Vorst. 1997. 'Mapping Out Fuzzy Buzzwords-Who Sits Where on Sustainability and Sustainable Development'. *Sustainable Development* 5: 87–93.

Parpart, Jane. 2014. 'Exploring the Transformative Potential of Gender Mainstreaming in International Development Institutions'. *Journal of International Development* 26, 3: 382–95.

Prugl, Elisabeth. 2010. 'Feminism and the Postmodern State: Gender Mainstreaming in European Rural Development'. *Signs: Journal of Women in Culture and Society* 35(2): 447–75.

Reddock, Rhoda. 1989. Report on the evaluation of the Dominica National Council of Women 1986–1988. Unpublished.

Rowley, Michelle. 2003. *Institutional Mechanisms for the Advancement of Women in the Caribbean: Regional Assessment.* Barbados: UNIFEM.

Sardenburg, Cecelia M.B. 2007. 'Back to Women? Translations, Resignifications and Myths of Gender Policy and Practice in Brazil', in *Feminisms in Development: Contradictions, Contestations and Challenges*, edited by Andrea Cornwall, Elizabeth Harrison and Ann Whitehead, 48–64. London: Zed Books.

Squires, Judith. 2007. *The New Politics of Gender Equality.* London: Palgrave MacMillan.

Subrahmanian, Ramya. 2007. 'Making Sense of Gender in Shifting Institutional Contexts: Some Reflections on Gender Mainstreaming', in *Feminisms in Development: Contradictions, Contestations and Challenges*, by Andrea Cornwall, Elizabeth Harrison and Ann Whitehead, 112-122. London: Zed Books.

Tinker, Irene. 1990. 'The Making of a Field: Advocates, Practitioners and Scholars'. In *Persistent Inequalities: Women and World Development*, by Irene Tinker, 27–53. New York: Oxford University Press.

Walby, Sylvia. 2005. 'Gender Mainstreaming: Productive Tensions in Theory and Practice'. *Social Politics: International Studies in Gender, State and Society* 12(3): 321–43.

Weaver-Hightower, Marcus B. 2008. 'An Ecology Metaphor for Educational Policy Analysis: A Call to Complexity'. *Educational Researcher* 37(3): 153–67.

Woodford-Berger, Prudence. 2007. 'Gender Mainstreaming: What is it (about) and should we continue doing it?' in *Feminisms in Development: Contradictions, Contestations and Challenges*, edited by Andrea Cornwall, Elizabeth Harrison and Ann Whitehead, 122–34. London: Zed Books.

Chapter 7

Masculinities and the Practice of Dominica's National Gender Policy

Ramona Biholar

INTRODUCTION

Masculinism, 'an ideology that justifies and naturalizes male domination and power, accepts heterosexuality and the existing division of labor as normal, and is resistant to change and not subject to fluctuation over time' (Reddock 2004, xxiii), has profound implications for modern societal structures (Nurse 2004, 3). Caribbean feminist scholarship has long pointed to the negative impact of masculinist ideologies for both women and men. While continuing to critique the reproduction of the ideological and material relations of gender (Barriteau 2001, 29–30), and thus women's inequality, some scholars have indicated that gender inequality is reproduced partly by the invisibility of masculinity (Kimmel 2004). Along with challenging the myth that 'men are neither a problem nor have problems' (Rutherford 1988; Nurse 2004, 3), Caribbean scholarship has also challenged both the invisibility of masculinity as well as ways that masculinity has been included in state and popular discourses of gender equality in the region (Rutherford 1988; Nurse 2004, 3).

Understanding the *life* of feminist strategies for gender equality, such as gender policies in practice, is the overarching concern of this chapter. I discuss the contradictions between instantiations of gender at individual, interpersonal, institutional and ideological levels, pointing out that patriarchal ideologies persist along multiple and competing interests, priorities and conveniences, and interpretations and discourses within and among institutions. Men are becoming more gender-conscious, while the idea of equity between sexes and the visibility of women in the public sphere are perceived as threatening male positions of authority and leadership (Reddock 2004, xiv); men and women are cooperating to end gender inequality, while women's empowerment is perceived as having 'too much equality' at the detriment of

131

men, who are now left behind; girls' achievements in education are seen as boys' 'disempowerment', while gendered occupational and decision-making differentiations are still more advantageous for males; masculinist ideologies are resilient despite being challenged by the state, women's groups, some men's groups, and individuals.

In such a contradictory context where 'success for men and for women is presented as inherently antagonistic' (Robinson 2003, 253), what can we expect of the implementation of gender policies, and what are therefore the implications for feminist strategies for advancing gender justice in the Anglophone Caribbean?

Premised on an in-depth case study I conducted in Dominica, the chapter shows that gender creates a contentious space of multiple and competing interpretations that influence feminist strategies, such as gender policies, within the state apparatus and CSOs. More specifically, rigid understandings of gender constructions and relations, and misreadings of gender as referring to women only, 'devoid of any understandings of hierarchies, power and privileges' (Barriteau 2001, 91) reinforce a masculinist approach to the policy implementation, hindering its potential to advance gender equality and justice. In fact, ideas of women's inequality are contested and feminist strategies for gender equality are resisted while men occupy the contentious space gender creates to claim their 'disempowerment'.

This is facilitated by the persistence of asymmetric relations of power between women and men. If pre-existent patterns of gender inequalities in the patriarchal state are not addressed, seemingly gender-neutral policy can have a discriminatory effect. In other words, indirect discrimination is fostered, despite good intentions of eliminating discrimination. Although masculinities are included as a basis for creating gender-neutral policy and challenging masculinism, it turns out that policy interpretations and implementation are actually shaped along the paradigms of masculinism and the myth of male marginalization.

I therefore suggest that the resilience of the material and ideological relations of gender must be challenged in order to transform unjust gender systems. In particular, the hierarchies carried by the constructions of femininity and masculinity should be confronted so that material changes (distribution of resources, for example) do not reproduce ideological biases (relations of domination) (Barriteau 2001, 33).

CONCEPTUAL FRAMEWORK AND METHODOLOGY

In an effort to achieve gender equity and equality, much attention has been given throughout the Caribbean to the design of national gender policies, as well as to their approval by national cabinets. The Commonwealth of Dominica (hereinafter Dominica) drafted the National Policy and Action Plan for Gender Equity and Equality in the Commonwealth of Dominica (hereinafter the DNGP or the gender policy). In 2006, Dominica was the first in the Caribbean to approve its policy. Since then, Dominica has undergone a process of policy implementation.

Generally, there is insufficient understanding of the *life* of the policy after its drafting (Mosse 2004). Lessons still remain to be learned about policy in practice, about the actors involved and the politics of alliance they subscribe to, about the synchronicity of multiple and competing agendas and interests, about negotiations taking place and, not lastly, about the relationship between policy and practice. The question that has been posed by scholars and is still valid to ask is: 'What if, instead of policy producing practice, practices produce policy?' (Mosse 2004, 640).

The process of policy implementation is conceptualized in this chapter as complex, challenging, and versatile, compelled to resonate to the reality on the ground. Its ultimate results are the realization of policy intentions for the beneficiaries.[1] I am also guided by Barriteau's definition of gender as 'a complex system of personal and social relations through which women and men are socially created and maintained and through which they gain access to, or are allocated status, power and material resources within society' (Barriteau 2001, 26). Relations of gender entail an asymmetry of power with 'differential material and ideological outcomes' (Barriteau 2001, 27). This chapter focuses on the ideological dimension of gender, and more precisely on constructions of masculinity (Barriteau 2001, 30).

I understand the concept of masculinity as a spectrum of representations that draw on patterns of behaviour, attitudes and choices (Biholar 2013, 8–9, 190) that become tangible through social action in different social contexts (Connell and Messerschmidt 2005, 836). By no means universal nor homogenous, masculinity is diverse, depending on the specificities of particular contexts; fluctuating, depending on the specificities of 'new historical conjunctures' (Demetriou 2001, 355; Connell and Messerschmidt 2005, 846, 852; Plummer 2010, 5); and plural and hierarchical. Hence, scholarship refers to multiple *masculinities*. Among this plurality and hierarchy, hegemonic masculinity stands as the standard for evaluating other identities (Plummer 2010, 8). In fact, hegemonic masculinity is a social and cultural construction (Lewis 2004; Mohammed 2004; Nurse 2004; Connell and Messerschmidt 2005) that ascribes identity codes and produces expectations of what it means to be/become a *real* man in different settings. *Being* or *becoming* a *real* man is thus premised on prescriptive and normative frameworks of how he should behave, express himself, perform his manhood and ultimately live his life irrespective of his personal characteristics, qualities, capabilities, circumstances, needs and preferences (Plummer, 2010, 8; Biholar 2013, 8–9). Existing in relation to feminine identities (Reddock 2004, xxiii), the *real* man 'should not associate in any way with feminine characteristics' (Biholar 2013, 223–24; also Dowd 2008, 209; Plummer 2010, 6). Instead, he should subscribe to heteronormativity and assert control over women so that their subservient position within the gender hierarchy is preserved. Proving manhood according to the paradigms of hegemonic masculinity opens access to power, authority, control, privilege and status.

Applying an ethnographic case-study method suits the intention of the research in this chapter to offer a thorough understanding of the *life* of the gender policy in the national context of Dominica (Biholar 2013, 111). Information was gathered through forty semi-structured, in-depth interviews, three focus group discussions (FGDs), various participatory and unobtrusive field observations, informal discussions, text and audio data.[2] The field research was conducted in 2013. Therefore this chapter discusses the practice of the gender policy until that point in time.

DISEMPOWERED MEN?

'While acknowledging women's progress, finding a space today to have a meaningful conversation about the ways in which women continue to be systematically disadvantaged is often like navigating a minefield' (Robinson 2003, 253). For a gender policy addressing equality and women's issues to be attractive, the concerns about men and masculinities need to be visible and addressed publicly. The policy intentions to transform patriarchy and advance women's rights are thus legitimized by androcentrism. In fact, men use gender equality to exercise agency, negotiate their perceived loss of power and resist woman-centred feminism, by using a feminist agenda.

The DNGP, a strategy that is part of the feminist agenda for advancing women's rights and gender equality, brings to attention and engages with the discourse(s) on masculinities, and on boys and men. Acknowledging that some men rely on perceptions that 'there is a direct relationship between women's advancement and the displacement of, or worsening in the status of men' (DNGP 2006, 11) and feel 'threatened by the idea of equity between the sexes' (DNGP 2006, 11), the document emphasizes the 'collaboration between men and women' as essential for achieving gender equality (DNGP 2006, 10). In engaging with the concept of gender, it pinpoints the detrimental effect that asymmetric relations of power between women and men have on the sexes. According to the policy, 'central to the understanding of gender is the recognition of an inequity in existing male-female relations that are characterized by the subordination of women and the devaluation of anything or anyone defined as feminine. At the same time, traditional notions of masculinity and manhood can be a problem for men themselves, as well as for women' (DNGP 2006, 13).

Although the policy's goals and strategic objectives parallel the issues faced by women and men, the DNGP is concerned with, and places emphasis, on boys' and men's issues. For example, it recognizes that 'by 2005 the underperformance of males in the education system relative to that of females, coupled with a burgeoning academic and popular discourse around issues related to masculinity have raised serious concerns for policy makers and planners' (DNGP 2006, 62). The document identifies gender differentials in Dominican education performance as an alarming area, as it leads to 'a generation of males who are ill prepared to take on some of the occupations and positions which should be shared between men and women in society' (DNGP 2006, 83). Referring to men as an 'increasingly "disempowered" gender' in the education area, the policy raises the question of the construction of masculinity, rather than limiting the focus on educational achievement alone (DNGP 2006, 82–83). However, can we really talk about men as a 'disempowered' gender?

Men's 'disempowering' in the education area is not mirrored by reduced male participation in decision-making positions. Although Dominican women take more advantage of education opportunities than men, this does not translate fully into equal opportunities for political leadership roles. The Commonwealth of Dominica Millennium Development Goals Assessment of 2010 indicates that women occupy the majority (61.5%) of permanent public administration and managerial-level positions, such as permanent secretaries. However, they are the minority when it comes to parliamentary and decision-making processes (18.5%) (MDGs Assessment 2010, 33). This reveals the persistence of gendered occupational stereotypes where men occupy mostly leadership positions (Bailey 1997; Chevannes 2001) and women occupy administrative positions.

Indeed, boys' issues are real, as the policy text reflects as well. However, popular explanations that boys' disempowerment is linked to boys being neglected, while girls receive more attention and thus achieve more in school, trivialize the essence of the boys' issues and undermines the importance of the socialization process which supports the ideological dimension of gender relations. Basically, femininity is policed and the female is hyper-disciplined into *becoming* the docile mind and body, while at the same time nurturing a free, public-oriented masculinity. In truth, the privileging of males as the dominant actors in the gender hierarchies renders them (as well as females) vulnerable, although their vulnerability may manifest differently (Figueroa 2004). Boys' individual vulnerability does not undermine the connection of their masculine identity to status, power and material resources (Barriteau 2001, 26).

As Robinson indicates, 'Men are the paradigm of a citizen and women are included as citizens through their relationship with men' (Robinson 2003, 253). Concerns over the possible disruption of this model explain the popular appeal and 'tenacity of the claims of male marginalization' (Robinson 2003, 253).

The public interpretation is that women have arrived at a 'safe' space of equality while leaving men behind. They have secured educational and professional achievements, which give them the freedom to decide on their relations with men. In fact, as Robinson points out, 'woman questions' became 'so contentious that they can hardly be discussed' (Robinson 2003, 253). The reality of male marginalization claims and the backlash against feminist work has delegitimized feminist efforts for women's empowerment in the Caribbean by arguing for an equal focus or more focus on men and boys. Now that *gender* has replaced 'women' and 'woman questions', key concepts such as equity and empowerment risk being emptied of their feminist critical analysis. Moreover, as respondents indicated, a lack of understanding of the term gender and the novelty of a gender policy suggests the return to family. Yet, women run the risk of becoming invisible under this category, which is the patriarchal, domestic space where they have been historically relegated and confined to and thus, is problematic. This suggests a retreat from the feminist approach to advancing women's empowerment and gender equality, while nonetheless having in place feminist strategies like the DNGP.

SOCIETAL CONCERNS ABOUT MEN, BOYS AND MASCULINITIES

Societal concerns about men, boys and masculinities are confirmed by the research data. Respondents representing the Bureau of Gender Affairs (BGA), Caribbean Male Action Network (CariMAN), DACAMEN, the UWI Open Campus, and the Grammar School explained during interviews and FGDs that Dominican men are 'disempowered' as a consequence of the socialization process. The fixed constructions of femininity and masculinity, and the socialization along asymmetric sex-linked roles are more detrimental to boys than girls nowadays. One discussant explained the disadvantage faced by boys and consequently men:

> When I say disadvantage is that they [boys] do not really get the kind of attention that they should get. To me, we place more emphasis on the girls. At home, we would actually have rules for these girls. As a girl, you don't do this and you don't do that, and you need to do that. With the boys, oh … they are boys. From small, we let them have their way. They go out, they have their way. (Group interview, Grammar School teachers)

Another teacher supported this view. She stressed that the issue of boys' underachievement is a consequence of parents' attention and restrictions being disproportionately applied to girls. This translates into girls becoming more compliant and diligent (Group interview, Grammar School teachers). As a result, they pursue education, while boys enjoy freedom from rules and get an early sense of independence. They turn into men who 'are more laid back' and spend most of their time at the rum shop. The side effect of such asymmetry, as a male education officer at the Ministry of Education pointed out, is that 'females are taking equal opportunities and running away with [them]. So the males are left in the dark' (Interview, male policy officer, Ministry of Education, hereinafter MOE).

One reaps what one sows. As Chevannes stresses, this socialization and its resultant constructions of gender have asymmetric results (Chevannes 1999). Yet again, the data collected in Dominica confirm what was revealed by earlier theoretical insights into the connection between male privileging and academic performance (Figueroa 2004), the division of labour along sex lines (Chevannes 2001), hegemonic masculinity (Connell 1995; Plummer 2010) and peers' policing of manhood (Plummer 2010): that gender inequalities affect negatively not only girls, but also boys. Both girls and boys are rendered vulnerable within patriarchal arrangements of gender (Biholar 2013, 9), though their vulnerability may manifest differently and unequally. Boys' individual vulnerability does not undermine their ideological and institutional authority or the association of masculine identity with status, power and material resources (Barriteau 2001, 26). This leads to multiple discourses of empowerment and vulnerability for both women and men, which concur and compete.

For example, during consultations on the DNGP conducted by the BGA with Portsmouth grassroots women, informants expressed concern that men are at a disadvantage vis-à-vis women. Because the strides women have made are not paralleled by a similar advancement of men, some informants suggested that it is women's responsibility now to facilitate men's progress by backing up and allowing men to go further. 'We find our boys more back. We should push them. Not leave them like that, because women are more advanced' (Researcher's field observations, BGA grassroots consultation session, Portsmouth). Yet, other women from the same area rhetorically questioned this argument during a group interview: 'Men are left behind by whom, marginalized by whom?' (Group interview, grassroots women, Portsmouth). They pointed out that it is not about men being left out, but about the choices they make: their interest in short-term, more lucrative activities, such as hustling, gang affairs and drug trading, rather than going through the lengthy education system (Researcher's field notes, Roseau).

The encoded division of labour, which runs along gender roles, supports an economic system that allows men's involvement in 'the shadowy world of illegal activity' for income generation (DNGP 2006, 64) to the detriment of their achievement in education. Anchored in, and perpetuating underlying gender stereotypes, the economic system allows men to make a living out of minimal jobs, while it forces women to go through the education system in order to gain a decent living (Group interview, grassroots women, Portsmouth; FGD men, Roseau).

Actually, the Dominica case study confirms that the detrimental effect of gendered socialization on girls and women should not be disregarded. While expectations of girls and women are high, putting them under a constant pressure to excel in order to prove themselves, boys and men are entitled to positions of excellence. By virtue of being male, they have a *natural* entitlement to status, authority, respect, leisure, public presence and institutional power, whether in politics, the economy, the family or the sphere of religion. This historical privileging of males, as Figueroa (2004) explains, fuels boys' academic underperformance and underachievement. The education and socio-economic systems, both structured on and mirroring the unbalanced gender arrangement, allow the asymmetric construction of gender roles and expectations, and provide yet another reason for the frequently interrogated issue of male underachievement in the Caribbean. In other words, the structures in place enable boys to choose occupations, which are more lucrative and which do not require intensive schoolwork. Reminiscent of earlier scholarly work (Bailey 1997), Chevannes stresses that men persist in dominating positions of power:

> Girls choose the clerical and service areas, but boys choose the technical and vocational, the ones perceived as bringing higher levels of income – both types of choices determined by prevailing gender ideas; outside of it they generally fare better than girls, when employed, and undertake more own-account business and high risk crimes. (Chevannes 2001, 224)

These analyses compete with the male marginalization theory, which states,

> The description of Caribbean societies points to lower-strata men's marginal positions in the family, role reversal in a small but increasing number of households, boys' declining participation and performance in the educational system, the greater prospect of men inheriting their fathers' position in the social structure, the decline in the proportions of men in the highest-paying and most prestigious occupations and the decrease in men's earning power relative to women's especially in white collar occupations. (Miller 1991, 97)

These competing theoretical discourses are mirrored by the Dominican public discourse. While disputing women's struggles for equality, the idea that men are at a detriment because of women's advancement is a contested issue. The public discourse suggests in fact that the marginalization of men is illusory. On the one hand, the argument people commonly use to support male marginalization relates to women's achievement in education, pointing at the 40 women graduates at the UWI Open Campus in Dominica versus the three male graduates (Interview, 'Talking Gender' radio programme moderator). On the other hand, this argument focuses on the symptoms of what is actually a structural problem emerging from gender constructions and the socialization of ascribed, patriarchal and therefore asymmetric roles for women and men (Researcher's field notes, Roseau). Masculinities and men's and boy's responsibilities in society need to be understood in connection with the wider socio-economic context. The dynamics between the economy, family, and the construction of gender roles during the aftermath of Hurricane David are explained by respondents thus:

> The younger boys fall into the trap of earning money illegally. It is not so much the rising women, but the declining men. In terms of formal education, women increased their participation at a greater level than men. It is a decline of men as economic power…. Hurricane David broke up families, dislocated people. We're still in social rebuilding phase. People migrated, farms were destroyed, farms collapsed and the market crises in Europe also [had] influence. There was major dislocation. That aspect of society was not really addressed. A lot of people were put in a certain position because of this disruptive situation. The model of the father, however, weakened [and] became more dispersed. Mothers drifted to university teaching. Within the traditional model of father working, mother rearing of children, fathers declined, mothers surfaced and the family collapsed. Rebuilding houses was addressed. Farming was addressed. The main reconstruction of family was not addressed. (Interview, DACAMEN)

Thus, public opinion also reflects the understanding that the loss of power for men corresponds to Dominica's rapid loss of economic power. The slide of boys into illegality appears to be a consequence of their fathers' loss of economic power, especially in farming, after natural disasters caused by Hurricane David in 1979. This disrupted not only the economy, but men's families and occupational identities. As the respondent stressed, 'It is not so much the rising women, but the declining men' (Interview, DACAMEN). Such multiple, competing discourses highlight the importance of attending to, through national gender policies, competing interpretations of and approaches to the role of men in challenging gender inequality and achieving social change (Barriteau 2000).

CONTESTATIONS OF GENDER

The shift from women to gender, using the concept gender in the title of the policy, the focus on men and the change in the Bureau's name set the ground for policy implementation. One respondent from BGA clearly indicated, 'Perhaps if we didn't introduce gender, perhaps the policy wouldn't have been passed' (Interview, director BGA). Another respondent explained, 'When it was the Bureau of Women's Affairs (BWA), the name alone would not encourage men to go. Their concerns were not attended as they liked' (Interview, teachers' union member).

> So it was felt that to reach [to men], you need to really have men be a change in focus. So men's organizations, women groups as well, even the National Council of Women were already thinking: 'let us have a focus on [family]'. Perhaps some of them weren't quite understanding of the whole term gender, not looking for why a gender policy. It's just that some of them were thinking: 'There's concern that our men are being disadvantaged, there's concerns of violence and perhaps that due to women achieving and men feeling threatened'. Those were the type of discussions going on [when deciding on the gender policy]. (Interview, director BGA)

In essence, the methods mentioned above emerge as a feminist strategy to advance gender equality in a contradictory terrain where gender is still interpreted as referring to women's issues only, instead of an 'arena of tensions' (Connell and Messerschmidt 2005, 853), hierarchies and power relations between and among women and men. Certainly, this does not translate into an overall transformation of power between women and men. The DNGP disputes women's enjoyment of equality by pointing out, for example, that the gender differentials in education do not translate into gender differentials in the distribution of poverty (DNGP, Section 5.4, 2006, 88). In its preamble, the policy indicates that although the status of women is 'relatively good' (DNGP 2006, 61), 'visible achievement of successful women masks the reality of those who are unable to break out of the cycle of childbearing, unstable relationships with men and endless poverty. It is evident that the majority of women labor long hours both inside and outside of the home, tolerating incredible uncertainties' (Mohammed and Perkins 1999 in DNGP 2006, 61).

Consequently, by replacing women with gender, the policy enables a space for multiple, and competing, masculinist interpretations of women's and men's gendered realities to challenge feminist ones, and, in implementation, to delegitimize feminist interpretations of the gender relations of power in the policy document and in public discourse. Gender thus offers a space for men to join the equality struggle. Once attention is given to men's issues and their perceived 'disempowerment', a discussion of gender equality including women as well may not be that controversial.

MASCULINIST RESISTANCES TO FEMINIST STRATEGIES FOR GENDER EQUALITY

Concerns have been expressed about the name change from the Bureau of Women's Affairs to Gender Affairs. Many perceive it as a surface initiative, by which the content and the attitudes of the bureau remain the same – unilaterally dedicated to women's issues. CariMAN respondents explained, 'We may have had women affairs before, but then there's still some men who still do not see it as if it is gender; the perception is that the BGA is really catering for women' (FGD CariMAN). Yet again the data confirm that by perceiving gender as simply referring to women and men without understanding its hierarchical power dynamics and tensions, it leads for women to a *jeopardized equality* or an equality stripped of its equity dimensions. Addressing gender inequality requires more than simply treating women and men the same. It is also about recognizing and addressing the differences between their gendered realities and ensuring equality of opportunities and results. Equality appears to be more acceptable and understood because it is seemingly less biased against men. However, equality entails a three-pronged model of approaches to ensure justice that comprises, but also goes beyond, (1) *formal equality* of identical treatment. As human beings 'free and equal in dignity and rights' (UDHR 1948, Article 1) women and men should be afforded equal rights in and before the law. Nonetheless, given the differences between women and men, their different contextual positioning and experiences, identical treatment may reinforce inequalities. (2) Equity approaches that take into consideration de facto life realities should be used so that both men and women can enjoy equal opportunities to material resources and can equally achieve results. Therefore, *equity* is part of ensuring *substantive equality*. (3) Furthermore, ideological barriers usually impede taking up opportunities – even when they are afforded – and thus achieving results, and consequently can foster indirect discrimination. As I mentioned elsewhere, full realization of 'equality is achieved only when social structures and power relations that perpetuate subordination are modified' (Biholar 2013, 25). Opportunities, institutions and systems are 'grounded in historically determined male paradigms of power and life patterns' (CEDAW General Recommendation, 24, 2004, para. 10). Therefore, the transformation of asymmetric relations of power between women and men (transformative equality) is an approach that must be considered and taken concomitantly with formal and substantive equality (Biholar 2013, 24–25). Yet again, although the DNGP reflects the importance of using both equality and equity approaches for advancing gender justice, misrepresentations of gender and equality dominate public discourses, negatively impacting the interpretation and practice of the policy.

The Bureau has been heavily criticized that although it added gender to its name, in reality, it does not look at gender, because it has no male staff and does not involve men in its work. One male activist said, 'We hear a lot about women, but what about men?' He used a rather sarcastic tone to talk about feminist work, the BGA and the gender policy, implying that 'women's gain is commensurate with men's loss' (Robinson 2003, 253). In explaining that the Bureau is not concerned with men's issues, he mentioned that despite taking a gender name and pushing for a gender policy, 'they still are a bunch of feminists' (Interview, sexual minority rights activist). Such negative connotations attached to the notion of feminism indicates the hostility to feminism within Dominican society. In struggling for the maintenance of power, feminists and their work are discredited (Connell and Messerschmidt 2005, 852) to the point that many hide their feminist identity behind the title of women's rights activists in order to circumvent the backlash (Interview, former DNCW president).

The significance of the Bureau's work is minimalized within the governance institutional infrastructure. The Bureau has little power to determine the priority given to its initiatives, including the DNGP. It shows that misunderstandings of gender and resistances to feminist strategies are reflected in the practice of the gender policy. The policy is treated much as gender is conceived and treated – as 'an outside runner to the political stage on a "minority position"' (Mohammed 2014, 23). Furthermore, the Bureau is one of those governmental departments which are insufficiently funded and to which human resources are sparsely allocated from the wider governmental financial and human pool. Consequently, initiatives spearheaded by the Bureau, such as the gender policy implementation, do not represent an immediate and tangible interest for government officials. As Mohammed explained,

> [The] use of the term gender instead of women in public documents has not convinced majority popular opinion that it is inclusive of the gendered condition faced by men themselves, nor that women are capable of creating policies and programs that enhance the economic fortunes or more efficient governance that might ultimately benefit all. (Mohammed 2014, 5)

Clearly, the notion of gender creates a contentious space of multiple interpretations and contradictions, making it 'a social category that is ripe for manipulation' (Comments, Mohammed 2013). As a result, the gender policy opens up a space of strategic political manoeuvre, in terms of satisfying certain types of constituencies at a certain time and place, without the government taking any concrete, sustainable action – failing the decades of Caribbean feminist analysis and advocacy. (Researcher's field notes 2013; Interview, member of DNCW & the Ministry of Agriculture (hereinafter MOA) gender focal point (hereinafter GFP)).

MALE ALLIES AND THEIR GENDER NEGOTIATIONS WITHIN THE MASCULINIST STATE

The 'what about men' question prompted men's organizations engaging with concepts of gender and equality. CariMAN, is a regional male organization. The organization's purpose is 'to provide a forum for discussion on masculinity; design and develop interventions to facilitate communication around gender and manhood, and to share best practices' (Holmes 2011). In order to achieve these goals, CariMAN undertakes 'a multi-sectoral approach to engage boys and men, and individuals and groups who work with them through different learning methods and partnering with existing male and female groups and organizations' (Holmes 2011, 2).

In its work, CariMAN takes account of and builds on the strides and experiences of women's groups. Executive board members of CariMAN explained that the organization entered the gender equality discourses through the alliance with women's rights, building up on women groups' experiences, and through work on the elimination of violence. In fact, it seems that CariMAN takes women's work and their achievements as models of action for working on men's issues.

> When we look at the women's groups, we must applaud that the women have made good strides. They have succeeded in many areas and hence, probably, the poor perception of males as related to gender. Because even the women admit [that that's] why gender has been mentioned all the time about women's rights. Even if the women have made that much strides, have succeeded, we are starting afresh. Other than that, we are starting on our own to collaborate with them. They can help us make the strides that they made, how they got to where they got to and we could get there and have collaborative work together.... They have made good head way, hence the reason why I think it is even more forceful on men to come in line with women. (FGD, CariMAN)

It cannot be overlooked that the account also points fingers at the success of women as shadowing the presence of men in the gender space, which has facilitated the misinterpretations of gender. Rather than opposing feminist advancements, CariMAN uses the space that feminism has created to accommodate men within. For that, they not only partner with women's organizations, such as the DNCW and the BGA, but also the Planned Parenthood Association or the MOE for the gender policy implementation in order to give men a voice within the gender equality conversation. Members of the CariMAN executive board explained,

> We've been taught in our culture that men are supposed to be 'macho', and that is what is messing up most of our men ... that they become very weak in terms of trying to be strong. So when you confront [them] by violence, because they are confronted by violence, they can't deal with it because it would make them seem less a man. So the men are saying the gender policy is gonna turn things around for us as men, and give us a voice that is better heard and we'll go for it. So I believe the fact that the identity of men in the policy is more palatable, and I can say basically even for myself as a male. (FGD, CariMAN)

The policy thus creates a platform for men to challenge traditionally ascribed masculine roles, debunk stereotypes related to the constructions of masculinity and un-silence men's issues. It recognizes that men undergo structural discrimination as well, and that they can be vulnerable within a masculinist environment.

It becomes clear that being central to the patriarchal arrangement of gender, men cannot see beyond the marginal (women) moving towards their *dominating* space, and once near, they feel disempowered. This indicates that within a patriarchal context, men struggle to occupy the position of power that they feel they have allegedly lost and use an equality discourse to highlight it (Researcher's field notes, Roseau). Within this sexist context, CariMAN carefully negotiates the feminist approach, and engages with the gender equality discourse.

> We as CariMAN, as a male organization, need to be careful because some of the reaction we get is that people may say CariMAN is giving more power to the women because when you say: listen, look at the relationship with women, stop violence and so on, those who do not understand it will say: look at what they doing to us, they talking about women, women, women.... That is why we have to be so careful of how we bring it up. But at the same time we have to educate the population what is the focus here, we need to educate [on] what is gender. (FGD CariMAN)

Ironically, not only women but men also fall victim to a context in which the balance of power weighs heavier on men's side. What emerges is that for both women and men, the policy is an instrument of negotiation within the state, and between the state and society, still androcentric in readings of women's rights.. Not only women, but also men are now struggling for power in a masculinist environment. They use gender equality to exercise agency, negotiate their loss of power and resist woman-centred feminism by using a feminist agenda.

Competing interests become clear as CariMAN builds on the feminist agenda. For women, and the Bureau in particular, as the central implementer of the policy, the gender policy and the alliances with men for its implementation become a space for bargaining in order to continue the work on women's issues. To make a policy on equality and women's issues attractive, the concerns about men and masculinities need to be visible and addressed publicly. It thus appears that androcentrism legitimizes the project of transforming patriarchy and advancing women's rights intended in the national policy document.

THE *LIFE* OF THE GENDER POLICY – DIVERGENT POLICY PRACTICES

Clearly, the gender policy provides a space for the regional discourse on equality and gender justice for women and men, which is meant to influence state policy. However, this discourse becomes about who is more marginalized, while it is clear that materially, ideologically and structurally power has not shifted yet, or rather it is far from being balanced, even in relation to the implementation of the policy.

In reality, the policy is neither given much attention nor carefully considered among relevant stakeholders in the country, let alone practised. What becomes then of the DNGP implementation process? Personal gender consciousness and commitment of individuals in particular positions in certain departments or agencies of the government or in civil society organizations guide professional interests and priorities, and become factors that give 'life' to the policy. One respondent explained, 'The policy on its own is a beautiful document. What drives the policy is the people who are implementing it' (Interview, member of DNCW & MOA GFP). For example, at the time of drafting the gender policy, the Minister of Social Services, Community Development and Gender Affairs understood the societal importance of a gender policy and supported its approval by the country's cabinet. Such political will proved to be a crucial ingredient for the 'push' for a gender policy in Dominica (Interview, PS Ministry of Social Services). Moreover, the Bureau was viewed, among civil society and government circles, to be one person who took the work of policy implementation as personal, and this was explained as the driving force behind the gender policy initiative. Therefore the personal commitment of the BGA director to the policy implementation process reveals the format that feminist activism tends to take within the state apparatus in Dominica: *the political becomes personal.*

The marginality of the state's gender machinery and the oversight of the DNGP by state actors require feminist activists within the gender machinery (institutional) to engage in extensive personal networking and advocacy (personal) in order to be able to give life to the gender policy. Respondents explained that the Bureau worked hard, 'pushed and pushed' and largely disseminated the policy, especially at the ministerial level (Interview, civil society activist and top-level civil servant, Ministry of Health, National Drug Abuse Prevention, hereinafter MOH). The MOE GFP confirmed that the 'team' of gender focal points had numerous meetings and consultations spearheaded by the director of the BGA in an effort to 'get the gender policy off the ground' (Interview, MOE GFP). Moreover, it was those that had a prior awareness of the importance of a gender policy stemming from personal conditioning and interests in advancing gender equality that facilitated the life of the policy.

> It was disseminated everywhere, as far as I know, to a lot of ministries. They [BGA] had meetings with different sectors. Because of my involvement, I'd go to the meetings. The way you are socialized and conditioned ... if I hear 'gender policy' I'd run because of my background. However, someone who never heard of the gender policy would hesitate before they participate. (Interview, MOH)

Lack of such personal conditioning, interests, priorities or circumstances makes the policy *a forgotten text gathering dust on a shelf*, although it has been made available. It seems to be retrieved from the shelf if and when circumstances so require. It is known if and when it is required to be known, which reveals the contradictory condition of the policy as an instrument of action. For example, the policy text becomes useful to support fundraising proposals. Drawing on local and regional documents to frame such proposals, and particularly referring to national gender policy and the data therein, would raise the chances for gaining grants (Researcher's field notes 2013). The policy gains significance when meetings focused on it summon the participation of governmental officials. For example, one respondent confessed,

> Actually we have a meeting tomorrow to discuss the gender policy.... I'm going to bring it home to read it in preparation for the meeting with the consultant tomorrow.... I wasn't aware of it. I have to read up on the gender policy to see what it says. (Interview, top-level civil servant, MOE)

Obviously, interests, priorities and personal conditioning can open up opportunities for the implementation process. These contradictory accounts are indicative of the contradictory life of, and value given by, different stakeholders in Dominica to the DNGP. Despite the proposition in the policy document itself that the institutional framework should entail policy implementation that is 'an important concern for all citizens', and the removal of 'the popular idea that national policy and plans, when formulated, will gather dust on a shelf' (DNGP 2006, Section 1.6, 16), the policy is generally limited to a written text only. It becomes a living instrument at the level of practitioners' reality (civil society representatives or civil servants) only when it is required or when it can help achieve a goal, depending on interests, priorities, personal conditioning or circumstances.

As indicated at the MOE, the visit of an international gender consultant and the urgency of meetings and consultations for the updating and acceleration of the policy implementation became one of those circumstances when the policy was conveniently taken out from the shelf and brought to life. It encouraged decision makers at the MOE to learn about the policy and appropriate its content when it was necessary. Conversely, the lack of interest, priority, circumstance or personal conditioning may impose blocks to the policy practice. The Dominica case study confirms therefore that the state engages in what Mohammed coined as 'politics of convenience'. In practice, governments and their representatives do not just deliver policy, rather they 'seem to be invested in a democracy of convenience – whether that convenience benefits the individual politician, or the collective sentiment of an influential group' (Mohammed 2014, 23).

Evidently, the policy represents multiple priorities and divergent practices. They consist of both personal and institutional interests, and understandings of what is necessary to be achieved in reality. Once approved and launched, the policy has a life of its own. As aforementioned, the Dominican government contracted an international gender specialist to update the policy so that life realities of constituents were acknowledged and incorporated in the policy, making it 'more relevant' (Director BGA, Dominica GIS 2013). The policy practice seems to involve a continuous updating of the policy text according to the lived realities on the ground and to alliances, priorities and entrenched interests.

The policy reflects, therefore, a combination between policy goals on paper, and a vivid update of those goals to resonate with current realities. Its text becomes a system of representation of lived realities. Resonance of the policy with such realities renders its implementation feasible. What the policy provides therefore is a narrative of what has occurred in practice, instead of being a guideline for the practice. As a consequence, it is the realities of relevant stakeholders on the ground that circumscribe and determine the policy practice, rather than the policy text itself.

CONCLUSION

Lessons for the Caribbean feminist advocacy for national gender policies should take into account the fact that policy intentions do not necessarily translate into policy practice (Mosse 2004). Successful implementation of gender policies requires, in essence, the acquisition and production of meaning at the levels of governmental agencies, civil society organizations, and individuals as the policy beneficiaries. This makes it possible to internalize, process and practice the policy itself (Biholar 2013). In the particular context of Dominica, the gender policy acquires and generates meaning by incorporating in its text concerns about masculinities, men and boys. This creates a policy resonant to the concerns in the country. Moreover, such an approach opens up the understanding of gender as being inclusive of men. The chapter argued that such understanding of gender enabled a space for multiple and competing interpretations of women's and men's gendered realities and relations of power in both the policy document and in the public discourse. Therefore, (a) interpretations of men as disempowered and silenced in their gendered experience, coexisting with perceptions of men as the powerful sex and masculinities as the gender identities associated with power; (b) interpretations of women as advanced and empowered at the detriment of men, competing with understandings of women as the subject of gender inequality, still having a subordinate position; (c) male organizations' priority to provide spaces for men to discuss their issues in order to 'un-silence' them, prevailing over men's critique and transformation of their unequal status, competing with (d) men organizations' priority to ally with women activists to transform men's unequal status, form the discursive terrain which shaped the process of policy implementation in Dominica. This confirmed that policy implementation is not a single, homogenous process. Instead, it is a complex discursive terrain shaped by diverse social, economic and political forces (Li 2007). Alliances, competing, entrenched interests, networks, priorities – either personal or institutional – convenience and negotiations, rather than the gender policy text, guide its practice. Implementing gender policies seems to be rather a continuous updating of the policy text so that it represents the reality on the ground. To answer Mosse's question, practice indeed produces policy.

While belonging to the transnational feminist agenda for women's empowerment and gender justice, the gender policy represents a space for men's contestation of women's inequality. The chapter argues that the social category of gender used by the policy becomes an entry for men to join the equality discourse. It equips men with agency to pay attention to their identity, voice their issues and negotiate with the patriarchal state for reconsideration of their societal position. This is because the masculinist nature of the state and society, through the centring of men, partly obscured their gendered experiences and condemned them to invisibility.

The Dominica case study reveals that gender represents a space for strategic manoeuvers, enabling 'men to feel less threatened and speak about their issues' (Interview, MOH). The policy goals of gender equality, however, are not necessarily met through the shift in focus to men and masculinity. Although women's advancements are visible and men are included in the gender equality discourse, the hegemony of patriarchal ideologies and asymmetric power relations remains invisible, hence difficult to grasp. The discourse surrounding the policy implementation has become that women are dominant and men are marginal, even though data reveals otherwise. The competing interpretations and interests entailed by the policy in practice have led, in fact, to the perpetuation rather than eradication of 'asymmetries of access to status, power and material resources' (Barriteau 2001, 26). Shifts in material resources must correspond to shifts in ideologies in order to challenge structural inequalities and appease gender tensions (Barriteau 2001, 28; CEDAW, Ciudad Juarez Report, 2005, para. 35).

When interests, priorities and conveniences are coupled with fixed understandings of gender constructions, asymmetric gender relations and resilient misreadings of gender, we should not be taken by surprise by resistances to the implementation of the gender policy as an important state instrument. It is only when society truly addresses rigid constructions of femininities, masculinities, and power imbalances, can gender justice be achieved and real transformation of gender relations brought about.

NOTES

1. The notions of (policy) implementation and practice are used interchangeably throughout this chapter.

2. The research respondents are indicated in the research report Biholar, Ramona. "Politics, Power and Gender Justice in the Anglophone Caribbean: Women's Understandings of Politics, Experiences of Political Contestation and the Possibilities for Gender Transformation" IDRC Research Report 106430-001, by Principal Investigator Gabrielle Jamela Hosein and Lead Researcher Jane Parpart. Ottawa, ON Canada: International Development Research Centre, 2014.

REFERENCES

Bailey, Barbara. 1998. *Introduction to Curriculum Studies*. Edited by Charmaine McKenzie. Distance Education Centre, University of the West Indies.

Barriteau, Eudine. 2001. *The Political Economy of Gender in the Twentieth-Century Caribbean*. Hampshire, New York: Palgrave.

———. 2000. 'Re-examining Issues of "Male Marginalisation" and "Masculinity" in the Caribbean: The Need for a New Policy Approach'. Barbados: Centre for Gender and Development Studies, University of the West Indies.

Biholar, Ramona. 2013. 'Transforming Discriminatory Sex Roles and Gender Stereotyping. The Implementation of Article 5 (a) CEDAW for the realisation of women's right to be free from gender based violence in Jamaica'. Utrecht: School of Human Rights Research/Antwerp: Intersentia.

Chevannes, Barry. 1999. *What We Sow and What We Reap. Problems in the Cultivation of Male Identity in Jamaica*. Kingston, Jamaica: The Grace, Kennedy Foundation.

———. 2001. *Learning to Be A Man. Culture, Socialization and Gender Identity in Five Caribbean Communities*. Kingston, Jamaica: University of the West Indies Press.

Commonwealth of Dominica Millennium Development Goals Assessment of 2010.

Commonwealth of Dominica. 2006. National Policy and Action Plan for Gender Equity and Equality in the Commonwealth of Dominica.

Commonwealth of Dominica, Government Information Service. 2013. 'Bureau of Gender Affairs Reviews National Policy for Gender and Equality', July 2, 2013.

Connell, Raewyn. 1995. *Masculinities*. Sydney: Allen and Unwin.

Connell, Raewyn and James W. Messerschmidt. 2005. 'Hegemonic Masculinity: Rethinking the Concept'. *Gender and Society* 19(6): 829–59.

Demetriou, D.Z. 2001. 'Connell's Concept of Hegemonic Masculinity: A Critique'. *Theory and Society* 30(3): 337–61.

Dowd, Nancy. 2008. 'Masculinities and Feminist Legal Theory'. *Wisconsin Journal of Law, Gender and Society* 23(2): 201–48.

Figueroa, Mark. 2004. 'Male Privileging and Male "Academic Underperformance" in Jamaica', in *Interrogating Caribbean Masculinities. Theoretical and Empirical Analyses*. Edited by Rhoda E. Reddock, 137–66. Kingston, Jamaica: University of the West Indies.

Holmes, Thomas. 2011. Speech at the Launching of CariMAN (Dominica) Chapter, June 3, 2011.

Kimmel, Michael. 2004. 'Men, Masculinities and Development', the 2004 Lucille Mathurin Mair Public Lecture, March 11, 2004.

Lewis, Linden. 2004. 'Caribbean Masculinity at the *Fin de Siècle*' In *Interrogating Caribbean Masculinities. Theoretical and Empirical Analyses*. Edited by Rhoda Reddock, 244–66. Kingston, Jamaica: University of the West Indies Press.

Li, Tania. 2007. *The Will to Improve. Governmentality, Development, and the Practice of Politics*. Durham: Duke University Press.

Miller, Errol. 1991. *Men at Risk*. Kingston: Jamaica Publishing House.

Mohammed, Patricia. 2014. 'Gender Politics and Global Democracy: Insights from the Caribbean', in *Global Democracy: An Intercultural Debate*, edited by Jan Aart Scholte, University of Warwick, Building Global Democracy Project (Manuscript at Palgrave Macmillan, Elgar and Zed).

Mosse, David. 2004. 'Is Good Policy Unimplementable? Reflections on the Ethnography of Aid Policy and Practice'. *Development and Change* 35: 639–71.

Nurse, Keith. 2004. 'Masculinities in Transition: Gender and the Global Problem-tique', in *Interrogating Caribbean Masculinities. Theoretical and Empirical*

Analyses. Edited by Rhoda Reddock, 3–37. Kingston, Jamaica: University of the West Indies Press.

Plummer, David and Stephen Geofroy. 2010. 'When Bad Is Cool: Violence and Crime as Rites of Passage to Manhood'. *Caribbean Review of Gender Studies* Issue 4, p. 17.

Reddock, Rhoda. 2004. 'Interrogating Caribbean Masculinities: An Introduction', in *Interrogating Caribbean Masculinities. Theoretical and Empirical Analyses*, edited by Rhoda Reddock, xiii–xxxiv. Kingston, Jamaica: University of the West Indies Press.

Robinson, Tracy. 2003. 'Beyond the Bill of Rights: Sexing the Citizen', in *Confronting Power, Theorizing Gender. Interdisciplinary Perspectives in the Caribbean*, edited by Eudine Barriteau, 231–61. Kingston, Jamaica: University of the West Indies Press.

Rutherford, Jonathan. 1988. 'Who's That Man', in *Male Order: Unwrapping Masculinity*, edited by Rowena Chapman and Jonathan Rutherford, 21–67. London: Lawrence & Wishart.

Chapter 8

The National Policy on Gender Equality of Jamaica

(En)Gendering Equity in Neo-liberal Times

Maziki Thame and Dhanaraj Thakur

INTRODUCTION

In 2011, the Jamaican government approved the National Policy for Gender Equality (NPGE). Among other things, the policy sets a vision for gender equality and equity across all aspects of public and private life. It provides guidance for developing solutions to specific problems such as gender-based violence, the limited political representation of women in local and central governments and the unequal social and economic status of men and women. Implicit in our examination of the NPGE is the question, what should such policies be expected to achieve as tools for effecting gender justice? We find Eudine Barriteau's argument that gender justice eschews hierarchies of men in relation to women, and of masculinities and femininities, a useful starting point (Barriteau 2004, 438).

We begin from the premise that in addition to contesting existing structural sources of gender-based inequities, gender policies should seek to change notions of masculinity and femininity that sustain patriarchy. This chapter seeks an understanding of the relationship between the NPGE and the patriarchal state through a critical reading of the policy, its aims, ideologies and strategies. We examine the intersection of the dominance of neo-liberalism in the region, with its increasing emphasis on gender as an aspect of liberal human rights, and the contradictions that emerge within that frame. The NPGE emerged when neo-liberalism was cemented in Jamaica and was justified as part of the state's economic imperatives, rather than an initiative to increase rights, freedoms and social justice. This is not to suggest that economic imperatives are not critical to gendered power and to realizing 'justice' and freedoms more broadly, but that the framing of what constitutes development can itself be problematic and detrimental to gender justice.

We argue that the NPGE's potential for promoting gender equality is limited, even while we note that the process behind the final policy document did not seek to imitate prevailing gender ideologies. It was the result of an extensive consultative process, but it did not include many of the alternative views of gender relations that were part of its initial consultations, such as alternative notions of sexuality or women's rights which are also present in national gender troubles. This, we suggest, points to an opportunity to expand the discourse on gender relations in Jamaica by building on the initial consultative process behind the NPGE. This can be part of an overall review of the policy that would perhaps go further in promoting gender equality in the country. Among the concerns of this chapter is how contemporary politics, embedded ideologically in neo-liberalism, can reinforce masculinism and gender inequality while simultaneously providing a public policy airing for gender equality.

BACKGROUND

The State and the NPGE

The NPGE of Jamaica emerged as an initiative from the Bureau of Women's Affairs (BWA).[1] The process began in 2004 with a series of public consultations on the substance of what was to eventually become the NPGE. The bureau was supported in this regard by an advisory body (the Gender Advisory Committee),[2] which the government established. The policy was approved in 2011, which meant that both major political parties in Jamaica, during their respective tenures in government, supported the policy. The bureau, though dedicated to matters of gender equality, exists in the midst of the patriarchal state and is curtailed in its powers with respect to the larger power of the state. The policy is meant 'to transform gender ideologies, inequitable gender relations and gendered governance practices at all levels of public sector organizations'.[3] It privileges a multisector approach with an emphasis on bridging the public/private divide, but the policy is directed mainly at the public sphere. Among the NPGE's three objectives, two are focused on behaviour change at institutional and public levels. Its objectives are:

- To reduce all forms of gendered discrimination and promote greater gender equality and social justice;
- To strengthen institutional mechanisms and develop the skills and tools required to mainstream gender in cultural, social, economic and political institutions, structures and systems and

- To promote sustainable behaviour change and improve organizational effectiveness and the capacity of public sector entities to develop, implement and monitor gender responsive plans, projects, programmes and policies (Bureau of Women's Affairs 2011, 19).

The NPGE approaches change in the public sector through gender mainstreaming, the implementation of gender-responsive costing and budgeting, gender-aware monitoring and evaluation and the establishment of GFPs throughout the sector. GFPs are expected to direct public bodies towards gender sensitivity and planning for gender equality. The GFPs do not have any specific powers of implementation and they have no resources available to them. Taitu Heron, who acted as a GFP at the Planning Institute of Jamaica (PIOJ), argued that their success is dependent upon the specific dynamics of the public entities and the mechanisms of support within them (Heron August 29, 2013, Interview with Thame). One hundred and nine GFPs exist to date. Faith Webster, then executive director of the BWA, indicated that while they are eager and diligent, the momentum can be lost. She argued that institutionalization is required since currently there is an emphasis on specific people, which raises the problem of sustainability (Webster, August 14, 213, Interview with Thame).

The People and the Problem of Representation

The bureau engaged in a wide consultative process in the making of the NPGE, including NGOs, community groups, the medical fraternity, security forces and faith-based organizations. The bureau also observed Jamaica's commitments to international and regional bodies and agreements on gender matters. At the same time, most of the stakeholders we interviewed about the NPGE formulation felt the process was top-down and largely manufactured by the BWA. This is perhaps not unexpected as other research on policymaking processes in Jamaica suggests that they are often centralized and exclude marginalized groups (Acosta 2006).

The limited voice of 'grassroots' Jamaicans in the consultative process has also been a concern. Women's advocate Linnette Vassell[4] argues that this was inevitable given the nature of the participatory process and its emphasis on a written product (Vassell August 16, 2013, Interview with Thame). Clinton Hutton, who participated in the consultative process as a scholar of gender, felt that women's groups dominated the process, and that specifically middle-class and educated female voices prevailed (Hutton August 23, 2013, Interview with Thame). In that regard, Vassell concluded that the policy would favour women across class, but that middle-class women would benefit especially given that this strata has the greatest access to decision making

(Vassell August 16, 2013, Interview with Thame). Hutton held that the policy's focus on the state ensured that those women closest to the centre of power would benefit most (Hutton August 23, 2013, Interview with Thame). Indeed, these types of arrangements determine which issues are prioritized within the policy.

Moreover, the consultative process was marked by the under-representation of men, which resulted in insufficient attention to their concerns and interests (Hutton August 23, 2013; Heron August 29, 2013, Interviews with Thame). Where men were represented, Vassell posits that the focus tended to emphasize male marginalization and that this had to be contended. She argues that it was difficult to have a conversation around that issue because the men would not respond to contrary data. Masculinity was not seen as a problem, and it was on the offensive. She argues that male marginalization became the source through which to incorporate men, and consequently consultations did not deal with how men's power constrains the behaviour of women (Vassell August 16, 2013, Interview with Thame) and, we could add, men themselves.

We note that the policy does not aim to end patriarchy, but since it is a policy on gender equality we expect that at its core, it should address male domination in Jamaica, including how it impacts the position of vulnerable men such as homosexuals and those in the working class. In exploring the extent to which the policy meets such expectations, it is important to consider the ways the policy negotiates the patriarchal reality in which it exists, as well as the broader socio-economic environment, including the dominance of neo-liberalism. It is important also to think through the ways in which the policy reproduces or seeks to change broad societal norms.

A NOTE ON PATRIARCHY IN JAMAICA

Our concern with patriarchy in this chapter is with the ways in which men dominate the private and public spheres, and in which patriarchal masculinity is privileged and hegemonic in Jamaica. We are concerned specifically with the state, its insertion into the private sphere through legislation and the ways in which legislation and policies that challenge unequal gender relations can explode patriarchy. Along with the nuclear family, the state is historically and contemporaneously the most critical purveyor of patriarchy. Its institutions, practices and discourses are inextricably bound up with the prerogatives of manhood (Brown 1992). The Jamaican state is no different. This is attached to its relationship with religion and the church, business and other interest groups and how it expresses Jamaican cultural norms. We begin from the premise that Jamaica, like most modern societies, is patriarchal. Indeed, we observe in parliamentary debates on matters related to women's rights, political representatives' keenness to silence women's needs or frame them within economic imperatives of the state, hide men' s unequal access to power and protect heterosexuality, even when it is violent. In this way, the state helps to reproduce hegemonic masculinity. What, therefore, should we expect when the state engages in the production of a national policy on gender equality? Even though the NPGE framers and stakeholders may be undeniably committed to gender equality, implementing it becomes an important challenge when the state is itself steeped in patriarchal understandings and practices.

The Jamaican state's male-centredness is evidenced most powerfully by the over-representation of men in government – in 2013 only 14% of parliamentarians were women. At the same time, it is important to note that a woman, Portia Simpson Miller, headed the Jamaican government. This does not however detract from the fact that the state is ideologically male-centred and patriarchal in orientation. In addition, the Jamaican state is representative of, and central to, male dominance in broader society. Hence even women in parliament often betray patriarchal sentiment and their prerogatives remain limited or curtailed by patriarchal norms. In discussions on the Sexual Offences Act for instance, Olivia 'Babsy' Grange, MP and former minister responsible for women's affairs, implored women, mothers, girlfriends, wives and sisters thus: 'You know your men best, you know the things that bother them…. We know that women have the power to stop a lot of the crimes taking place'. Women, she said, should be 'more proactive in helping to stop and solve crime' (Jamaica Hansard 2009, 268). Patriarchal sentiments ultimately find a way of imposing the burden of responsibility for male 'misbehavior' on women.

We argue in this chapter that the patriarchy of the Jamaican state is most concerned with the domination of a specific group of men – middle-class, heterosexual men – over society. From its inception, the postcolonial state was captured by the Jamaican middle-class and brown male,[5] and control over it was later extended to the black middle-class male. Middle-class masculinity imposed itself as *the* legitimate power base within the state through symbolic manipulation and violence whenever it deemed necessary. The patriarchal character of the state was therefore determined by that class and its vision of respectability.[6] It currently faces direct challenges from the masculinity of the urban underclass, which often uses violence against the state and within informal structures of power in politics and the economy.[7] This challenge emerged from early independence; but the state now finds itself unsure of its powers over that segment of the population.[8] The increasing presence of women in important sectors of the economy also presently challenges patriarchy. Keeping these challenges in mind, this chapter will question whether there is a crisis or resilience of patriarchy existing in Jamaica, and how the state deals with these challenges, especially considering the adoption of policies such as the NPGE and other legislative manoeuvres in favour of women. We will also explore how and which groups become beneficiaries of this process.

PATRIARCHY AND GENDER EQUALITY
IN NEO-LIBERAL TIMES

The NPGE is constructed on the premise that 'Jamaica is an egalitarian society, which values equality and dignity of each citizen by affording and facilitating their human rights' (Bureau of Women's Affairs 2011, 19). This is a curious position given that it is a policy meant to address the problem of gender inequality in Jamaica. It blinds us to the deep inequities which prevail in Jamaica, be they around class, race or gender matters. The liberal foundations which this proclaims, and which Jamaica as a nation claims to uphold, are not consolidated. If the policy is built on this premise, how is it then justified? While it claims to be dedicated to a human rights framework, the policy is most critically grounded in a desire for development. It claims, 'The cornerstone of Jamaica's development is our people; therefore eliminating barriers to equal participation at all levels of society for women and men will translate into meaningful and sustainable human and national development' (Bureau of Women's Affairs 2011, 7).

The NPGE is rationalized as contributing to the larger goal of national development. It states:

> A national policy on gender would encourage the Jamaican community to recognize that development, as a multidimensional process, must involve the reduction of gender inequalities as an integral element of achieving broad based equitable growth. This would contribute to good governance by highlighting and integrating the concerns of women and men in all of the Government's development policies, plans and programmes. (Bureau of Women's Affairs 2011, 17)

Within that vein its vision is 'a society in which men and women have equal access to socially valued goods and are able to contribute to national development' (Bureau of Women's Affairs 2011, 17). This understanding of citizenship places a certain burden on nationals to contribute to development. Citizenship then becomes contingent upon this contribution and human potential is tied to the state and its ambitions, in this case 'development'. The imperatives of the state become the imperatives of the citizen so much so that the policy hopes that it can 'create a socio-economic, political and legal environment free of discrimination on the basis of sex; where females and males, at all stages of the life-cycle, can enjoy their full human rights and develop their *full potential as citizens*' (Bureau of Women's Affairs 2011, 19, (our emphasis)). The approach is consistent with the economism of neo-liberalism in which 'gender equity is related to the ways that inequities interfere with the goals of efficiency, stability, and growth'. Gender equity therefore becomes a means to an end, rather than an end in itself (Beregon 2006, 135). Further, the state is here constructing a vision of citizenship attached to its own failure to produce development. Ong points out that 'market driven logics have infiltrated the thinking and practice of governing', and while the state is withdrawing from its welfare role, it wants citizens 'to act as free subjects who self-actualize and act on their own behalf' (Ong 2006, 8). The state therefore becomes 'concerned with instilling behavior of individual self-management' where, 'the neoliberal ethical regime requires citizens to be self-responsible, self-enterprising subjects' (Ong 2006, 11, 12).

Neo-liberalism produced certain negative effects, including the deepening incapacity of the state to fulfil its goal of development. Because the Jamaican economy has fared poorly in the climate of neo-liberal globalization, the burdens especially on women as the main caregivers and heads of families in Jamaica and on the poor have intensified. State failures are partly filled by an inflow of remittances from Jamaicans abroad, which provide a cushion to those at the bottom and a main source of foreign exchange earnings for the economy.[9] The failing of the formal economy is also seen in the growth of the informal sector. This sector and deepening poverty have been associated with high levels of crime and violence among men at the lower socio-economic level.[10] The state is presented with crises on a number of levels. Middle-class men who control the state cannot rely on working-class men for the sustenance of middle-class patriarchy because many men are pushed out of the formal economy where traditional patriarchal roles are played. The pursuit of education, jobs and salaries does not seem a sure route to social mobility because neo-liberalism tends to elevate those who have economic means, and men have therefore opted out of that process. Society also views the state as failing in its fight against crime and violence (associated with Jamaica's economic decline and the growth of the informal sector) creating a crisis of credibility for the state in its seeming inability to control the population, and, in particular, 'wayward' boys and men of the urban underclass. It also faces a crisis in that the state seems to be losing the battle against poverty and development. In the face of this decline, Jamaica's development model has not been re-charted and the state must explain why it fails to meet public expectations. State officials often seek to turn the public's attention to those citizens who have failed to be self-sufficient/responsible, such as poor single mothers who have too many children and burden the state, or criminal elements among the poor who supposedly divert investment and scare tourists away.[11] Indeed, this response is arguably also a response to the 'crisis of masculinity' embodied in the notion of the marginalized male in the Caribbean.

The contemporary perceived imminent threat of female takeover of the nation highlights the character of gendered power in Jamaica. Presumably today, Jamaican males face marginalization because of their failure to meet

patriarchal standards of manhood and because of female progress in education and the labour market, and their role as household heads. Female progress is popularly taken as an indicator of male decline in Jamaica, even while
Keisha Lindsay and others have debunked the myth of male marginalization
in the Caribbean. Lindsay presents empirical evidence which shows that
women's status as household heads should not be interpreted as an indicator
of their social, economic or psychological power, but instead as an indication that they are further marginalized by the burdens associated with their
status as household heads. Additionally, decision making in such households
continues to revolve around conventional norms of masculine and feminine
authority in which women control domestic tasks and men determine decisions on expenditure, solely or jointly with women. Lindsay notes that while
female enrolment in education and literacy rates have increased, girls and
women continue to be over-represented in traditionally 'feminine' spheres
(Lindsay 2002, 63–64). Women also dominate traditionally female employment spheres, face higher levels of unemployment and are employed in low-
ranking positions in most sectors, which translate into low wages (Lindsay
2002, 66–69). Women's wholesale involvement in the economy therefore
does not indicate their economic independence or access to power.

Some Jamaican men, particularly working-class men, experience marginalization as the Jamaican economy declines and as the state eschews a
'welfarist' role. However, men are not marginalized relative to women as a
whole. Rather, structures of power treat these men as women in relation to
the power of the state and groups above them in the class structure, thus reinforcing the equation of femininity with weakness and subordination. Indeed,
while middle-class Jamaican women may be making progress, they rarely
displace middle-class men in power. Women across classes are still subject to
patriarchal power. This frame broadly protects patriarchy, heterosexism and
the economic status quo while making space for middle-class women who
have emerging power within the Jamaican state to have a say without critical
disruption of the status quo. As Hutton notes, some women are close to the
seat of power, and therefore have a voice. Middle-class women in particular
are able to wield power through their class status, marked by their progress
in the professions and in their participation in institutions such as marriage,
which gives them access to power through their husbands. Within that context, an idea of gender equality could be mobilized to protect the state and
those groups which serve its interests. Yet, we should acknowledge that there
is no substantive decline in patriarchal masculinity in Jamaica, and that most
middle-class women are working within patriarchal power systems. Second,
where society presumes patriarchy to be failing – the family (for working-
class men), the classroom and certain spheres of the economy – there are also
shifting expressions of patriarchy. Indeed men are responding to challenges

to patriarchy which emerged in the neo-liberal era and which emerged with deepening poverty and a decline in the formal economy. At the same time, these shifts represent a crisis of masculinity within the middle class. If men are not opting for the 'civilizing' forces of education, who will be the allies of the men presently in power who have defined their masculinity through colonial and elite tropes of respectability?[12]

When considering indicators which are associated with men failing to live up to expectations of manhood, it is necessary to deconstruct the cultural norms and structural dynamics that produce them. These norms and dynamics provide a deeper understanding of why, for instance, men may opt out of education and the formal economy, which are often regarded as feminized precisely because men are rarely able to play patriarchal roles within them, given the low wages in these sectors and the declining faith in the dream of social mobility through education. Within the NPGE, these dynamics are not critically engaged but rather are presented as a part of the problem of male marginalization, which is taken as a given that requires public attention. The policy does not sufficiently interrogate popular readings of male and female socio-economic conditions in contemporary Jamaica and therefore becomes part of the body of flawed and popular understandings of current realities. The NPGE's situational analysis acknowledged that women are under-represented in positions of power economically and politically, and despite their over-representation in education at tertiary levels, face more unemployment (Bureau of Women's Affairs 2011, 10–11). It does not disaggregate by class, so we are not made aware if these indicators apply across class differences. We do not know therefore whether female attendance and performance outstrips boys in the middle class as opposed to the poor.[13] Yet the policymakers respond to the under-representation of men in the classroom with the solution that 'they should be provided with incentives to enter the teaching profession' (Bureau of Women's Affairs 2011, 11). Why, we might ask, do men need to be present in the profession and how will such incentives impact the status of women in it? We could argue that the thrust of the NPGE aligns with the popular belief in the need to restore men to their appropriate place within society. Indeed, alarm around male decline is embodied in the policy which calls for making special provisions for men over women.

Women of the underclass are stereotyped in the wider society, especially in their roles as mothers. They are routinely called out as being inclined to irresponsible 'breeding' causing themselves and their offspring to be a burden on the nation. Motherhood has become a powerful avenue to deepen women's alienation from power, not simply because of the domestic demands it involves but because of the way in which it has been seen as a route to social decay in Jamaica. On the one hand, the Jamaican setting allows motherhood to be potentially empowering, given the ways in which mothers become the centre of the home through matrifocality, and because it is considered to be an important function of citizenship. Tracey Robinson points out that motherhood is the mechanism through which women do service for the nation, which is seen as the basis for citizenship (Robinson 2003, 246). It is nonetheless a limited citizenship as its potential is curtailed by the burdens associated with it. A specific type of motherhood is valued in the Jamaican context: the burden-bearing and virtuous mother, socially responsible for her offspring, with no additional pressures on the state or on men, and a mother who can be held up as a paragon of virtue, who is passing on high moral codes to her offspring. Crime has come to be associated with failing mothers, both through their decisions to reproduce in spite of their poverty, and because they are presumed to have failed to pass on ideals of moral responsibility to their children, especially sons. They become stigmatized by the state, which calls them out as reckless and irresponsible in bringing children into a world they cannot afford. The single, impoverished mother ultimately becomes a powerful symbol of a force undermining national stability. In an instant, her subordinate place is cemented in 'unplanned' motherhood.

In 2013, Lisa Hanna, the minister of youth and culture, brought a motion to reopen the debate on abortion and did so by presenting such a viewpoint as a rationale for abortion. She expressed more of a concern for the state's capacity to manage the care and consequences of 'unwanted children' than for women's freedoms and rights as citizens in a democratic political association. Hanna noted that it cost the state $1.7 billion a year to fund the Child Development Agency, and some $436 million to operate government-run homes. She highlighted problems such as inadequate parenting skills employed by 'child' mothers and the neglect and abuse of children, which would presumably encourage social decay given the 'direct correlation between crime and unwanted children' as reasons to pursue pro-choice legislation (Luton 2013).

Minister Hanna's rights claims are in keeping with and are central to the advancement of neo-liberalism in local politics and economics. Her arguments reflect a morbid prioritizing of finance over people's well-being. She reduced women's concerns regarding their control over their bodies to a means to purging the nation of 'undesirables'. This represents a significant ideological shift over previous attempts to change the legislation. Under the Offences against the Persons Act, abortions are illegal in Jamaica under all circumstances, but changes to the laws have been considered since the 1970s. In 1975 Minister of Health Kenneth McNeil, 'impatient of the gross social injustice', called for reform of legislation impacting abortions, but could not advance the legislation in parliament given 'the power of religious institutions that rallied against it'. 'Frustrated by the noise, McNeil simply enacted a policy of providing safe abortion services in a public health clinic on Eureka Road in Kingston 13' (Ministry of Health 2008, 9). This period represented a marked ideological difference from the present. The socialist rhetoric of the 1970s expressed concern for the freedoms of the Jamaican people. To make sense of the attempts at improving the quality of, and access to, rights for women at that time,[14] we must appreciate that the understandings of freedom which prevailed within the public and the state merged liberal individual rights, socialist ideas of redistributive justice (social and economic rights) and racially based claims for justice in Jamaica. At the same time, the struggle for women's rights and freedoms during this period faced significant challenges. The turn to neo-liberalism in the 1980s[15] shifted away from questions of economic justice and required that the expansion of rights be seen in economic terms. Liberal individual rights could be preserved if they could remain while removing or reducing the state's socio-economic responsibilities to its citizens, regardless of their so-called contributions to the nation.

While it is important that Hanna raised the matter of women's rights to abortion, and her attempt might be read as a strategic intervention given the power of patriarchy to deny women's issues an airing, the way in which she entered the debate had no far-reaching implications for women's empowerment. Instead, it relieved the state of responsibilities to protect girls and women who may be unable to navigate their bodies as empowered beings. Abortion was presented critically as a means of cutting the state's costs. The arguments occur in the context of men's control over the formal sphere of the economy, and deepening neo-liberal focus posited against women's 'control' over the domestic sphere but not their bodies. Women do not control state policy or its effects on their bodies and their families. While society expects women to manage the domestic sphere, they do not have control over the economic policies which determine their capacity to cope. Despite the well-known negative effects of neo-liberalism on women's worlds,[16] the Jamaican state hastens its neo-liberal commitments. Women's absence from control over the economy is intimately connected to their ambiguous control over their bodies. The overburdening of women is accepted and projected as a virtue in Jamaica and is consistent with neo-liberal logic.

Indeed, 'there is no illusion that women's commitment to the family should preclude paid work or other income-generating activities' (Robinson 2003, 237). Women's labour in the Caribbean made them significant contributors to the public sphere, but this is experienced as an additional burden because they also 'bear a disproportionate amount of the burden of work in the home' (Robinson 2003, 250). Within the NPGE, there is a definitive sense that women's integration into the economy is needed, and there is little that is meant to relieve their burdens. It devises no innovations to ease the burdens on women, such as compulsory childcare provisions by state agencies, though this would hardly be considered in a climate of economic decline and the dominance of neo-liberal thinking. It makes no attempt to rescue the non-nuclear families which prevail in Jamaica, and destigmatize Jamaican women and men who fail to live up to patriarchal expectations.[17] On the other hand, the feminization of certain sectors of the economy such as education is seen as part of a threat to men's power.

As it is, the state's attempts to recentre middle-class patriarchy are expressed in hopes and efforts for men's return to the classroom and boys' enhanced performance in education; for men's return to the workforce and entry into marriage for those who have seemingly opted out of their bread-winner role; and for women to marry and continue the work of mother-ing the nation, in effect, bearing the burden of a lack of development. As neo-liberalism shifts the burdens of dealing with poverty to women around the globe, the Jamaican state also consolidates and legitimates its failure to provide welfare to its citizens by explaining poverty through the lens of absent fathers, criminal, violent, working-class men and single mothers. We are expected to believe that marriage, the consolidation of the nuclear family and the 'restoration' of men to patriarchal masculinity will rescue the nation. As the effects of neo-liberalism deepen the shift away from developmental imperatives within the state, the NPGE and its promise of gender equality can shift the goal of development to the citizenry. The NPGE can be used to bring women more deeply into the project of development supposedly as its beneficiaries, but the nation also benefits if they can act as engines of growth through their incorporation. It can bring fallen men back to the classroom, to respectability and as contributing citizens. The state's hope that marriage and the nuclear unit will triumph in Jamaica is consistent with this expectation from the NPGE that we be 'good' citizens. It is also consistent with the state's need to reproduce and legitimize itself, and the men who have power in it.

THE NPGE, BOURGEOIS PATRIARCHY AND THE PROBLEM OF HETERONORMATIVITY

We find a certain weakness in the policy's questioning of gendered norms in Jamaica given its state-based, institutional and structural focus. We believe that tackling ideological structures is critical to arriving at gender equality because even while institutional mechanisms may follow equitable gender guidelines, it is people who manage institutions, and patriarchal biases at individual levels can damage efforts at structural reform. While the discus-sion of the consultative process, especially evident in its appendices, gives some indication that people questioned understandings of masculinity and femininity at that level, the policy does not seek to deconstruct Jamaica's gen-der culture and there is no attempt to tackle problematic norms in the strate-gies developed to effect gender equality. Indeed, the policy at times suffers from a reproduction of the heteronormative strains which prescribe men's and women's roles. We gain insights into the gendered ideas of policymakers in statements such as 'the role of women in the criminal activities is disturbing' (Bureau of Women's Affairs 2011, 59) and 'the role of women in "protecting" male criminals is disturbing' (Bureau of Women's Affairs 2011, 63). Why should we be disturbed by women's role in criminality? Is this a general concern with criminality in Jamaica or of women's participation in it? Unless we have specific understandings of male and female relations and hierarchies, in a society with high crime rates, there should be no specific alarm about women's participation in criminal activities. Does this concern reflect an anxiety about a decaying femininity? In its discussion of the problem of crime in Jamaica, the policy notes that men are over-represented as victims of crime and in the criminal justice system, specifically as a result of the patriarchal status quo (Bureau of Women's Affairs 2011, 10–11). However, the NPGE does not provide insights into how to undermine this status quo. Among its targets and strategies, it charges the Ministry of National Security to:

- design and implement a comprehensive crime plan that includes strategies to address gender-based violence and other forms of violence against women;
- establish a safe house and 24-hour hotline to temporarily assist people who are the victims of human trafficking; and
- employ temporary special measures to increase the representation of women in the Jamaica Constabulary Force (JCF) (Bureau of Women's Affairs 2011, 27).

While the NPGE distinctly views violence as a problem of male perpetrators, (Bureau of Women's Affairs 2011, 49) and women as their victims, it does not consider the problem of violence against men by other men. Heron notes that the policy is blind to violence against boys and to homophobia (Heron August 29, 2013, Interview with Thame). The policy also does not engage with a view of crime and violence as symptoms of the domination over working-class and poor men in the power structure. Its view of violence and the role of the security forces is limited, and it consequently recommends few measures to shift masculinities away from an acceptance of violence as a part of manhood. Indeed, the NPGE's failure to further interrogate the problem is extended to the attempt to pursue gender equality by incorporating more women into the JCF. The JCF is constantly called out for its own use of violence against the population. Why then would we wish to increase women's representation in it? For the women represented in the force, what protections are being offered against its patriarchy? Also, as with women in politics, women in the force can conceivably become actors wielding patriarchal power over more subaltern women. The emphasis on gender equality becomes problematic when it simply seeks to insert women into situations which are inherently unfavourable. They are unfavourable because the undergirding ideas which shape them are not tackled. This is why gender justice is the more transformational goal. Transforming masculinities and femininities is at the core of that project.

The policy is shaped by heteronormative ideas which do not significantly challenge the power structure that favours middle-class men in politics, heterosexual masculinity or virtuous, burden-bearing womanhood. Its heteronormativity is especially seen in its failure to tackle matters of sexuality (Heron August 29, 2013, Interview with Thame). Whereas the government of Jamaica is clear in its understanding of homosexuality and rights based on sexual orientation, the NPGE makes no such statement.[18] It notes that a view emerging from public consultations was that the 'police [are] reluctant to investigate violence between heterosexual couples – they do so more readily in cases of violence between two men if they are in a homosexual relationship' (Bureau of Women's Affairs 2011, 12), but that domestic violence is derided in same-sex unions and there are no avenues for redress in the justice system as a result of homophobia (Bureau of Women's Affairs 2011, 14). Nonetheless, there are no named strategies to destigmatize homosexuality or to encourage tolerance and protection within the Jamaican community. Silence on matters of sexuality suggests an unwillingness to challenge the homophobia which prevails within the state, reflected in current legislative debates, such as the Sexual Offences Act. While neo-liberalism is consolidated in the economic sphere, the emphasis on human rights in liberalism is not embedded in Jamaican politics and this is reflected in approaches to gender equality. Norms are not challenged if they do not disrupt the pre-eminence of the market and if they empower those who already have power.

The nature of heteronormativity in the Jamaican case is also attached to understandings of male and female roles in the family. The view prevails that the failure to consolidate nuclear families is a national failure, since it is understood as being replaced by insecure, mainly female-headed families that are not able to bring up 'good' citizens. As indicated earlier, women who are unmarried and procreating share a significant amount of blame in explanations of 'national crises' in Jamaica. The sustenance of patriarchy in Jamaica depends on the construction of gendered power through the stigmatization of prevailing family structures, especially female-headed ones, and the promotion of marriage. Alexander argued that the household is an important ideological instrument of the state and 'because it has been an important space in which a particular kind of hierarchical, patriarchal power has resided, the state must move to rehabilitate this sphere' (Alexander 1994, 19). It is the middle-class male who emerges as powerful in the context of the nuclear unit and the state's stigmatization of dominant family structures in Jamaica. In the usually middle-class context of marriage, men enjoy patriarchal status as the head of the family. Men's presence in the nuclear unit not only gives them power over women but also over men, usually those in the Jamaican underclass who do not marry and do not enjoy status as responsible males in the larger society, partly because of their absence from the nuclear unit. Given that marriage has not cemented itself among most Jamaican women who often assume positions as heads of households in the absence of men, the domestic sphere can represent a potential place for women's power. The promotion of the nuclear family by the state is important therefore to the consolidation of men's power in general, but the stigmatization of non-nuclear families is specifically important to consolidating middle-class patriarchy.

CONCLUSION – THE NPGE AND THE FUTURE

The NPGE has been severely encumbered from its genesis in two ways. First, it was insufficiently radical to challenge the patriarchal status quo. Second, as an instrument of the state it has paradoxically been tasked with changing the same organizations and institutions that are responsible for its implementation. These factors have inevitably been shaped by the period during which the policy came into being, when neo-liberalism dominated the nation. Gendered power thus has to be understood as specific to historical periods. This fact helps to explain the observation that no popular commitment or agitation emerged to sustain and implement the policy. With the primacy of the market and ideas that sustain it, social opposition has declined in the Caribbean. Indeed, as Vassell points out, we should see the absence of popular engagement with the policy as part of the absence or weakness of an activist movement that could push for change. Vassell points specifically to the weakness of the women's movement, its lack of ideological clarity and backlash from a turn to the right in the wider society (Vassell August 16, 2013, Interview with Thame). It is important to note that this gives the state enormous room to wield power over instruments that should, if we think as feminists, be mechanisms for transforming the state itself. It means that measures to hold the state to account will, at best, be weak.

We can argue that the state has a critical role to play as a potential change-making institution in any society, but if the state is not radicalized, it is unlikely to serve this function. If the state is most concerned with self-preservation as a patriarchal institution, it will first defend the interests of patriarchy and in this case, the power of middle-class men. While the approach to gender equality taken within the NPGE tends towards changing the state, the capacity for change is undermined by a public demobilized in the neo-liberal era. A popular agenda is critical because as a part of the project of reproducing the state, the state must contend with opposition to it and seek it as it were to balance interests. We should ask, what would a popularly driven document look like? Since we are concerned with patriarchy, the public most important to that process is women. Vassell argues that women have to play a vanguard role because 'the people with the trouble know best how to change it'. She believes that women need to show men how gender inequality harms them and how hegemonic masculinity damages men. Women should seek to validate their humanity through partnership with them (Vassell August 16, 2013, Interview with Thame). Indeed mobilization for change in Jamaica has to be considered in terms of the need for feminism and feminist perspectives.

We believe our discussion provides insights that can assist efforts to take up openings provided by the NPGE. The support given to the process by the state indicates a willingness to engage with gender matters. We should be careful to question what is at stake for those that run the state, and therefore what strategic means feminists or anyone affected can employ to disrupt the flow of power in the interest of unseating patriarchy. Inclusion at the negotiating table is not open to all. Class impacts not only battles between male patriarchs, but also women who are allies of the state. Women who are able to acquire the 'requisite' skills will have to push to open spaces further, and where they are unable to do so they must seek to get at the heart of the norms that inform policymaking processes. They must seek popular alliances that can sustain a national dialogue for change and action towards gender equality in tandem with the NPGE.

A lack of awareness about and even opposition to gender equality among men and women is an important obstacle to realizing the goals of the NPGE. However, Tafari-Ama suggested that the initial debates around the policy often hinted at more equitable visions of Jamaica and encouraged nuanced rather than monolithic views about gender among men and women 'so that we could talk about how gender really cuts across class, time and space and other forms of identity' (Tafari October 4, 2013, Interview with Thakur). Indeed, in revisiting the NPGE and considering how to move it forward, the time may be right to initiate a similar moment of national self-reflection on gender justice and women's rights in Jamaica. Gender is not divorced from other ideological frames, and if development is part of a gendered and NPGE goal, the place of neo-liberal economics in contemporary Jamaica, whom it burdens and how it genders the nation must ultimately be transformed.

NOTES

1. The bureau is undergoing change that would lead to the creation of a Bureau of Gender Affairs.

2. The Gender Advisory Committee was established by the government in 2005 with the aim of developing a national gender policy. It consisted of fifteen members from various sectors in society and was chaired by Professor Barbara Bailey (The UWI, Mona).

3. Bureau of Women's Affairs, 'National Policy for Gender Equality', 19.

4. Vassell is a long-standing advocate on women's issues. She has written on gender in Jamaica and served on the Committee of Women for Progress, which won gains for women in the 1970s and birthed the Women's Resource and Outreach Centre (WROC).

5. We are using middle class as both elite and as the middle strata. For an elaboration of this see C. L. R. James's characterization and critique of that sector in 'The West Indian Middle Classes'. Also see Lindsay, *The Myth of Independence: Middle Class Politics and Non-Mobilization in Jamaica*; James, *Party Politics in the West Indies*; Lewis, 'Masculinity, the Political Economy of the Body, and Patriarchal Power in the Caribbean'. See Thame, 'Reading Violence and Postcolonial Decolonization Through Fanon:' for a discussion of the ways in which that masculinity imposed itself on the working class through garrison politics.

6. For a discussion of citizenship and respectability politics, see Anthony Bogues, *Postcolony, Nation: Caribbean Inflections*.

7. For a discussion see Obika Gray, *Demeaned but Empowered: The Social Power of the Urban Poor in Jamaica*.

8. For a discussion, see Thame, 'Reading Violence and Postcolonial Decolonization Through Fanon'.

9. Remittances are presently Jamaica's first main source of foreign exchange earnings and come in direct inflows to individuals and families.

10. See for example Francis, *Crime and Development: The Jamaican Experience*. For a discussion of violence and poverty in Jamaica, see Levy, *They Cry Respect!: Urban Violence and Poverty in Jamaica*.

11. See Hanna's discussion on the state's responsibilities for 'unwanted" children on page 162. Numerous such statements are made by public officials, for instance National Security Minister Peter Bunting's statement at the launch of the Jamaica Employers' Federation's (JEF) 31st annual business and workplace convention and expo, suggesting that crime and corruption was preventing *rapid* growth and development in Jamaica – see http://www.caribbean360.com/news/jamaica_news/657583.html#ixzz2xk1r71Qz

12. For a discussion see Linden Lewis, 'Nationalism and Caribbean Masculinity'.

13. Evidenced in *National Policy on Gender Equality*, Appendix 5, 59–60.

14. Legislation was passed during the period on equal pay, maternity leave and to secure access to financial support for the offspring of unwed mothers.

15. For a discussion of Jamaica's neo-liberal turn see Kari Levitt, *Reclaiming Development: Independent Thought and Caribbean Community*.

16. For a discussion of how feminist economists have responded to the effects of structural adjustment on women, see Bergeron, *Fragments of Development*, 130–39.

17. See for instance, parliamentary debates on the Matrimonial Causes Act of 1988 where Member of Parliament A. Johnson held that he hoped the Bill would receive publicity so that 'people would get out of the whole habit of being afraid of marriage and not entering into it in the numbers which are needed if we are to have more and better families properly speaking in our shores'. Jamaica Hansard, 'January 4–April 26, 1989' 14, no. 3 (1989): 13.

18. Successive Jamaican governments have remained committed to maintaining legislation that criminalises same-sex sexual relations. See parliamentary debates on the Sexual Offences Act. In the 2009 debates, then Minister of Education Andrew Holness argued that there is 'an inconsistency with the penalty structure [that] would suggest a greater crime is being committed in terms of rape versus buggery'. Then Prime Minister Bruce Golding noted: 'there were offences in the law which were nowhere as serious as anal abuse, but were carrying a more serious penalty because the legislation approach that question with timidity'. He said, 'We had to be very careful to make sexual intercourse as defined in law very specific, which means a man in relation to a woman. Any relaxation of that definition would take us onto a promenade on which it was not felt by me, that we want to go'. Jamaica Hansard, 'January 13–March 31, 2009', 221, 352.

REFERENCES

Acosta, Andres. 2006. *The Policymaking Process in Jamaica.* Washington D.C.: Inter-American Development Bank, 2006.

Alexander, M. Jacqui. 1994. 'Not Just (any) Body Can Be a Citizen: The Politics of Law, Sexuality and Postcoloniality in Trinidad and Tobago and the Bahamas'. *Feminist Review* 48(1): 5–23.

Barriteau, Eudine. 2004. 'Constructing Feminist Knowledge in the Commonwealth Caribbean in the Era of Globalisation'. In *Gender in the 21st Century: Perspectives, Visions and Possibilities*, edited by Barbara Bailey and Elsa Leo-Rhynie, 437–65. Kingston, Jamaica: Ian Randle Publishers.

Bergeron, Suzanne. 2006. *Fragments of Development: Nation, Gender, and the Space of Modernity.* Ann Arbor: University of Michigan Press.

Brown, Wendy. 1992. 'Finding the Man in the State'. *Feminist Studies* 18(1): 7–34.

Bureau of Women's Affairs. 'National Policy for Gender Equality (NPGE), Jamaica'. Kingston, Jamaica: The Bureau of Women's Affairs, 2010.

Francis, Alfred. 2009. *Crime and Development: The Jamaican Experience.* Kingston, Jamaica: Sir Arthur Lewis Institute of Social and Economic Studies, The University of the West Indies.

Gray, Obika. 2004. *Demeaned but Empowered: The Social Power of the Urban Poor in Jamaica.* Kingston, Jamaica: University of the West Indies Press.

———. 2001. 'Rethinking Power: Political Subordination in Jamaica', in *New Caribbean Thought: A Reader*, edited by Brian Meeks and Folke Lindahl, 224–25. Kingston, Jamaica: University of the West Indies Press.

Jamaica Hansard. 'January 13 – March 31, 2009'. 34, no. 3 (2009).

James, Cyril Lionel Robert. 1962. *Party Politics in the West Indies*. Vedic Enterprises.

Levitt, Kari. 2005. *Reclaiming Development: Independent Thought and Caribbean Community*. Kingston and Miami: Ian Randle Publishers.

Levy, Horace. 1996. *They Cry Respect!: Urban Violence and Poverty in Jamaica*. Centre for Population, Community and Social Change, Department of Sociology and Social Work, University of the West Indies, Mona.

Lewis, Linden. 2002. 'Envisioning a Politics of Change within Caribbean Gender Relations', in *Gendered Realities: Essays in Caribbean Feminist Thought*, edited by Patricia Mohammed, 512–30. Kingston, Bridgetown, Port of Spain: University of the West Indies Press and The Centre for Gender and Development Studies.

———. 2004. 'Masculinity, the Political Economy of the Body, and Patriarchal Power in the Caribbean', in *Gender in the 21 St Century: Caribbean Perspectives, Visions and Possibilities*, edited by Barbara Bailey and Elsa Leo-Rhynie, 236–61, Kingston: Ian Randle Publishers.

———. 2000. 'Nationalism and Caribbean Masculinity'. In *Gender Ironies of Nationalism: Sexing the Nation*, edited by Tamar Mayer, 261–83. U.K.: Routledge.

Lindsay, Keisha. 2002. 'Is the Caribbean Male an Endangered Species'. in *Gendered Realities: Essays in Caribbean Feminist Thought*, edited by Patricia Mohammed, 56–82. Kingston, Bridgetown, Port of Spain: University of the West Indies Press and The Centre for Gender and Development Studies.

Lindsay, Louis. 1975. *The Myth of Independence: Middle Class Politics and Non-Mobilization in Jamaica*. Institute of Social and Economic Research, The University of the West Indies.

Luton, Doraine. 2013. 'Hanna Wants Abortion Laws Reviewed'. *Jamaica Gleaner*. June 18, 2013.

Ministry of Health. 2008. 'Report of the Advisory Committee on Abortion, Ministry Paper No. 6/08'. Kingston, Jamaica: Government of Jamaica.

Mosse, David. 2004. 'Is Good Policy Unimplementable? Reflections on the Ethnography of Aid Policy and Practice'. *Development and Change* 35(4): 639–71.

Ong, Aihwa, 2006. 'Experiments with Freedom: Milieus of the Human'. *American Literary History* 18(2): 229–44

Robinson, Tracy. 2003. 'Beyond the Bill of Rights: Sexing the Citizen', in *Confronting Power, Theorizing Gender: Interdisciplinary Perspectives in the Caribbean*, edited by Eudine Barriteau, 231–61. Kingston, Jamaica: University of the West Indies Press.

Simpson-Miller, Portia. 2011. 'Statement to Parliament on International Women's Day - March 8, 2011'. Kingston, Jamaica: Government of Jamaica.

Thame, Maziki. 2011. 'Reading Violence and Postcolonial Decolonization Through Fanon: The Case of Jamaica'. *Journal of Pan African Studies* 4(7): 75.

Thomas, Deborah A. 2011. *Exceptional Violence: Embodied Citizenship in Transnational Jamaica*. Durham: Duke University Press.

LIST OF INTERVIEWS

Heron, Taitu (former gender focal point representing the Planning Institute of Jamaica).
Interview, August 29, 2013.
Hutton, Clinton (Lecturer, University of the West Indies, Mona, member of the Board of Gender Studies). Interview, August 32, 2013.
Tafari-Ama, Imani (Lecturer, University of the West Indies, Mona and consultant who worked on the initial consultation exercises for the BWA). Interview, October 4, 2013.
Vassell, Linnette (Women's Resource and Outreach Centre, WROC). Interview, August 16, 2013
Webster, Faith (former executive director, Bureau of Women's Affairs). Interview, August 14, 2013.
Wedderburn, Judith (director of the Friedrich Ebert Stiftung (FES) in Jamaica and participant in stakeholder consultations during the drafting of the NPGE). Interview, November 1, 2013.

Chapter 9

Feminist/Womanist Advocacy for Transformational Leadership in the Anglophone Caribbean

Individual and Collective Agency

Shirley Campbell

This chapter analyses the strategies, processes, practices, structures and contestations[1] experienced by feminists/womanists and their male allies seeking to promote a transformational style of leadership in the Anglophone Caribbean beginning in the 1990s. The Caribbean office of the UNIFEM – now UN Women – has supported efforts to foster a 'different kind of leadership' in the region that would position women as agents of change at every level of society. A combination of factors influenced this goal. These included the 1995 Beijing Platform for Action, which encouraged using the strategy of mainstreaming gender to increase women's rights.

Acting on the Beijing mandate, UNIFEM Caribbean took a consultative approach and a historical and cultural perspective to developing interventions for promoting a transformational style of women's leadership in the region. They based these interventions on research findings and analyses of the region's geopolitics, economic development models and a 'crisis of leadership', including widespread disillusionment with the political system (West Indian Commission 1992). A multiplicity of concepts and theories including feminist/womanist definitions of transformational leadership (TL), power and authority, patriarchy and masculinity, feminist advocacy and social movement (SM) theories influenced the approach to the proposed interventions.

The feminist/womanist activists' philosophical approach to social transformation also informed the movement's recommendations. Their opposition to sexism and their action to change social hierarchies (Antrobus 2004, 24–25; hooks 1984, 10) shaped the proposed interventions. Additionally, womanist activists highlighted the importance of addressing the intersection of sexism with oppressions such as racism, classism, ethnocentrism, universalism, location and the discursive exercise of power, which they addressed simultaneously, (Hill Collins 2000, 97–100; hooks 1984, xii; Mohanty 2003, 501–4).

Some Anglophone Caribbean women claim a variety of feminisms (mainly radical, socialist and liberal)[2] and womanisms. Although 'womanism' emerged from US black feminist theorizing, this chapter focuses on a Caribbean women's rights' movement that is diverse in ethnicity, race, class, education, location, religion and culture.

Additionally, the movement's activism played out at the personal, organizational, institutional, national, regional and international interface. Women's interaction at these levels inspired and catalysed their advocacy strategies for interventions to advance TL in the region.

Against this background, the chapter aims:

- to analyse the historical background and macro-regional context within which feminist/womanist advocacy in the region sought to create a transformational type of leadership;
- to explore the experiences and understandings of women to determine the factors that enabled or impeded the transformation of leadership and gendered power relations; and
- to describe advocacy strategies emerging from an analysis of the data that suggest democratic practices that could enhance women's rights and gender equality in state and non-state sectors under a transformational style of leadership.

In addition to these broad objectives, this chapter explores issues related to the historical and regional context within which feminists/womanists struggles for TL emerged and developed. The enablers and obstacles encountered, the advances and setbacks experienced and the negotiation of tensions between the women's movement and women and men in politics to influence systemic changes to the concept and exercise of power and leadership are also discussed. Recommendations for advancing women's rights and social justice under TL concludes this chapter.

Further, the chapter outlines an integrated feminist analytical framework developed by the author to evaluate the chapter's data. The framework integrates several theoretical concepts to analyse advocacy strategies for enhancing TL. It uses a qualitative research methodology that employs content analysis of texts, as well as interview data from nineteen participants. The analytical framework helped to identify the main themes emerging from the research findings. The research concludes that although women are making significant social advances, they continue to be, for the most part, excluded from top public leadership in politics and the corporate boardroom. A central force undergirding the continuing power of gender inequality is the ideological persistence that justifies male privilege and women's subordination (Barriteau 1997, 2–4). The chapter therefore focuses on this dichotomy between the ideological continuities of women's subordination in the domestic (private) sphere, and advances in their material (public) conditions, which act to produce and reinforce their exclusion from top positions of public leadership (Barriteau 1998, 191–205).[3]

THEORETICAL FRAMEWORK

Multiple issues operating at several levels in the Anglophone Caribbean region influenced women's actions to advance TL. To accommodate this diversity, the author developed an integrated feminist analytical framework hybrid to analyse the data in this chapter. The framework intersects the theoretical concepts of feminist TL, power and authority; gender hierarchies; patriarchy and masculinity; and social movement (SM) theory. The framework also reflects the cyclical and non-linear nature of the women's movement's advocacy and situates it within the historical context of the political economy of the Caribbean region.

Feminist TL[4] is an important element of the framework. It is values-driven and challenges hierarchical relationships, especially patriarchy, to advance gender justice at all levels of society. It seeks to redress women's general exclusion from positions of top public leadership and authority, challenges the status quo and takes risks, including the possibility of personal losses, to create radical social change (Antrobus 2002, 49). Leadership is based on legitimate authority (consensus) and the consultative sharing of power, authority and decision making that exercises power 'with', not 'over' others. Leadership is transparent and accountable, relational, and dialogical (Batliwala 2011, 22–27; Barriteau 2001, 7–14).

Feminist TL acknowledges that leadership exists at every level and creates opportunities for enabling that leadership. It inspires excellence, productivity that exceeds expectations, and creates opportunities for self-actualization that merges personal and organizational goals. TL models desired behaviours, and facilitates development opportunities such as training, coaching, mentorship and sponsorship. Additionally, TL builds networks of alliances and coalitions for advancing social justice (Batliwala 2011, 22–27).

The process of attaining TL begins with personal transformation and risk taking directed at equitable social change (Antrobus 2002, 47–51; Antrobus 2004, 166–74; Barriteau 2001, 2–4; Barriteau 2004, 2–5; Batliwala 2011, 18–28; Vassell 2001, 5–19). Such leadership resists patriarchal dominance within households and public spaces, and builds broad alliances for advocacy that includes male allies. Personal transformation is associated with experiences of deep personal crisis from which people emerge spiritually strengthened and with a commitment to influencing others to arrive at their epiphany (Vassell 2001 revised).

TL aims to democratize institutional structures (Antrobus 1999, 9; Vassell 2001, 7). Research participants Peggy Antrobus and Andaiye, both veterans of the Caribbean women's movement, emphasized the need for transformational change grounded in mass advocacy. They believe that political parties are constrained from making radical changes in the interest of the mass of the people by their history, structures and liberal parliamentary democracy philosophy and processes. Consequently, they recommended that broad alliances of women and their male allies organize outside of political parties to pressure party leadership to exercise political will. Both agreed that these external alliances are essential for lobbying and supporting women within political parties who refuse to promote women's issues unless they benefit the interests of their party (Skype™ Interview, May 23, 2012).[5] Hazel Brown, another veteran of the women's movement, who leads a broad alliance of non-governmental organizations in Trinidad and Tobago, argued that a critical mass of activist women demanding change within political parties is also necessary to effect radical change (Andaiye 2009, 17). Both perspectives are valid and arguments such as these have motivated the Caribbean women's movement to strengthen women's roles in political leadership.

Additionally, the framework addresses the idea that power – legitimate authority to influence decision making – exists discursively. Transformational leaders, as Barriteau (2001, 169–70) posits, apply power consultatively, transparently and decisively, 169–70. Barriteau argues further that transformational leaders are comfortable with acquiring and exercising power (Barriteau 2001, 5–6; Barriteau 2004, 3–4). These characteristics are evident among a variety of transformational Caribbean women leaders (Barriteau 2004, 2). These include the internationally acclaimed late Ruth Nita Barrow[6] (Barriteau 2001, 170), the late Eugenia Charles, Prime Minister of Dominica (Miller 2006, 256), the late Clotil Walcott, veteran trade unionist and relentless advocate for valuing unremunerated labour (Global Women's Strike 2007).

Ruth Nita Barrow displayed this comfort with power as secretary general of the Young Women's Christian Association (World YWCA). She acted decisively to fundamentally change the course of the organization. Unpopular as the changes were, she was uncompromising in exercising professionalism and commitment to realizing the mission of the organization (Barriteau 2001). Eugenia Charles, in fact, developed a reputation for, and admitted to enjoying, the exercise of power (Miller 2006). Clotil Walcott relentlessly lobbied the Trinidad and Tobago government to value unremunerated work and to record it in the national accounts. The law passed in 1996 (Global Women's Strike 2012). These outstanding achievements of some women in the regional movement were used as case studies in TL training to demonstrate that while leadership was predominantly the domain of patriarchal men, women, although comparatively few, have the ability and political will to lead decisively.

In relation to patriarchy and masculinity, the TL framework addresses social relations that position heterosexual men as the main source of authority and decision making in the family and the public domain of leadership. On the one hand, patriarchal ideology privileges the social attributes associated with hegemonic masculinity – provider, protector, leader, athlete, patriot, tall, dark, handsome, wears a suit and tie and publicly displays the most recent technological gadget (Kimmel 2004). Driving a powerful car that is attractive to a bevy of beautiful women completes the stereotype. These characteristics may be displayed by women, but much less often than males. In contrast, the attributes associated with women, less privileged men and other subaltern groups are devalued and feminized. Simultaneously, the framework acknowledges the contribution of male allies who champion the cause of women's rights.

The framework also highlights the importance of networks, alliances and coalition building that advance women's rights and social justice. Collaborations such as these were organized by Caribbean feminists/womanists at different levels and catalysed their action towards TL in the region. A distinctive feature of this movement-building includes demonstrating the connections among, and the need for changing, institutional structures and cultures that perpetuate women's subordination (Evans 2005, 11–12).

Finally, the chapter's analytical framework includes social movement theory, which is concerned with the collective action of independent social groups using various strategies to demand social change. The global women's movement falls into this category; it is diverse, informed by feminist/womanist politics and perspectives, driven by local issues, but supported globally (Antrobus 2004, 9). It addresses a broad variety of issues including the political economy, peace and the environment (Jaquette 1994, 1–5). The framework provides the point of departure for analysing the findings and making recommendations that could advance gender justice and democracy under TL.

METHODOLOGY

Content Analysis

A qualitative methodology – content analysis – was used to cross-reference texts to identify explicit and implicit meanings that women activists assigned

178   *Chapter 9*

to their advocacy for TL in the Anglophone Caribbean. Three types of texts were analysed to obtain data for this chapter – online (soft copies); printed (hard copies); and transcripts of an FGD, telephone and Skype™ interviews and e-mailed responses to a questionnaire. These texts were drawn from speeches, magazines, books, research papers, journals, conference papers, meeting reports, project proposals and newspaper articles about women's TL advocacy. The FGD included eight participants and follow-up interviews, conducted via telephone and Skype™ with nine participants. Two people submitted completed questionnaires via email. A total of nineteen participants contributed to the research, providing insights into the political economy and gender hierarchies affecting public discourse about the importance for TL in the region.

FINDINGS AND DISCUSSION

Macro-Regional Political Economy and Sociocultural Context

Discussions regarding the need for TL emerged in the Caribbean region in the late 1990s and were articulated in the UNIFEM Caribbean (now UN Women) Strategy and Business Plan (1997–2000). The plan, among other issues, outlined the organization's commitment to implementing a TL project that would change the 'paradigm of leadership in the Caribbean'[7] by creating a gender-sensitive, community-based, human-centred, sustainable development programme to advance women's involvement in public leadership as agents of change. The search for a non-hierarchical, non-authoritarian, collective style of leadership differed from the traditional hierarchical approach practised in organizations. The desire to be more inclusive, consultative, respectful and equal was a sentiment derived from SMs of the 1960s and the 1970s such as the Black Power and the civil rights and peace movements (Focus Group Discussion, April 5, 2012, Kingston, Jamaica).

Women's advocacy for transformational change was also influenced by a desire to disrupt patriarchal norms within political parties that subordinated women's rights issues to the national political agenda (Molyneux 1985, 233–35). This led women to form alternative organizations such as the Caribbean Association for Feminist Research and Action (CAFRA) and to strengthen the autonomy of the women's arms of liberal political parties. Their struggle for change was also an attempt to recover (and create new) spaces for women's advocacy and transformative action. These spaces were dislocated by the setbacks experienced by the democratic movements in the 1970s and 1980s, which included the US invasion of Grenada and the killing of Prime Minister Maurice Bishop, the assassination of Walter Rodney in Guyana and the decline and fall of the progressive government of Michael Manley in the 1980s in Jamaica (Focus Group Discussion, April 5, 2012,

Kingston, Jamaica). The outcomes of these events continue to shape the responses of SMs in the region in the contemporary period. They also signal that the democratic movements underestimated the importance of the geo-politics of the region to its allies in the North Atlantic (Ibid.).

The desire for TL that would be more responsive to people's needs was also a way of contesting the negative impacts of the demands of the neo-liberal economic model imposed by international financial institutions on beneficiary governments. These demands, by liberalizing economies and cutting social services, aimed to reverse the gains and memories of the democratic movements of the 1970s. They also strengthened the desires of women's movements for a more caring and responsive leadership, especially because women so often filled the social service gaps resulting from cuts in government spending (French 1994, 165–82; Raaber & Aguiar 2008, 1–23; Sparr 1994, 1–39). The increased demands on women's time and energy reduced their capacity to offer themselves for public leadership, even if they had the desire. Additionally, although women's training and access to services increased their autonomy, and better positioned them for leadership, the results were often limited (Henry-Wilson 1989, 241–52; Henry-Wilson 2004, 587–89).

Ideologues who believed that social services were a burden on an impoverished state also acted to erase the memory of the gains of the 1970s and 1980s by focusing exclusively on a non-historical and selective analysis of state failures. Neither did they connect these explanations to the unequal global power structure nor to the national cultural and socio-psychic challenges emerging in an increasingly global era, including those linked to postcolonial conditions. Members of the women's movement resisted this broad brush by shifting their internal governance structures to making them more efficient, equitable and responsive to people's material needs. These attempts at equity were, however, undermined by tensions resulting from differences, inside and outside of the organizations, relating to competencies, class, ethnicity, race, political party loyalties and the demands of international donors that were contradictory to local priorities (Ford-Smith 1989; FGD, April 5, 2012).

The Influence of WID and GAD Discourses

The meetings and outcomes of UN conferences and other bilateral and multilateral gatherings energized and catalysed the efforts of leading Caribbean women activists to advocate for transformative change. The 1990s discourse on TL in the region coincided with the global shift from the WID to the GAD paradigm. WID focused on integrating women into the market economy; GAD aimed to deconstruct gendered power relationships and hierarchies that treated and valued women and men, masculinity and femininity, unequally.

The GAD strategy for advancing social justice focused on mainstreaming gender into development planning, design, implementation and monitoring and evaluation of all policies, projects and programmes at all levels (Connelly Li, MacDonald & Parpart 2000, 56–64; Rathbeger 1989, 1–6). The expectation was that GAD would increase opportunities for women's advancement in public leadership. However, this did not happen to the extent expected because of the persistent dichotomy between the liberal ideology justifying women's subordination and progress in their material condition (Barriteau 1997, 3–6).

The History of the Idea and Movement: Debates and Strategies around Women as Transformational Leaders in Public Life

The feminist movement's history of struggle for a non-authoritarian leadership at the local and regional levels also occurred globally (Batliwala 2011, 21). The experiences of these local and global issues inspired Joselyn Messiah, then director of UNIFEM Caribbean, to lead the movement for implementing TL in the region. She was influenced by the Beijing 1995 conference mandate to position women for public leadership; the regional search for an indigenous, culturally relevant and responsive, transparent and accountable Caribbean leadership; and the outcomes of the setbacks in the 1980s, discussed earlier. Messiah's leadership of the research team in the Women in the Caribbean Project (WICP)[8] between 1979 and 1982 increased her exposure to the oppressive conditions of women's lives and strengthened her desire for transformed governance (Massiah 1998, 1; Senior 1991, 1–2). Roberta Clarke, her replacement as director of UNIFEM Caribbean, continued the tradition of advocacy for TL. Clarke's experience from leading the CAFRA research project on sexual violence in the region (CAFRA News 1992) also equipped her for continuity.

UNIFEM Caribbean's internal document on the proposed TL project provides valuable insights into the organization's approach to the project. It outlined its commitment to using strategies that would radically, but incrementally, change the paradigm of leadership across the region. These strategies included conducting research to identify the historical, psychosocial, political and economic barriers preventing more women from participating in public leadership. The research results would inform the development of interventions to advance TL. UNIFEM Caribbean commissioned secondary and primary research from Barriteau (2001) and Vassell (2001 revised) to explore the global and regional thinking about TL and its practice. Both researchers provided insights regarding the definition, core content, and the location and practices inherent to TL. Vassell also examined training projects to determine their potential to advance TL.

The UN body sponsored meetings of leading Caribbean feminists and womanists to get their ideas for a Caribbean TL framework. One meeting was in Barbados in May 1999. There, Peggy Antrobus, the keynote speaker, along with 25 other women, concluded that a TL paradigm for the region should be non-authoritarian, culturally relevant and should reform institutions (Antrobus 1999).

UNIFEM Caribbean also agreed to integrate leadership skills training into all of its activities, structures and processes because it viewed leadership as a cross-cutting theme that affected every level. For this reason, the researchers documented best practices of exemplars for use as cases in TL training. They also identified regional countries with the best learning communities for leadership training (Changing the Paradigm of Leadership in the Caribbean UNIFEM Caribbean, n.d.).

The UNIFEM document also defined the desired competencies of transformational leaders. These included people experiencing a paradigm shift at the personal level resulting in increased self-awareness and self-confidence grounded in spirituality. This enhanced state involved continuing critical reflection on action, taking responsibility for the current state of affairs and acting to transform situations at the personal, community and societal levels. Risk taking was another TL competency, even if it involved the loss of personal power. Other personal competencies identified included viewing challenges as opportunities, and envisioning and acting on the possibilities for change by being creative and innovative (Ibid.).

The UNIFEM TL programme targeted women at three levels – community, local politics and formal leadership – to identify best practices that were transferable. The rationale was to identify how women exercised and sustained leadership where they served. Women engaged in local politics represented a pool of leaders experienced in public service and familiar with public policy and change processes, and therefore positioned for movement into top public leadership. Women in formal leadership positions in representational politics, trade unions, the media and the private sector presented opportunities for increasing their numbers at the local, national and regional levels of formal politics, and had possibilities for challenging the political system to change qualitatively (UNIFEM Caribbean, n.d.).

Influencing Women [and Men] in Politics, Institutions and Systems to Practice Transformational Leadership

The strategies, processes and practices used in TL advocacy and training facilitated women's empowerment to behave differently and to exercise power in consultative, broad-based, compassionate and non-authoritarian ways. Actions to achieve these outcomes included recruiting women with

TL potential of different ages, experiences and professions across diverse groups and political parties. This broad-based mobilization demonstrated that collaboration for change was possible in spite of differing worldviews. Cross-party recruitment also demonstrated possibilities for collaboration in spite of the divisive nature of partisan politics and that others, apart from expert power, had the capacity to lead.

The pedagogical approach focused on a critical reflection of praxis to achieve conscientization (Freire 2007). Curriculum instructors validated people's lived experiences by using their personal narratives as tools of analyses. After each round of training, facilitators reviewed and updated documents and shared content material. This strategy enabled learners to review material at will, and share them with a wider community. This strengthened personal and institutional capacities for sustainability. The audiovisual material used in training was circulated to the media for promoting candidates and for advancing the concept of TL in the public domain. How to win elections and engender public policy were two of the main documents shared.

To encourage systemic changes, the movement encouraged women in politics to focus political campaigns on issues and integrity rather than personality and to be accessible and act to engender public policies. Women's manifestoes, plans of action and lists of high profile, committed and qualified women willing to serve in public leadership were presented to politicians, institutional leaders and at public forums. Other strategies aimed at systemic changes included petitions, media and communication campaigns and broad-based national consultations. These actions that included lobbying governments and private sector entities to support women in public leadership encouraged popular participation, transparency and accountability.

Regional symposia, such as Engendering Local Government (1997), inspired participating countries to intensify national campaigns for local government reform. The movement viewed local government as a strategic entry point for honing women's experience in electoral politics. Women's intense use of services provided by local authorities positioned them for this interface.

The regional women's movement also influenced institutions through advocacy, networking and coalition building at the local, regional and international levels. For example, women pressured governments to honour their obligations under UN conventions such as the CEDAW. This advocacy resulted in enactments, such as domestic violence bills, in all Anglophone Caribbean countries (ECLAC: Caribbean Synthesis Review 2010, 1, 3).

To advance further the movement for women's leadership, broad-based alliances of academics, government officials (policymakers) and activists collaborated. They conducted joint research to obtain empirical evidence to strengthen their demand for gender-sensitive public policy. The women trained parliamentarians, policymakers and other political activists in how to use research data to lobby and build coalitions to engender development planning. The CARICOM model legislation on sexual violence was influenced by the research findings in the 1979–1982 WICP study on women's lives (Senior 1991). The CAFRA study on sexual violence provided national and regional databases that informed CARICOM's model legislation on sexual violence (CARICOM Model Legislation on Sexual Offences 2011). Under the CAFRA project, police and paralegals were trained to assist survivors of sexual violence (ECLAC/UNIFEM: Eliminating Gender-Based Violence 2003, 3–4, 10).

The women's movement also sought to influence political outcomes and the performance of politicians and state and non-state actors by submitting petitions, holding private meetings with women candidates and one-on-one meetings with politicians to lobby them to support legislation for women's rights (Andaiye 2009, 9). The movement also used advocacy strategies such as rallies, demonstrations and media campaigns, nationally and regionally, to influence shifting the political culture away from male dominance and towards women's public leadership (Catalysts for Change: Caribbean Women and Governance 2004).

Feminist Strategies in Political Life: Cross-Party, Cross-Class, Cross-Ethnicity Training and Organizing

The women's movement sought to further influence political outcomes and institution building by implementing cross-party trainings on how to win elections. They taught women politicians and their supporters how to conduct electoral campaigns – how to fundraise, canvass, build networks and allies within and outside of political parties and cultivate congenial relationships with media representatives. These trainings were held between March 2002 and December 2005 under the Women's Political Participation (WPP) Training in Governance and Democracy project (UNIFEM: Catalysts for Change 2004).

The WPP project also developed a regional plan of action to build alliances, networks and coalitions at the national, subregional and regional levels. The plan included conducting research and advocacy, using a media and publicity campaign to increase public awareness of viable women leaders and convening pre-planning and start-up consultations at the national and subregional levels. They established subcommittees at the subregional level to monitor the implementation of planned activities (Ibid.).

Another example of influencing institution building and political outcomes included 'The Ten Points for Power Action Plan' developed by the women in Trinidad and Tobago in the aftermath of the Beijing Conference and the tensions generated by the calling of early elections in 1995. The plan called for an end to ethnically divisive politics, which was an important attempt to democratize the political culture. The plan also called for an economy more responsive to people's needs and a code of ethics for the conduct of public servants, a gender analysis of public policies and programmes, and increasing women's representation to a minimum of 30% of political party candidates (Network of NGOs 2010; Reddock 2004, 38–39).

Creating a Critical Mass of Women to Change the Content and Conduct of Leadership

In seeking to transform the 'content' and 'conduct' of women's leadership in the region, UNIFEM Caribbean acted to create a critical mass of gender-sensitive women who were knowledgeable, competent and committed to running for political and other public leadership positions. In addition to training in how to win elections and engender public policy, they were trained in TL practices. Curriculum developers and facilitators included veteran women politicians who shared their experiences during training. They also mentored and coached participants. Beneficiaries were expected to offer themselves for public leadership, encourage other women to do the same and contribute to providing an alliance and network of support, nationally and regionally. They were expected to assist in broadening and strengthening a constituency of public support for women's leadership and a demand for good governance practices by current leaders (UNIFEM 2004).

Managing Difference in and Outside of the Regional Women's Movement

The women's movement acted to transform relationships relating to race, ethnicity, class, culture and masculinity. In Trinidad and Tobago, Women Working for Social Progress (Workingwomen) collaborated with the HWO to launch an anti-racism (including internalized racism) campaign in 1995 (Wells, cited in Reddock 2004: 19–39). This collaboration responded to the tensions in the aftermath of the national elections in which an East Indian majority government replaced an African majority government for the first time since political independence in 1962. A cross-class, cross-ethnic group of women, and their male allies, acted to manage the situation with an anti-racism campaign that envisioned transformational possibilities.

A similar envisioning of revolutionary possibilities occurred with the launch of Red Thread in Guyana, a cross-class, cross-ethnic, cross-party collaboration. Red Thread, an income-generating group brought African, East Indian and Amerindian-Guyanese women together, many for the first time. By leading this collaboration women in the Working People's Alliance (WPA) were fulfilling one of the party's founding principles, which was to build cross-group alliances to overcome a fractured body politic (Hinds 2000). Red Thread demonstrated how people could collaborate around their common oppressions, in spite of their differences (Nettles 2007, 57–59; Kempadoo, 2013, 6–7). Training women in cross-party TL sessions had a similar intent.

Addressing another issue of difference, the near absence of working-class women from the leadership of the Caribbean women's movement, veteran womanist activist Andaiye (2002, 13) considered this lacuna an indictment on the movement's middle-class leadership. She suggested that its failure to create a paradigm shift in its class base was reminiscent of the failure of their liberal and left-leaning parties to address the woman question in the 1980s (Andaiye Ibid.).

Rhoda Reddock's (2007) response to Andaiye's critique was that consider-able efforts by the movement to integrate working-class women into its lead-ership were stymied by a socio-historical context that fostered a formidable and persistent 'mistrust of the "Other"', a legacy engendered by the ideology of white supremacy that justified the enslavement of Africans and the inden-tureship of East Indians in the region. This mistrust, institutionalized in social relationships, is difficult to overcome, she opined (Ibid.). This difficulty may explain the loss of momentum in the anti-racism alliance between Working-women and HWO. Exposing women to TL theory and practice and imple-menting strategies to build their self-confidence and to exercise emotional intelligence in leadership were important responses to these considerations.

The women's movement also critiqued the definitions and behaviours asso-ciated with the binary opposites of womanhood and manhood and femininity and masculinity, and called for their transformation (Barriteau 2003, 334–38; Mohammed 1996, 6–24; Mohammed 1998, 27; Lewis 2007, 1; Lewis & Carr 2009, 1–2). The tensions within popular discourse on shifting gender roles, including the misogyny directed at women and the male marginalization the-sis, were placed on the agenda. Focus on the destructive nature of hegemonic masculinity, personally and socially, came under the microscope (Tang Nain 1993, 19–20). One of the outcomes, increased violence directed against women and children – and other marginalized groups such as homosexual men by heterosexual men – also entered the conversation (Lewis 2007, 1; Lewis & Carr 2009, 1–2).

Managing Tensions between The Women's Movement and Women in Politics

To ease tensions existing between the feminist movement and women politi-cians, members such as the Network of NGOs in Trinidad and Tobago, apart from training women in how to win elections and engender public policy, held 'frank and open' private meetings with women politicians. They petitioned and lobbied them and their male allies to build cross-party alliances, attend forums organized by the women's movement, support legislation in parliament and incorporate women's issues into their political platforms. The consensus is, however, that elected women have little or no contact with the women's movement and do not advocate women's issues unless they favour their political parties' interests (Andaiye 2009, 17).

Sheila Roseau, coordinator of the CIWiL admitted to the gap between the women's movement and women politicians. This continuing gap inspired a move to send a delegation to a meeting of the Commonwealth Women Parliamentarians to discuss ways of collaborating. The parliamentarians expressed empathy for the gender agenda but admitted that they were fully occupied 'surviving' the male-dominated environments of parliament and their political parties (Sheila Roseau, interviewed, October 19, 2012). This focus on vigilance for 'survival' and reservations about championing the gender agenda may be explained by the preference for inexperienced male politicians by party leaders and their women allies. Henry-Wilson (1989, 241–52; 2004, 587–89) explained how this practice led to males being recruited to top political leadership positions, given access to party patronage, placed in winnable seats and mentored by veteran males, ahead of women with years of experience in party work and gender consciousness.

Experience has shown that women who defy the limitations of patriarchal party orthodoxy pay a high price through marginalization and removal from ministerial posts, party positions or candidature. For example, Portia Simpson-Miller, then Jamaica's minister of local government, was vilified by party colleagues in 2004 because she abstained on an opposition-sponsored parliamentary vote criticizing her government for its underfunding of the fire services for which she had ministerial responsibility (Simpson 2004). Verna St. Rose in Trinidad and Tobago was allegedly fired in 2012 because she advocated legislative changes on abortion and gay marriage (Ramdass 2012).[9] Gail Texeira, former minister of health in Guyana, was sidelined to the Ministry of Youth and Sports by the late president Janet Jagan, presumably because she supported the Medical Termination of Pregnancy Act (1995) (Nunes 2012, 87).

Advances and Setbacks in the Regional Women's Movement

Like all advocacy efforts, advances and setbacks occur. The women's movement succeeded in incrementally sensitizing the public to the quality and viability of women politicians. Progress towards building a critical mass of women exposed to TL theory and practice and supportive of women's candidature is evident. The seven Caribbean Policy Development Centre

(CPDC) training interventions implemented in Jamaica, Barbados and the OECS countries trained approximately one hundred and ten women from different political parties. Two of the participants subsequently became cabinet ministers in Antigua and Barbuda. One participant became the minister of education in Grenada; two participants from Dominica, who were local government representatives, became candidates in their national elections. One woman from St. Vincent and the Grenadines launched an internal party campaign calling for 30% of the party's candidates to be women, and one woman planned to run for the presidency of her trade union (Isiuwa Iyahen, n.d.).

In relation to setbacks, the sanctions against those who defy the party line, described earlier, the 'currents' of 'misogyny' and associated gender-based violence is unfortunate (Barriteau 1997, 1–4). These responses remove evaluation away from the construction of masculinity, male socialization and male privilege (Figueroa 2004), issues that need urgent attention and solutions to advance the development of the region.

Recommendations and Discussions Based on the Analytical Framework

For the future, coalition building and outreach that mobilizes broad alliances of women and men to pressure leaders to exercise political will for implementing transformative change is essential. Civil society groups such as the Jamaica Civil Society Coalition (JCSC) and the 51% Coalition in Jamaica[10] work with private sector entities to support women's public leadership. This work demonstrates the flexibility and multi-group alliances that may be necessary for creating transformational change in the future (Carol Narcisse, Interview, August 14, 2012). The analytical framework stresses the importance of broad alliances and coalitions of women, and their male allies, advocating inside and outside of political parties.

A longitudinal comparative analysis study of project beneficiaries' uses of the skills gained in TL interventions to measure the effectiveness of the use of scarce resources is clearly needed. The framework identifies the characteristics of TL that could provide a standard for evaluating such progress. The movement needs to engender ways that encourage the broad mass of people to practice TL principles, individually and collectively, and to demand good governance from leaders. Multimedia strategies such as mobile applications, animation, and engaging face-to-face conversations at the community level are some possibilities. One research participant explained that transformative change is possible even with only one woman in parliament, with none, or only with those supportive of transformation. She cited the examples of the passing of the abortion law in Barbados's parliament when Billie Miller was the lone woman representative in government and the passing of the

Maternity Leave Law in Jamaica, pushed from outside the political party by a broad coalition.

The most obvious approach suggested for encouraging mass support for TL is modelling desired behaviour – being the change you desire. Leaders must also address solutions to the macroeconomic issues that preoccupy constituents (CAFRA News, Vol. 2, 19–22). These include alternative development strategies, the crippling debt burden, unemployment, family life and chronic non-communicable, lifestyle-associated diseases. The rejection of divisive politics that deepens the historical racial and ethnic divide is also urgent.

Consistent and high-quality community-based caring and safe support will make women more comfortable about leaving their families to take up leadership posts. With this support, politically minded women will be able to transition seamlessly from serving as teachers, nurses and social workers to serving as politicians (Marshall-Burnett, interviewed, April 14, 2012). Syringa Marshall-Burnett, former president of the Senate – Jamaica's upper house – suggested that cross-class, cross-gender, cross-ethnic community meetings, could be the base for this care service. These spaces, she suggested, could transition to using truth and reconciliation strategies to discuss issues of domestic and sexual violence, including incest. In a similar vein, she suggested that parliaments needed to become parent-friendly and cited the South African parliament as the standard to be emulated.

Detailed research of outstanding women leaders in the Caribbean and Latin and South America needs to continue. Best practices could be culled from these studies to prepare a culturally relevant list of TL characteristics that aspirants could use to check their personal progress towards achieving TL (Carol Narcisse, interviewed, August 14, 2012).

CONCLUSION

Advocacy for a woman's transformational style of leadership that emerged in the Anglophone Caribbean region in the 1990s built on a tradition of activism to situate the locus of power in non-authoritarian, collective, organizational structures that promoted equality and respect for everyone and placed women's experiences and voices in public discourse. For 20 years, the women's movement has implemented strategies, structures, processes and practices to advance a culturally relevant, transparent, accountable, responsive and compassionate style of change leadership at different levels.

The movement has made progress; greater public awareness of the quality and viability of women's leadership exists, and in a number of spaces, more women are offering themselves for top public leadership positions. However, as was the case with WID and GAD, the momentum of change has not happened to the extent expected. Early indicators are that a number of trends may be emerging. One is a backlash aimed at maintaining patriarchal privilege which is surfacing in many parts of the Anglophone Caribbean. The other is an alliance of women, and their male allies, who are determined to continue and strengthen advocacy, not just for advancing women's rights but for advancing the rights of all of humanity, including the most marginalized groups. This point may be where the conversation needs to continue.

NOTES

1. Strategies are planned activities – short, medium or long term. Processes are the methods used to implement activities. Practices are actions taken. Contestations identify differences and attempts at resolution.

2. The majority of Caribbean feminists is liberal and focuses on reforming the capitalist state to advance women's rights. Nonetheless, the roots of second-wave Caribbean feminism emerged among radical and socialist feminists (Reddock 1998, 62–63).

3. This chapter builds on a Rapid Assessment of Projects on Women's Political Participation in the Caribbean Region (n.d.) prepared by Isiuwa Iyahen's for UNIFEM Caribbean, and Andaiye's (2009) assessment of women's political participation in electoral processes in the Caribbean in the period 2007–2009.

4. This discussion of feminist leadership draws heavily on Batliwala's 2011 study on leadership.

5. Antrobus headed Jamaica's Women's Bureau (1974), The UWIs Women and Development Unit (1979), and is a founding director of Development Alternatives with Women for a New Era (DAWN). See http://www.caricom.org/jsp/projects/personalities/peggy_antrobus.jsp?menu=projects. Andaiye, another outstanding Caribbean transformational leader, is highly respected regionally and internationally. She is a founding member of the Working People's Alliance and Red Thread. See http://www.selmajamesbooktour.net/node/3.

6. Ruth Nita Barrow was the UN Convener of the NGO forum for the third World Conference of Women, one of the seven secretary-generals of the World Council of Churches, a governor general of Barbados and its permanent representative to the UN.

7. 'UNIFEM Caribbean Office Summary Proposal: Changing the Paradigm of Leadership in the Caribbean: Transformational Leadership Project' (n. d.).

8. Messiah led the WICP's research team as head of the UWI's Institute for Social and Economic Research (Eastern Caribbean). It was the first major regional project that researched women's lives and subsequently informed major policies.

9. Anna Ramdass, 2012, 'Anil: Verna fired for gay/abortion rights', *Trinidad Express Newspapers*, at http://www.trinidadexpress.com/news/anil__verna_fired_for_gay_abortion_rights_-182475091.html. Accessed May 9, 2013.

10. The 51% Coalition is the broad alliance of women's organizations in Jamaica that advocates women's and men's directorship on boards and commissions to be no less than 40%, or no more than 60% of each group.

REFERENCES

Andaiye. 2009. 'Critical Review of Selected Interventions in Support of Women's Participation in Electoral Processes in the Caribbean in the period 2007–2008'. The University of the West Indies Institute for Gender and Development Studies: Nita Barrow Unit. Accessed October 27, 2012. http://networkngott.org/networkngott/images/pdfs/ciwil_document_2009.pdf.

———. 2002. 'Towards Building a Movement: A Critique of Feminist Politics and Organising in the Caribbean'. Lecture presented at the biennial Lucille Mathurin Mair Lecture, University of the West Indies, Mona Campus. March 6, 2002.

Antrobus, Peggy. 2004. *The Global Women's Movement: Issues and Strategies for the New Century*. London: Zed Books.

———. 2002. 'Feminism as Transformational Politics: Towards possibilities for another world'. Society for International Development. London & New Delhi. Thousand Oaks CA: SAGE Publications: 46–52.

———. 1999. 'Walk Slowly in the Wind Together'. *Dawn Informs: Development Alternative with Women for a New Era 2/99*. Accessed October 29, 2012. http://www.dawnnet.org/uploads/newsletters/1999-June.pdf.

Barriteau, Eudine. 2004. 'Women and Leadership: Some Strategies of Transformational Women Leaders in the Caribbean'. Address delivered at the Centre for Management Development, Cave Hill, Barbados, December 2, 2004. Accessed October 29, 2012. http://www.cavehill.uwi.edu/gender/archives/library/women_leadership_barriteau_2004.aspx.

———. 2001. 'Historical Concepts and Paradigms of Leadership and their Relevance to Strengthening Women's Transformational Leadership in the Caribbean'. Accessed April 13, 2010. http://www.sputtr.com/read/historical-concepts-and-paradigms-of-leadership-and-their--d41d.html?f=1qeXpurpn6Wih-SUpOGunKanh7TY6d-nj2s7T09WOt9Xj0Mrc4-mF1dbJkMLK4NXK3tTS34_ly5S0ytHWzuDnzt7d-hc3d2oXo0MrZ5ImcopSXqNimoLCH2oqg46ygn66I3eHZ3KmllOvf3J7V0uX-d0qPc19Oe5trW1M7T093X49TonLXb4t_Z3dfTlaSZvtXW2t-Knp-8zuLJ0ZWkmbPpyt7byprf2suWo-I

———. 2001. 'The Challenge of Innovative Leadership of a Traditional Women's Organization: The World YWCA and Ruth Nita Barrow', in *Stronger, Surer, Bolder Ruth Nita Barrow: Social Change and International Development*, ed. Eudine Barriteau and Alan Colby, Cave Hill, Barbados: University of the West Indies Press.

———. 1997. 'Are Caribbean Women Taking Over? Contradictions for Women in Caribbean Society'. Inaugural Dame Nita Barrow Women in Development and Community Transformation Visitorship Lecture, OISE and the University of Toronto, Toronto, Canada.

Barriteau, Eudine and Alan Cobley, (eds). 2006. *Enjoying Power: Eugenia Charles and Political Leadership in the Commonwealth Caribbean*. Jamaica: University of the West Indies Press.

Batliwala, Srilatha. 2011. 'Feminist Leadership for Social Transformation: Clearing the Conceptual Cloud'. Creating Resources for Empowerment in Action (CRE)

– Association for Women's Rights in Development (AWID). Accessed May 7, 2013. http://web.creaworld.org/files/f1.pdf.

CAFRA. Accessed November 10, 2012, at http://www.cafra.org/spip.php?article25.

Caribbean Regional Symposium: 'Engendering Local Government'. 1997. Rex St. Lucian Hotel, Castries, St. Lucia, 30 June – 3 July.

Caribbean Community (CARICOM) Secretariat. 2011. Model Legislation on Sexual Offences. Accessed September 16, 2013. http://www.caricom.org/jsp/secretariat/legal_instruments/model_legislation_sexual_offences.jsp.

CARICOM Plan of Action to 2005: Framework for Mainstreaming Gender into Key CARICOM Programmes. Accessed December 17, 2011. http://www.caricom.org/jsp/community_organs/gender_and_development/plan_of_action.pdf.

Catalysts for Change: Caribbean Women and Governance: Projects and Activities: Regional Programme of Action. http://cfcportal.net/artman/publish/article_50.shtml.

CIWiL. 2012. Advancing Women's Transformational Leadership across the Caribbean, at http://www.ciwil.org/.

Connelly, Patricia, M., Tania Murray Li, Martha MacDonald, and Jane L. Parpart. 2000. 'Chapter 3 Feminism and Development: Theoretical Perspectives', In *Theoretical Perspectives on Gender and Development*, ed. Janc L. Parpart, M. Patricia Connelly, and V. Eudine Barriteau. Ottawa: IDRC.

ECLAC. 2010. 'Caribbean Synthesis Review and Appraisal Report in the Context of the 15th Anniversary of the Adoption of the Beijing Declaration and Platform for Action'. LC/CAR/L.259, May 14, 2010. Accessed January 6, 2014. http://www.eclac.cl/publicaciones/xml/2/39542/LCARL.259.pdf.

ECLAC/UNIFEM: Eliminating Gender-Based Violence, Ensuring Equality. 2003. ECLAC/UNIFEM Regional Assessment of Actions to end Violence against Women in the Caribbean. 3–4, 10). See http://www.cepal.org/publicaciones/xml/0/38620/lcarg764.pdf.

Evans, Kristy. 2005. 'A Guide to Feminist Advocacy'. Gender and Development, 13 (3), 10–20. Accessed November 14, 2011.

Figueroa, Mark. 2004. 'Old (Female) Glass Ceilings and New (Male) Looking Glasses: Challenging Gender Privileging in the Caribbean', In *Gender in the 21st Century: Caribbean Perspectives, Visions and Possibilities*, ed. Barbara Bailey and Elsa Leo-Rhynie, Kingston: Jamaica, Ian Randle Publishers, 134–61.

Ford-Smith, Honor. 1989. 'Ring Ding in a Tight Corner: A Case Study of Funding and Organizational Democracy in Sistren, 1977–1988'. Toronto: Canada, Women's Programme, ICAE (International Council for Adult Education).

Freire, Paulo. 2007. Pedagogy of the Oppressed. (New revised 30th anniversary ed.). New York: The Continuum Publishing Co.

French, Joan. 1994. 'Hitting Where it Hurts Most: Jamaican Women's Livelihood in Crisis', in *Mortgaging Women's Lives: Feminist Critiques of Structural Adjustment*, ed. Pamela Sparr, London: Zed Books Ltd., 165–82.

Gill, Margaret D. 2009. Some Thoughts on the Status of the Women's Movement in the Caribbean. See http://www.normangirvan.info/wp-content/uploads/2009/09/gill-womens-movement.pdf.

Global Women's Strike. 2007. 'For Clotil Walcott, beloved comrade'. Accessed June 29, 2012. http://www.globalwomenstrike.net/content/clotil-walcott-beloved-comrade.

Henry-Wilson, Maxine. 2004. 'Governance, Leadership and Decision-making: Prospects for Caribbean Women', in *Gender in the 21st Century: Caribbean Perspectives, Visions and Possibilities*, ed. Barbara Bailey and Elsa Leo-Rhynie, 585–91. Kingston: Jamaica, Ian Randle Publishers.

———. 1989. 'The Status of the Jamaican Woman, 1962 to the Present', in *Jamaica in Independence: Essays on the Early Years*, ed. Rex Nettleford, Kingston: Heinemann Caribbean, 75–104.

Hill Collins, Patricia. 2000. *Black Feminist Thought: Knowledge, Consciousness, and the Politics of Empowerment.* 2nd ed. New York: Routledge.

Hinds, David. 2000. 'Working People's Alliance (WPA): Brief History of the Working People's Alliance', April 7, accessed June 15, 2012. http://www.guyanacaribbeanpolitics.com/wpa/history.html

hooks, Bell. 1984. *Feminist Theory: From Margin to Center.* Boston: South End Press.

Jaquette, Jane, ed. 1994, 2nd ed. *The Women's Movement in Latin America: Participation and Democracy.* Boulder, CO: Westview Press.

Kandiyoti, Deniz. 1998. 'Bargaining with Patriarchy'. *Gender and Society*, 2, no. 3, (September Special Issue) in Honor of Jessie Bernard, 274–90. Accessed February 17, 2014, http://www.smi.uib.no/seminars/Pensum/kandiyoti,%20Deniz.pdf.

Kempadoo, Kamala. 2013. 'Red Thread's Research: An Interview with Andaiye'. *Caribbean Review of Gender Studies: A Journal of Caribbean Perspectives on Gender and Feminism*, 7, 1–17, http://sta.uwi.edu/crgs/december2013/journals/CRGS_7_Kempadoo.pdf.

Kimmel, Michael. 2004. 'Men, Masculinities, and Development'. Lecture presented at the biennial Lucille Mathurin Mair Lecture, University of the West Indies, Mona Campus. March 11, 2006.

Lewis, Linden. 2007. 'Man Talk, Masculinity and a Changing Social Environment'. *Caribbean Review of Gender Studies: A Journal of Caribbean Perspectives on Gender and Feminism*, 3, 1–22. Accessed December 17, 2011. https://sta.uwi.edu/crgs/april2007/journals/Linden_Lewis_pm_07.pdf.

Lewis, R. Anthony and Robert Carr. 2009. 'Gender, Sexuality and Exclusion: Sketching the Outlines of the Jamaican Popular Nationalist Project'. *Caribbean Review of Gender Studies: A Journal of Caribbean Perspectives on Gender and Feminism*, 3, 1–22. Accessed December 17, 2011. http://sta.uwi.edu/crgs/november2009/journals/Lewis_Carr.pdf.

Massiah, Jocelyn. 2001. 'Foreword'. in *Stronger, Surer, Bolder Ruth Nita Barrow: Social Change and International Development, ed.* Eudine Barriteau and Alan Cobley. Kingston, Jamaica: University of the West Indies Press.

Miller, Carmen Hutchinson. 2006. 'Stereotyping Women's Political Leadership: Images of Eugenia Charles in the Caribbean Print Media'. in *Enjoying Power: Eugenia Charles and Political Leadership in the Commonwealth Caribbean*, ed. Eudine Barriteau and A. Cobley, 239–57. Kingston: University of the West Indies Press.

Mohammed, Patricia. 1998. 'Rethinking Caribbean Difference'. *Feminist Review* 59, (Summer): 1–5; 7–27.

————. 1996. 'Unmasking Masculinity and Deconstructing Patriarchy: Problems and Possibilities within Feminist Epistemology'. *Paper presented at the Symposium on The Construction of Masculinity: Toward a Research Agenda.* Centre for Gender and Development Studies, University of the West Indies, St. Augustine, Trinidad and Tobago, 11–13 January 1996.

Mohanty, Chandra Chalpade. 2003. 'Under Western Eyes Revisited. Feminist Solidarity through Anti-Capitalist Struggles'. *Signs: Journal of Women in Culture and Society 2002*, 28(2), 499–35.

Molyneux, Maxine. 1985. 'Mobilization without Emancipation? Women's Interests, the State and Revolution in Nicaragua'. *Feminist Studies* 11, (2) (Summer), 227–54.

Nettles, Kimberley. 2007. 'Becoming Red Thread Women: Alternative Visions of Gendered Politics in Post-Independence Guyana'. *Social Movement Studies* 6, (1) (May), 57–82, at http://courses.arch.vt.edu/courses/wdunaway/gia5274/nettles.pdf. Accessed March 18, 2014.

Network of NGOs of Trinidad & Tobago for the Advancement of Women: Network's Newsletter # 4. 2010. *Official Newsletter of the Network of NGOs, http://networkngott.org/networkngott/images/pdfs/network_news4.pdf.*

Nunes, Fred. 2012. 'Legal but Inaccessible: Abortions in Guyana'. *Social and Economic Studies, Special Issue on Women's Reproductive Health and Rights in Select Caribbean Countries*, ed. Taitu Heron and Sharika Maxwell, 61, (3) (September): 59–94. Accessed May 9, 2013. http://ssrn.com/abstract=2233860.

Raaber, Natalie and Diana Aguiar. 2008. 'Feminist Critiques, Policy Alternatives and Calls for Systemic Change to an Economy in Crisis'. Association for Women's Rights in Development (AWID). https://editorialexpress.com/cgi-bin/conference/download.cgi?db_name=IAFFE2011&paper_id=262.

Ramdass, Anna. 2012. 'Anil: Verna Fired for Gay/Abortion Rights'. *Trinidad Express Newspaper.* http://www.trinidadexpress.com/news/anil__verna_fired_for_gay_abortion_rights_-182475091.html.

Rathbeger, Eva. M. 1989. WID, WAD, GAD: Trends in Research and Practice. Dalhousie University, 4 (Summer) (3): 1–6.

Reddock, Rhoda. 2007. 'Diversity, Difference and Caribbean Feminism: The Challenge of Anti-Racism'. *Caribbean Review of Gender Studies. A Journal on Caribbean Perspectives on Gender and Feminism*, 1 (April): 1–24. Accessed February 27, 2014. https://sta.uwi.edu/crgs/april2007/journals/Diversity-Feb_2007.pdf.

————. 2004. Reflections on Gender and Democracy in the Anglophone Caribbean: Historical and Contemporary Considerations, SEPHIS-CODESRIA Lecture, January.

————. 1998. 'Women's Organisation and Movement in the Commonwealth Caribbean: The Response to Global Economic Crisis in the 1980s'. in Rethinking Caribbean Difference, *Feminist Review* 59 (Summer), 57–73.

Senior, Olive. 1991. 'Working Miracles: Women's Lives in the English-Speaking Caribbean'. Institute of Social and Economic Research, Cave Hill. Barbados, University of the West Indies Press.

Simpson, Lynford. 2004. 'Chastising Portia'. *Jamaica Gleaner*, April 12, 2004. Accessed January 6, 2014. http://jamaica-gleaner.com/gleaner/20040412/news/news3.html.

Sparr, Pamela, ed. 1994. 'What is Structural Adjustment?' in *Mortgaging Women's Lives: Feminist Critiques of Structural Adjustment*, ed. by Pamela Sparr. London: Zed Books Ltd.

Tang-Nain, Gemma 1993. 'Afro Caribbean Male Youth: A feminist analysis of the "problem"'. *CAFRA News: Newsletter of the Caribbean Association of Feminist Research and Action*, 7 (3), July–September.

The West Indian Commission. 1992. *Overview of the Report of the West Indian Commission: Time for Action*. The West Indian Commission. Christ Church, Barbados: Cole's Printery Ltd.

UNIFEM. 2004. Catalysts for Change: Caribbean Women and Governance, at http://cfcportal.net/. Accessed October 18, 2012.

Vassell, Linnette. 2001. 'Leadership Projects and Programmes for Women in the Caribbean: Towards Understandings of Transformational Leadership'. Prepared for UNIFEM Caribbean Office. Bridge Town: Barbados, at http://www.ciwil.org/publications/position paper final linette.pdf.

Women's Political Participation: Training in Governance and Democracy. 2004. http://cfcportal.net/artman/publish/article_50.shtml. Accessed March 18, 2014.

Chapter 10

Feminist Strategies, Masculinist Resistances and the Limits of Transformational Leadership

Denise Blackstock

INTRODUCTION

This chapter explores enactments of transformational leadership in the lives of two women leaders from St. Lucia in order to determine its effectiveness as a feminist strategy for advancing gender equality and justice, and women's rights and empowerment in the Caribbean. It draws on feminist scholarship and training relevant to transformational leadership carried out by the CIWiL, which trained the two women who are the main change agents in the chapter. The women underwent intense sensitization and awareness raising in key concepts such as democratic governance, gender-sensitive and ethical decision making, equitable and effective leadership approaches and partnership building with civil society for governance accountability. Keen attention was paid to principles of equality, transparency, fairness, mutual respect, cooperation and non-violence – traits considered to be anti-masculinist. These women were expected to assume leadership positions, and to personify and embody the characteristics of a transformational leader bringing positive changes in the lives of all with whom they come in contact, thus contributing to gender transformation. But, do they? What are the lived experiences of these women as they engage leadership in a 'new' way? Does training women in transformational leadership translate into practice in their personal and professional spaces? How does enacting transformational leadership transpose into transformed power relations between men and women? Are gender equality and justice and women's rights and empowerment being achieved? What are the implications for feminist advocacy and women's movement-building in the Caribbean, if these expectations are not realized?

The chapter provides answers to these questions by taking a narrative approach to the findings from two months of field research in 2013. Through

the themes that emerged, we can trace enactments, ambivalences, contradictions and the repudiation of feminist analyses of gendered structural, ideological and material power relations and how they should be confronted. To
facilitate this analysis, I first discuss the Caribbean's historical and theoretical
context for the pursuit of women's transformational leadership, including a
brief commentary on the chapter's specific contribution to the wider research
project being undertaken by the IGDS. Next, I present the methodology used
to answer the main research question and also provide some background
information on the women studied. I then present the main findings from
the fieldwork in St. Lucia, including an analysis of how the women leaders
investigated engage with these themes in their capacity as transformational
leaders. I conclude by arguing that while transformational leadership is being
enacted in a way that contributes to gender equality and equity in St. Lucia,
there is shift in the way gender, gender relations and gender equality are being
understood and acted upon. The women observed do not identify themselves
as feminists and seem to be searching for an identity that links the struggle
for women's rights within the broader context of the rights of men, children
and community.

WOMEN'S TRANSFORMATIONAL LEADERSHIP IN THE CARIBBEAN: HISTORICAL AND THEORETICAL CONTEXT

Research conducted by Campbell (2014) argues that the pursuit for a non-
masculinist style of leadership in the Caribbean emerged in the 1970s in an
attempt to promote equality and mutual respect for everyone and position
women's experiences and voices in public discourse. The gendered impact
of neo-liberal economic models of development pursued by Caribbean leaders, particularly on women and the most vulnerable in society, provided
the catalyst for the Caribbean women's movement activism calling for a
transformative leadership that was people-centred, non-hierarchical, inclusive and underpinned by gender equality (Campbell 2014; Antrobus 2004).
Campbell further argues that the quest was also driven by the post-Beijing
call for state and non-state sectors to promote women's public leadership as
a human rights issue and a necessity for advancing gender justice (Campbell
2014). To this end, and under the leadership of the Caribbean Office of the
United Nations Entity for Gender Equality and the Empowerment of Women
(UN Women, formerly the United Nations Development Fund for Women
(UNIFEM)), commitments were made to create and implement a gender-
sensitive, human-centred, sustainable development project for the region that
would involve women as change agents at every level of leadership in the
society (Campbell 2014). The financial and technical support provided to

women's organizations in the region, such as the CIWiL, to train women to be transformational leaders, launched the practical component of the quest to advance transformational leadership in the Caribbean.

Women's transformational leadership is underpinned by a critical feminist theoretical analysis of social relations of gender, which includes problematizing the role of patriarchal ideology in producing gender hierarchies that sustain gender inequalities (Campbell 2014). Writers such as Steans (2006) and D'Amico and Beckham (1995) argue that there is a gender hierarchy or ordering system that privileges masculine traits (for e.g. power, leadership, strength, aggression) over feminine traits (for e.g. nurturing, compassion, fragility, dependence), and which results in unequal gender power relations between men and women in social, economic and political spheres. Young, in Shepherd and Mohammed (1999) further argues that we acquire the social characteristics of masculinity or femininity through a process known as gendering. This involves acquiring an identity (masculine or feminine) and learning a set of differentiated behaviours and capacities appropriate to one's gender (Young 1999).

One of the earliest conditions challenged by feminist theorizing and activism was masculinist ways of leading. Feminists have worked to change patriarchal deployment of power, which is seen as a tool of oppression and the perpetuation of unequal gendered power relations (Barriteau 2001; Vassell, 2001). Thus, feminist transformational leadership has been concerned with influencing decisions to achieve outcomes that deconstruct gender hierarchies and advance gender justice (Campbell 2014). Gender justice is defined as the attainment of qualitative changes in women's and men's lives where neither is privileged, where masculinity and femininity are ascribed equal status and where women, men, girls and boys have equal opportunities, access to and control of society's resources (Barriteau 2007). In keeping with the objectives of the Caribbean's seminal transformational leadership project, the woman transformational leader is expected to intervene chiefly on two levels: (1) in the material realm of gender relations (improving the material conditions of women and men) and (2) in the ideological realm (mounting an active challenge to patriarchal norms and ideologies that keep women subordinated).

Built on the research project, 'Negotiating Gender, Policy and Politics in the Caribbean: Feminist Strategies, Masculinist Resistances and the Possibilities for Transformation in the Caribbean', this chapter presents a different perspective to the question of how gender equality and justice could be achieved in the Caribbean and the theoretical and empirical lessons that could be learned. Thus, whereas the quota system looks at the implications of getting greater numbers of women in parliament (Guyana); and women's political leadership at getting women in at the very top (Trinidad and Tobago);

and the Dominica and Jamaica cases at mainstreaming gender in policy, this chapter is concerned with a complementary issue because it explores the challenges of women's leadership, the resistances of the material and ideological relations of gender, the personal narratives of women in leadership and how they themselves negotiate with an ideal that women can provide a different but still effective form of leadership than the more patriarchal models. This chapter also fills the gap identified by Campbell (2014) to ascertain, through tracer studies, how the women who were trained to be transformational leaders are enacting the skills they acquired and to whose benefit.

METHODOLOGY

Determining the effectiveness of transformational leadership as a feminist strategy for gender transformation transported me into the lives and lived realities of two women who were trained to enact this type of leadership style by the CIWiL. These women are Jeannine Compton-Antoine and Brenda Wilson, natives of St. Lucia. St. Lucia was chosen as the research site due to preliminary research and also interviews with the then CIWiL coordinator Ms. Sheila Roseau, which revealed that CIWiL has been particularly successful in training women for political and civil leadership in that country. Ms. Una Mae Gordon, a CIWiL board member who was based in St. Lucia, was instrumental in identifying research subjects and in the final selection of these two women, who indicated their interest and availability to participate in the research. Through two months of intense shadowing, observations, personal interactions, conversations and interviews, I was able to ascertain what transformational leadership means for these women, how it has been demonstrated in their lives and the specific outcomes and implications of this form of engagement. This led me to interact with a wide cross-section of individuals (relatives, colleagues and beneficiaries of project and programme initiatives) in communities across St. Lucia who had first-hand contact and experience with the research subjects and who were willing to share their knowledge and perspectives. A total of 43 respondents, 24 females and 19 males, were interviewed. This diverse group was drawn from government agencies, CSOs, women and community groups and included senior government officials, education facilitators, programme and project beneficiaries, and persons with disabilities and their caregivers.

The research questions posed were geared towards determining whether transformational leadership was being enacted in a way that contributed to the achievement of gender equality and justice and women's rights and empowerment. They also sought to extract the real life narratives of how this transformation has been experienced by individuals, groups and communities and ascertain the strategies and techniques employed and also the opportunities and limitations of this particular leadership strategy. The qualitative data analysis software ATLAS.ti was used to systematically organize, code, and analyse the data collected. Themes emerged relating to (1) leadership approaches; (2) gender relations, male marginalization and feminist identity; (3) contributions of women transformational leadership; (4) challenges and resistances to transformational leadership; and (5) limitations of women's transformational leadership as a feminist strategy for gender equality and justice. The achievements and limitations were then inductively derived from the varied and sometimes overlapping strands of the emerging data. In presenting this data, the chapter relied extensively on the narrative approach, allowing the respondents to communicate directly their thoughts and feelings and then using these first-person perspectives and experiences as the point of departure for analysing the data in light of the main research questions and the theoretical framework on transformational leadership presented by Campbell (2014).

I will share some thoughts on reflexivity, how it played out in this ethnographic study and the potential impact on the study outcomes. According to Young (2008), reflexivity is where the researcher declares upfront how his or her personal opinions, beliefs and view of the participants may have impacted the research process and outcomes. As a fellow CIWiL trainee, I had a strong interest in transformational leadership and in ascertaining the viability of this feminist strategy for achieving gender equality and justice. This meant that I went into the research, not as a blank slate, but with prior knowledge of the issues and concerns. It also meant that I was able to easily establish rapport with the main research subjects who saw me as an equal, thus fostering open and honest communication. Also, while the other participants came from diverse social backgrounds and contexts, including social class, the trust and confidence they had in the main research subjects spilled over to me by virtue of association. This affected the knowledge production and outcomes in a positive way, as I was able to guide the research process towards advancing understandings of women's transformational leadership without the distraction that dealing with such a diverse group might have otherwise created.

BACKGROUND AND CONTEXTS – JEANNINE COMPTON-ANTOINE AND BRENDA WILSON

Jeannine is a marine biologist by profession and the general manager of the Soufriere Marine Management Authority (SMMA). The SMMA is a non-governmental organization based in Soufriere that manages the marine area of the west coast through a multi-stakeholder partnership comprised of government and civil society actors (fisher folk, divers, tourism interests, government agencies and private sector interests). Jeannine is also the first Caribbean representative to chair the International Whaling Commission (IWC). She is passionate about national development, which was mainly nurtured by her father, the late former prime minister of St. Lucia, Honourable Sir John Compton. A former parliamentarian herself, Jeannine has used that platform to advocate for policies and programmes to improve the lives of the people of St. Lucia. She is 43 years old, married and lives in Castries.

Brenda is from the small rural community of Mon Repos, St. Lucia. She is a social transformation officer in the Ministry of Social Transformation, Local Government and Community Empowerment and works throughout St. Lucia to secure the livelihoods of communities and build their resilience and sustainability. The seeds of community service were planted early in her life while in the care of her grandmother, who taught her the meaning of concern and care for the poor and underprivileged. These personal experiences have given her a focus, drive and passion for inclusive community development, which often inspires her to go beyond the call of duty, sometimes at great personal costs, in her quest to transform individuals and communities. Brenda is 49 years old and a single mother of one child, a son, whom she involves in her community work.

Focusing on these two women enabled me to explore enactments of transformational leadership in two different contexts, thereby facilitating an understanding of the specific contextual challenges faced in enacting a non-masculinist model of leadership. However, interestingly enough, when asked if they considered themselves transformational leaders, both hesitated to label themselves in that way. According to Jeannine, 'Being a transformational leader sometimes you don't even consider yourself as one because you do things because they mean something to you, that you see things going on in your country or society and you want to make changes'. Barriteau (2001) asserts that it is not necessary for a transformational leader to claim that identity. What is important, she argues, is that when researchers analyse women's approaches or the activities of the organizations which they head, or the environment in which they practice leadership, their work can be mapped on to the transformational leader conceptual framework, which will evaluate the transformational potential of their actions, behaviours and leadership approaches.

LEADERSHIP APPROACHES

Both women had a similar leadership approach, which integrated several elements of the transformational leadership model. For example, both women were described by colleagues and themselves as having a democratic or inclusive leadership style. Brenda opines, 'Democratic in that I seek consensus and I don't go out there enforcing my position. I know what I want to achieve, but I allow the community to see it as theirs and for them to own it'. Staff members of the SMMA describe Jeannine as a democratic leader because 'she doesn't just give directives. She would come and sit with you and ask, 'What do you think about that?' She's the kind of person that would take ideas from the line staff. She sits with us and we have that exchange of ideas and we sort through and then choose the best. So, that's what she does with us here and we didn't have that before' (C. Nicholas, SMMA accountant, Interview). Jeannine explains, 'I try to do the consultative thing … realizing that you can't just come and dictate. You listen, you talk and then you put forward your arguments. When I came in, I told them that they have to work together as a team. It is not just me; I am not just the bigger boss'.

This concept of not being 'the bigger boss' also emerges in Brenda's work with Broom Producers in La Pointe District. According to Paulina Ferdinand, 'Brenda is a lady who is down to the farmer when she has to meet with them. She wouldn't meet with us as an Officer, she would meet with us, and she would bring down herself low as being among us like a farmer. There is no boundary between the group members and her and we would interact in a meeting as all group members' (P. Ferdinand, president of Superior Broom Producers Inc., and Farmer, Interview). For Brenda, decision making under community development and social transformation is a collective process. For her, 'it's a community based approach, community owns it because the community knows their needs, know how to solve it, all they need are people to facilitate them in dotting their "i's" and crossing their "t's"'. She believes that 'the solutions are to be found internally, the community knows the solutions. My role is to facilitate them in identifying needs, to help them find sustainable and lasting resolutions. I do not work for you, I work with you. I am not there to do for you. I work with you so you can do for yourself. I am a facilitator. I am an enabler. Don't expect me to do for, expect me to do with'.

Vassell (2013) concurs with this approach arguing that the role of the transformational leader is to facilitate and engage others in the pursuit of individual and social transformation. She further argues that this should caution us not to see the transformational leader as the all-powerful agent or actor making things happen, but more as a way of doing and being. Mrs. Velda Joseph had this to say when queried about Brenda's leadership approach, 'Brenda has I think, understood very well the concept of community development. You don't go in and do things for people but you facilitate a process. Brenda has been very effective as a facilitator in that she helps you work through your ideas and she helps you implement your ideas' (V. Joseph, deputy director of community services, Ministry of Social Transformation, Local Government and Community Empowerment, Interview). For Mrs. Joseph, Brenda's approach to community development as a facilitator and enabler, and her belief that with the right tools and support individuals and communities can improve their social condition, makes her a transformational leader.

The foregoing insights highlight fundamental fissures between the traditional masculinist, authoritarian, hierarchical approach to leadership and the transformational leadership model being enacted by both women. Their non-hierarchal, consultative, people-centred leadership approach which deflects the spotlight away from the all-powerful leader to 'us', to the 'team', to 'inclusiveness' and to 'the collective' – not only in terms of decision-making processes but also in the implementation of agreed actions – is consistent with the transformational leadership theoretical framework presented by Campbell (2014) and CIWiL's transformational leadership training curriculum. Based on Brenda and Jeannine's philosophy of leadership and demonstrated actions with colleagues, their use of power and authority reflects the concepts of *power within, power to, power with* (Mosedale 2005; Luttrell and Quiroz et al. 2009), which is enabling, uplifting and inspiring. This approach is well received by all respondents and there is unequivocal acceptance of the trans-formational leadership style being enacted by both women.

GENDER RELATIONS, MALE MARGINALIZATION AND FEMINIST IDENTITY

Gender and gender relations manifest themselves in different and sometimes contradictory ways in these women's lives. The division of labour along gender lines is apparent in Jeannine's and Brenda's work environment. Men dominate the marine environment as fishermen, dive operators and marine rangers, while women play the lead role in community activities. Notwith-standing this, Jeannine breaks through the traditional gender roles in the marine environment by being a woman leader in this field. I questioned her on how she is using her position as a female transformational leader to improve the position of other women in this area and to transform the unequal gendered power relations. Jeannine expressed that she has tried to bring more women in but the main challenge is that women don't put themselves forward and so she is unable to recruit them. Jeannine asserts that 'you obviously speak to women and try to get them into more active roles in the area because there are possibilities for self-employment. However, as I said, the maritime industry, presently, in particular St. Lucia, is very male dominated'. Factors preventing a general breakthrough for women in this area include the prevailing cultural perception that 'only men work in the marine environment' and the inter-generational tradition of male grooming for active roles in marine life. The entrenchment of the traditional gender roles in this area poses a formidable adversary for Jeannine and as a woman transformational leader; she seems unable and ill equipped to challenge the embedded gendered assumptions and inequalities permeating this field in a way that can make a difference in the lives of other women. Jeannine's attempts at intervening in the material relations of gender for women are being constrained by the persistence of masculinist gender stereotypes that permeate the marine environment.

Brenda faces a similar challenge in community development, which has traditionally been an area dominated by women. She states, 'What has happened is that women are the greater activists in the communities that I've worked with than men and so women are a larger segment of the persons that I do my day-to-day activities alongside. Women are the ones driving community development'. Thus, unlike Jeannine, Brenda doesn't have to try to get more women involved as the majority of the persons she works with and who are actively involved in community development are women. The concern in this context is how to get more men involved in community activities. The initial reaction was to consider this a case of male marginalization as advanced by Miller (1994). However, a further review of the situation found that men did not participate even when invited to do so. According to V. Joseph (Interview), 'We recognize that the persons who come out when we call town hall and community meetings and the persons who form the majority of the membership in community based organizations are women'. Thus, there were no systematic and structural barriers (Barriteau 2003) hindering men's participation; but rather, male under-representation was seen by some respondents as a result of internalization of masculine stereotypes, which viewed community activism as a role of women (G. Wilson, Interview). Nevertheless, V. Joseph (Interview) highlighted the need to develop programmes geared towards increasing male involvement in community life. Both cases highlight the persistence and entrenchment of stereotypical gender roles based on heteronormativity and re-enforce the need for interventions into the ideological relations of gender to overcome these barriers. However, Brenda, like Jeannine, has been unable to successfully address these ideological dimensions of gender.

This is due in large part to the fact that their starting point for looking at and understanding gender equality differ from the feminist perspective. They do not self-identify with feminism and express sentiments such as, 'I try to balance everything so I wouldn't specifically look at my staff and say, ok, you're a woman, you're better, or I'll give you better privileges than men. I tend to look at everyone as human beings, male and female'. (Interview with Jeannine). Or, 'Not because you are female that benefits must come only to you. Males suffer some of the very disparities that women suffer too and so we need to understand that together men and women have to work for gender justice for both male and female, not one over the other' (Interview with Brenda). Both women take an egalitarian approach free from gender discrimination and inclusive of all groups in the society. This approach is supported by Barriteau (2007) who argues that in a gender-just system, there are no hierarchies of gender identities of men and women; or of the meanings society gives to masculinity and femininity; or asymmetries of access to, or allocation of, status, power and material resources in a society; 'or in the control over, and capacity to, benefit from these resources.

However, what appears to be missing from Jeannine's and Brenda's conceptions is due consideration to how the prevailing unequal gendered power relations in both their contexts can be addressed. A feminist reading of their approach to gender equality and justice could consider that by ignoring the active challenge required to patriarchy, they are in fact inadvertently supporting and enabling the masculinist systems that keep women subordinated and perpetuate gender inequalities. However, in her study on the women's piety movement in Egypt, Saba Mahmood (2004) calls for us to widen our understanding of women's agency on the question of gender equality and justice to consider the role of context in shaping the form women's agency and activism take. Both women originate from contexts where there is a strong focus on inclusiveness and non-discrimination as starting points. So for example, Jeannine grew up in a household with a father who was the prime minister of St. Lucia and in her words, 'seeing the role that my parents played, both mother and father, in trying to improve the lives of people in St. Lucia, you sort of take on some of the roles or similar attitudes'. For Brenda, growing up in a community setting with her grandmother, who inculcated in her the value of community service, and giving back, formed the basis for her own understanding of gender and gender relations and approach to working with men and women. These experiences have shaped, to a large extent, the way in which both women conceive gender relations and consequently how they enact transformational leadership.

Vassell (2013) asserts that many Caribbean women do not feel comfortable identifying with a feminist ideology because it is seen as not being sufficiently inclusive. As demonstrated by Brenda and Jeannine, they seek to link the struggles for women's rights within the broader context of rights of men, children and community. Vassell argues however, that self-identification is important for women's advocacy in the Caribbean, especially if the aim is to strengthen the path towards women in leadership and decision making on the basis that this can and will make a difference, not just for women but also for the wider society. This discourse has implications for feminist movement-building in the Caribbean and how women are organized individually and collectively, to enact transformational leadership and also challenge entrenched patriarchal norms for the achievement of gender equality and justice.

CONTRIBUTIONS OF WOMEN
TRANSFORMATIONAL LEADERSHIP

The data suggest that Jeannine and Brenda have made some important contributions in the areas of community livelihood and development and institutional building through projects and programmes that are gender-equitable. So for example, Jeannine has focused on improving food security for whaling communities in Alaska and St. Vincent in her work with the IWC. She advocates on their behalf because 'this is their livelihood and how they sustain themselves'. What Brenda does in her work with the Community After School Care Programme in St. Lucia is to ensure that the activities benefit boys and girls equally. According to her, 'I don't look at difference in terms of boys and girls.... We don't make a distinction between male and female. The subject areas being offered are for all of them'. This programme also provides employment and income for community members who are involved. Emphasis is also placed on promoting household economic independence and sustainability through skills development in kitchen gardening techniques. The Joy Sewing Project is another intervention that facilitates economic empowerment, but is specific to persons with disabilities, by building their capacity and skills in sewing clothes, which are then sold in the communities.

In the case of the St. Lucia Network of Rural Women Producers, the practical programmes in income generation characteristic of the WID approach also serve as the entry point to the redefinition of gender roles and gender power relations specific to the GAD approach in some cases as a result of the increase in women's awareness, self-esteem, autonomy and activism. One of the main objectives of the network is to bring women together who are housewives and unemployed outside the home in a supportive environment where they can build their income-earning capabilities. Through Brenda's support, women are trained in backyard gardening, craft, agro processing and livestock raising, which generate income to support their families. In an interview with Carmen Nurse, president of the Network, she highlights that this is a way of 'empowering women to develop skills and become independent, so they would be better able to support self and family' (C. Nurse, president of the St. Lucia Network of Rural Women Producers, Interview). The possibility of this spillover from interventions in material relations of gender (economic empowerment) to the ideological realm (change in unequal gendered power relations) was highlighted by Moser (1989), who points out that practical and strategic needs should not be seen as entirely distinct and separate, but rather as a continuum as demonstrated in this case. The increased self-confidence, independence and economic autonomy brought about by being able to earn a living for themselves and their families loosened the control their partners exercised over them due to financial dependence, hereby changing the power relations in the relationships.

Jeannine has also done some work in strengthening the institutional capacity of the SMMA through improvements in management, operational procedures and human resources. She has facilitated training of staff in the areas relevant for the organization and their own personal and professional development. As change agents, Brenda and Jeannine have been able to contribute to sustainability of livelihoods and individual, collective and organizational empowerment and transformation.

CHALLENGES AND RESISTANCES TO TRANSFORMATIONAL LEADERSHIP

Four main challenges were identified by Brenda and Jeannine as they seek to enact transformational leadership within the spaces they operate. These relate to: (1) the persistence of traditional gender stereotypes and women's perceived roles in society, (2) resistance to the bottom-up approach to community development, (3) personal struggles with balancing work and family life and (4) compromise of physical and mental health due to pushing oneself beyond the limit. Jeannine highlights, 'Well, it can be difficult, you know there are challenges and sometimes we don't even realize some of the blocks that we have because you are a woman. It is not until you are involved and you realize that you can't do certain things including when I come as General Manager. I am in charge of a group of men and some of them are stubborn you know, set in their ways and here comes this woman and telling them what to do'. As a result of this resistance, she found it is difficult sometimes to be taken seriously by men and to get them to listen to her as a woman. She highlights that 'as much as women have reached positions of power, influence and leadership, women are still looked at as a woman you know. It's a sexual thing and so it tends to be that challenge of how do you get people to see you not only as a woman but as someone who has a valuable contribution, not just Jeannine the woman but Jeanine that has a contribution to make, so that is a challenge I think not only for me but for women in general'. She emphasized the importance of having a support network for women, 'somewhere you can stand, people you can lean on'.

Brenda's non-hierarchical approach to decision making sometimes clashes with traditional masculinist ways of leading, to the detriment of people-centred community development. Brenda relates that she has had instances 'when you go out there promoting inclusion, promoting people-centered decision-making and to be told at the end of the day, here is what we're going to do and what we are going to do does not reflect the consulting process that took place'. Speaking on the impact of their work on family life, both women indicated that the family came out on the long end in most cases. Jeannine says, 'I tend to do things which sometimes drive my family crazy in terms of putting other people first. You tend to see them there as a stable force in your life so that they're always there you tend to abuse them just a little bit too much'. Brenda reflects on the impact of her community service on her son and says, 'In terms of my personal life on the level of Brenda the mother, my son is alone while I'm giving my time to community and so I often say that he becomes at risk while I'm trying to take away the risk from someone else. So I have to be very cognizant of that and it is stuff we discuss, he says while I'm available to everyone. I'm less available to him'. As Brenda the worker, 'I am always extending myself to get things done. Sometimes you feel exhausted, unappreciated because you want to see it happen. Sometimes it takes a toll on my health; many times I don't eat properly and so on it impacts me negatively that way. I guess I do need to remedy that'.

This notwithstanding, both women have developed strategies overtime to offset some of the challenges. These include adopting a consultative approach and building partnerships (alliances) which make it easier to resolve conflicts and advance issues. Brenda in particular focuses on community mobilizing and advocacy to counter top-down decision making for the communities. She states, 'Sometimes I want to throw my hands up in the air but then you empower the bottom people to effect the change at the top'. Jeannine adopts a non-confrontational approach when dealing with men because 'they automatically put up resistances when you come as a woman, especially one with an agenda and you don't get very much done. They will block you in every possible way'. As it relates to being invisible or ignored by men while being physically present, she indicates that it's about realizing that 'if I can't get it done through me, I can set up the forum where I bring everyone together. I put forward the idea, we argue about it and then I get someone else to do it'. Both women's experiences illustrate the persistence of masculinist power and the inherent challenges in launching a frontal attack on patriarchy. This is keenly appreciated particularly in Jeannine's experiences and what we see are the women devising coping mechanisms necessary to navigate their masculinist environments.

ACHIEVEMENTS AND OPPORTUNITIES OF WOMEN'S TRANSFORMATIONAL LEADERSHIP

However, notwithstanding the various challenges identified by Brenda and Jeannine, their enactments of a non-masculinist form of leadership has brought about positive changes and resulted in improvements in the lives of individuals, communities and organizations. For example, democracy is being enhanced and strengthened through the participatory, inclusive, non-hierarchical approach adopted by the decision-making processes. Whether it is the staff of the SMMA, the women of the St. Lucia Network of Rural Women Producers, the facilitators of the Community After School Care Programme, or women employed in the Joy Sewing Project, all are directly engaged in the decisions that will affect their lives. Jeannine and Brenda's non-discriminatory and inclusive approach to gender relations contributes to the achievement of gender equality and equity. The significance and necessity of transformational leadership for creating a gender-just and equitable society is reaffirmed when we consider that under masculinist forms of leadership, gender inequalities are reinforced and perpetuated. This makes Jeannine and Brenda's contributions as women transformational leaders even more significant as they are going against the tide of what has been normalized under patriarchal structures.

One of the most visible contributions these women have made is to improve the material conditions of all persons in the society. Their enact-ments of transformational leadership have contributed to poverty reduction in communities and households across St. Lucia through the economic empowerment of men and women through income-generating activities and a focus on sustainable livelihoods. For women in particular, specific gains in the area of practical gender needs within the framework of the WID approach have spilled over into the strategic gender needs raised by the GAD approach. Additional benefits to communities include resilience and adaptation to cli-mate change, behaviour modification in children to prevent future delinquent behaviours in the society, building and strengthening of government and CSOs for community and national development, and capacity development of community human resources. These processes build on the strengths of men and women in society characteristic of the transformational leadership style, hereby validating it as an effective strategy for the achievement of gender equality and equity, gender transformation and women's rights and empowerment in the Caribbean. These achievements should also provide the impetus for continued work throughout the Caribbean as we work towards building more democratic and equitable societies where there is an absence of discrimination on the basis of gender or other social qualifiers.

LIMITATIONS OF WOMEN'S TRANSFORMATIONAL LEADERSHIP AS A FEMINIST STRATEGY FOR GENDER EQUALITY AND JUSTICE

Women's transformational leadership as a concept and strategy for achiev-ing gender equality and justice has merit. Given its focus on demonstrating a non-hierarchical, inclusive and participatory type of leadership, respondents felt that this was what was required for genuine people-centred sustainable development. Nevertheless, despite its achievements, some challenges identified earlier as well as emerging contradictions in the actual enactment of transformational leadership undermine its effectiveness as a feminist strategy for advancing gender equality and justice in the Caribbean. These emerging issues require consideration in the context of the transformational leadership training conducted by CIWiL and how the programme and strategy could be strengthened to better achieve its objectives. The women studied did not appear to sufficiently grasp the critical feminist perspective underlining their training or the fact that they are expected to directly challenge unequal gendered power relations where found. Whether it is male domination in the marine environment or under-representation of men in community development, the women appeared ill equipped to address these gender inequalities.

Women leaders' invisibility and lack of agency in male-dominated environments, as highlighted in Jeannine's case, remain a challenge. This illustrates the difficulties in challenging the established gender hierarchies which remain embedded in Caribbean societies and pose a significant obstacle to feminist transformational leadership's vision of a direct confrontation with patriarchy as the only way to achieve gender equality and justice.

CONCLUSION

This chapter sets out to ascertain the effectiveness of transformational leadership as a feminist strategy for pursuing gender equality and justice in the Caribbean. The research revealed that while the enactment of transformational leadership is contributing to gender equality and equity in St. Lucia, there is a shift in the way gender and gender relations are being understood and acted upon. The women observed do not self-identify with politics and a feminist analysis and seem to be searching for an identity that links the struggle for women's rights within the broader context of the rights of men, children and community. The women were able to attain some achievements mainly in the material sphere of gender relating to economic empowerment of individuals and communities. However, it has been a challenge for them to transform unequal gendered power relations for gender justice. Masculinist ideologies remain embedded in the structures of civic leadership and render women leaders 'invisible' while being visible. In light of this, the chapter makes the following recommendations:

CIWiL's transformational leadership training curriculum needs to place a strong focus on Caribbean feminism and analysis of masculinism, including implications for transformational leadership in praxis. This focus will be geared towards promoting and building a common and collective understanding among trainees of how gender permeates the everyday lived realities of women and men and what is required to challenge patriarchal norms and ideologies in a way that advances the rights of men, women, children and community. Furthermore, a clearly articulated set of coping strategies and techniques for women transformational leaders to deal with gender discrimination directed at them and other women will be required, particularly in spaces where patriarchal ideologies remain embedded.

It is important to devise strategies and promote interventions that seek to alter established masculinist norms, but in a way that promotes gender equality and justice. The CariMAN has a number of initiatives in place throughout the Caribbean geared towards fostering positive, non-violent, cooperative, respectful masculinities and gender equality, and a partnership between CIWiL and CariMAN should be explored to establish strategies and joint activities for the pursuit of gender equality and justice for men and women within the context of transformational leadership. This inclusive approach could help break down barriers and ideologies that see the pursuit of gender equality as a zero-sum game, where women's gains are viewed as men's loss or vice versa.

There is a need for continued public sensitization, training and awareness on gender concepts and issues, particularly on women in leadership. As highlighted by Campbell (2014), organizations, such as the 51% Coalition in Jamaica, have been influential in gaining support from the government and the private sector for women's leadership, indicative of the type of alliances necessary to advance the transformational leadership agenda. CIWiL has undertaken similar initiatives and this should continue throughout the region. The importance of building partnerships and alliances with individuals and communities to foment the desire for participation and inclusion in decision-making processes was also underscored by Brenda (Interview). This is seen as a way to reject and counter hierarchical and top-down approaches to leadership with action originating from the bottom upwards. More of these efforts are necessary to promote transformational leadership at all levels in the society.

CIWiL should continue to provide a support network for women leaders to counter the isolation and loneliness they often feel when operating in a largely male-dominated context. In addition, it is important for future interventions and activism to look at the ways in which women's background and context influence enactments of transformational leadership and to connect individual empowerment with collective feminist movement-building. CIWiL's role in this process is to ensure that a critical analysis of patriarchal ideologies is fully integrated in its trainings and that trainees fully understand the necessity and implications for pursuing a style of leadership that will challenge established masculinist models, and to create collective, men-allied gender and feminist-conscious organizing for women's rights and empowerment and gender equality and justice for all.

REFERENCES

Antrobus, Peggy. 2004. The Global Women's Movement: Origins, Issues and Strategies. London: Zed.

Barriteau, Eudine. 2007. '30 Years towards Equality: How Many More? The Mandate of the Bureau of Gender Affairs in Promoting Gender Justice in the Barbadian State'. *Caribbean Review of Gender Studies Issue* 1, p. 17. http://sta.uwi.edu/crgs/april2007/journals/Eudine_Barriteau_Gender_Justice.pdf.

———— (ed). 2003. Confronting Power, Theorizing Gender: Interdisciplinary Perspectives in the Caribbean. Kingston, Jamaica: University of the West Indies Press.

————. 2001. 'Historical Concepts and Paradigms of Leadership and Their Relevance to Strengthening Women's Transformational Leadership in the Caribbean'. Background Paper: Transformational Leadership Project. UNIFEM Caribbean. http://www.ciwil.org/ Publications.aspx.

Campbell, Shirley. 2014. 'Feminist/Womanist Advocacy Toward Transformational Leadership in the Anglophone Caribbean: Enablers and Resisters'. St. Augustine: Institute for Gender and Development Studies.

D'Amico, Francine and Peter R. Beckman. 1995. *Women in World Politics: An Introduction.* Westport, Connecticut: Bergin & Harvey.

Luttrell, Cecilia, Sitna Quiroz, Claire Scrutton and Kate Bird. 2009. *Understanding and Operationalising Empowerment.* London, UK: Overseas Development Institute.

Mahmood, Saba. 2004. *Politics of Piety.* Princeton: Princeton University Press.

Miller, Errol. 1994. *Marginalization of the Black Male: Insights from the Development of the Teaching Profession.* Mona, Jamaica: Canoe Press.

Mosedale, Sarah. 2005. 'Assessing Women's Empowerment'. *Journal of International Development*: 243–57.

Moser, Caroline O. N. 1989. 'Gender Planning in the Third World: Meeting Practical and Strategic Gender Needs'. *World Development*: 1799–1825. http://www.china-up.com:8080/international/case/case/1296.pdf.

Steans, Jill. 2006. *Gender and International Relations: Issues, Debates and Future Directions.* Malden, MA: Polity Press.

Vassell, Linnette. 2013. Review of Draft Chapter. St. Augustine: Institute for Gender and Development Studies.

————. 2001. 'Leadership Projects and Programmes for Women in the Caribbean Towards Understanding of Transformational Leadership'. Prepared for UNIFEM Caribbean Office. http://www.ciwil.org/Publications.aspx.

Young, Kate. 1999. 'Notes on the Social Relations of Gender', in *Gender in Caribbean Development*, edited by Patricia Mohammed and Catherine Shepherd, 92–103. Jamaica: Canoe Press.

Young, Rebecca. 2008. 'What is meant by Reflexivity in the Context of Ethno-graphic Research? Does Reflexivity Have Limits?' Accessed June 2015. https://www.essex.ac.uk/sociology./documents./pdf/.ug_journal/vol1/.RebeccaYoung_SC203_2008.pdf.

LIST OF INTERVIEWEES

Anatole, Lucille. (Facilitator, Community After School Care Programme, Choiseul). Interview, March 20, 2013.

Antoine, Dave. (Husband of Jeannine Compton-Antoine). Interview, March 12, 2013.

Antoine, McQueen. (Marine Ranger, Soufriere Marine Management Association). Interview, March 8, 2013.

Compton-Rambally, Sian. (Daughter of Jeannine Compton-Antoine). Interview, April 3, 2013.

Butcher, Peter. (Chief Marine Ranger, Soufriere Marine Management Association). Interview, March 8, 2013.

Cadasse, Anthony. (Marine Ranger, Soufriere Marine Management Association). Interview, March 8, 2013.

Charlery, Eustacia. (Information Technology Facilitator, Community After School Care Programme). Interview, March 13, 2013.

Charlery, John. (Farmer, Superior Broom Producers/Latanye Farmers, La Pointe). Interview, March 23, 2013.

Charles, Vaughn. (General Manager, St. Lucia Fisheries Corporation; Board Member, Soufriere Marine Management Association). Interview, April 2, 2013.

Octave, Bernie. (Marine Ranger, Soufriere Marine Management Association). Interview, March 8, 2013.

Compton-Antoine, Jeannine. (General Manager, Soufriere Marine Management Association; Chair, International Whaling Commission). Interview, March 8, 2013; April 3, 2013.

Corisimie, Ronald. (Marine Ranger, Soufriere Marine Management Association). Interview, March 8, 2013.

Descartes, Ferina. (Cook, Community After School Care Programme, Mon Repos). Interview, March 13, 2013.

Descastes, Paul. (Farmer, Superior Broom Producers/Latanye Farmers, La Pointe). Interview, March 23, 2013.

Desroses, Cynthia. (Clerk, Micoud Village Council). Interview, March 21, 2013.

Dorleon, Leona. (Daughter of Broom Producer, Superior Broom Producers/Latanye Farmers, La Pointe). Interview, March 23, 2013.

Ferdinand, Paulina. (Farmer, Superior Broom Producers/Latanye Farmers, La Pointe; Member, St. Lucia Network of Rural Women Producers). Interview, March 23, 2013.

Ferdinand, William. (Farmer, Superior Broom Producers/Latanye Farmers, La Pointe). Interview, March 23, 2013.

Francilla, Cheledonia. (Facilitator, Community After School Care Programme, Choiseul). Interview, March 20, 2013.

Francois, Kerjacki. (Marine Ranger, Soufriere Marine Management Association). Interview, March 8, 2013.

Gordon, Una May. (Board Member, Caribbean Institute for Women in Leadership; Representative for the Eastern Caribbean, Inter-American Institute for Cooperation on Agriculture). Interview, April 2, 2013.

James, Lesley. (Sports Facilitator, Community After School Care Programme, Mon Repos). Interview, March 13, 2013.

Jean-Baptiste, Dion. (Close Friend of Brenda Wilson; Assistant Human Resource Manager, St. Jude Hospital, Vieux Fort). Interview, April 4, 2013.

Jean-Baptiste, Nicholas. (Cousin and Close Friend of Brenda Wilson; Lawyer). Interview, April 4, 2013.

Joseph, Shern. (Agriculture and Kitchen Garden Facilitator, Community After School Care Programme, Mon Repos). Interview, March 13, 2013.

Joseph, Sonia. (Member, Joy Sewing Project for the Disabled, Mon Repos). Interview, March 21, 2013.

Joseph, Velda. (Deputy Director of Community Services, Ministry of Social Transformation, Local Government and Community Empowerment). Interview, March 22, 2013.

Justin, Mario. (Marine Ranger, Soufriere Marine Management Association). Interview, March 8, 2013.

Moncherry, Bibianna. (Member, Joy Sewing Project for the Disabled, Mon Repos). Interview, March 21, 2013.

Nestor, Vernette. (Administrative Officer, Soufriere Marine Management Association). Interview, March 8, 2013.

Nicholas, Cleopha. (Accounting Officer, Soufriere Marine Management Association). Interview, March 8, 2013.

Norbert, Racha. (Life Skills Facilitator, Community After School Care Programme, Mon Repos). Interview, March 13, 2013.

Nurse, Carmen. (President, St. Lucia Network of Rural Women Producers). Interview, March 21, 2013.

Poleon, Anna Zilma. (Principal, Belle Vue Combined School). Interview, March 20, 2013.

Roseau, Sheila. (Coordinator, Caribbean Institute for Women in Leadership). Telephone Interview, October 31, 2012.

Smith, McClaude. (Music Teacher, Community After School Care Programme, Mon Repos). Interview, March 13, 2013.

St. Paul, Janieve. (Child Beneficiary, Community After School Care Programme, Mon Repos, Interview, March 13, 2013.

Wilson, Annabelle. (Child Beneficiary, Community After School Care Programme, Mon Repos). Interview, March 13, 2013.

Wilson, Brenda. (Social Transformation Officer, Ministry of Social Transformation, Local Government and Community Empowerment). Interview, March–April 2013.

Wilson, Elvinette. (Centre Coordinator, Community After School Care Programme, Mon Repos). Interview, March 13, 2013.

Wilson, Glen. (Master Trainer, St. John Ambulance; Cousin of Brenda Wilson). Interview, March 20, 2013.

Wilson, Lyle. (Son of Brenda Wilson). Interview, March 23, 2013.

Wilson, Phyllis. (Performing Arts Facilitator, Community After School Care Programme, Mon Repos). Interview, March 13, 2013.

Index

status of women;
  Dominica, 114, 140;
  Guyana, 93;
  Jamaica, 161;
  T&T, 121–22

transformational leaders, 176;
  Andaiye, 8, 189n5;
  Barrow, Ruth Nita, 176;
  Charles, Eugenia, 176;
  Walcott, Clotil, 176
transformational leadership, xv, 2, 4, 15,
    17–18, 34, 173–74, 178–79, 188,
    195–200, 202, 204–10;
  advocacy strategies, 174, 183;

factors that enabled or impeded, 174;
  history of movement, 180–81;
  personal transformation, 175, 181;
  training 181–82, 184, 185–86

WID, 112, 115, 125, 179, 188
women in parliament, 4–5, 11, 13, 46,
    58, 69–72, 76, 79–81, 89–92,
    94–106, 157
women's political education, 33
women's rights, 2, 11, 173–74, 177–78;
  Dominica, 116, 134, 144–45;
  Guyana, 68, 74–75, 78, 106;
  Jamaica, 154, 156, 163, 168;
  St Lucia, 196, 204, 208–9

About the Authors

Dr. Aleah N. Ranjitsingh is adjunct assistant professor, Brooklyn College of the City University of New York (CUNY). Department of Africana Studies, Caribbean Studies Program, 3304 James Hall, 2900 Bedford Avenue, Brooklyn, New York, 11210. Tel: (347) 869-6013. Aleahnr2@gmail.com.

Mrs. Deborah N. McFee is outreach and research officer, Institute for Gender and Development Studies, the University of the West Indies, St. Augustine Campus. Tel: 1-868-662-2002, ext. 83548. Deborah.McFee@sta. uwi.edu.

Dr. Ramona G. Biholar is lecturer, Faculty of Law at the University of the West Indies, Mona Campus. Faculty of Law, 1-3 West Road, the University of the West Indies, Mona Campus, Kingston 7, Jamaica. Tel: +1 876 587 3000; office: +1 876 927 1855; +1 876 977 4860, ext. 7419. ramona.biholar@ uwimona.edu.jm.

Dr. Maziki Thame is lecturer, Department of Government at the University of the West Indies, Mona Campus. Tel: 876-4570687. maziki.thame@gmail.com.

Dr. Dhanaraj Thakur is assistant professor, Department of Public Administration, College of Public Service and Urban Affairs, Tennessee State University. Tel: +1 615-963-7251. dthakur@tnstate.edu.

Dr. Natalie Persadie is assistant professor, Design and Manufacturing Engineering, University of Trinidad and Tobago, and part-time lecturer, the University of the West Indies, St. Augustine Campus. 59 Scotland Drive,

Cocoyea Village, San-Fernando, Trinidad, W.I. Tel: (868) 740 7127. npersa-die@hotmail.com.

Ms. Iman Khan is a consultant. 56 Church Road, Subryanville, Georgetown, Guyana. imzash@gmail.com.

Ms. Shirley A. Campbell is a gender specialist advisor with the University of the West Indies, Open Campus, Department of Foreign Affairs Trade and Development Canada/Strengthening Distance Education in the Caribbean (UWIOC DFATD/SDEC) Project. 11th Ave. Belville, St. Michael, Barbados W.I. Tel: 246-835-1311 or 246-417-7656. shirley.campbell@open.uwi.edu.

Ms. Denise Blackstock is an international development specialist, with a double Masters in International Relations and Development Studies from the University of the West Indies, Mona Campus. Lot 302, 7 West Aintree, Greater Portmore, St. Catherine, Jamaica W.I. Tel: 876-373-4598. deniseblackstock@yahoo.com.

Dr. Gabrielle Hosein is a Lecturer and Head of Institute for Gender and Development Studies, The University of the West Indies, St. Augustine Campus. Tel: 1-868-662-2002 ext. 83568. Gabrielle.hosein@sta.uwi.edu.

Dr. Jane Parpart is Adjunct Research Professor, University of Massachusetts Boston; University of Ottawa and Carleton University. UMB is in Boston, Massachusetts and University of Ottawa and Carleton University are both in Ottawa, Canada. 318 Selby Ave, Ottawa, Ontario K1Z 6R1. Tel: 343 883 1151 and 613 600 5491. Jane.parpart@umb.edu.